THE

Goulds

THE

Goulds

A Social History

by

EDWIN P. HOYT

Weybright and Talley

NEW YORK

Acknowledgment is made for permission to quote from
the following works: *Helen Gould Was My Mother-in-
Law*, by Celeste Andrews Seton as told to Clark
Andrews. Copyright 1953 by Clark Andrews and
Celeste Andrews Seton. Reprinted by permission of the
publishers, Thomas Y. Crowell Company, New York.
Jay Gould, 1867–1892, by Julius Grodinsky. The University of Pennsylvania Press, 1957.
Quotations of Count Boniface de Castellane are from
his book *How I Discovered America*, Alfred A. Knopf,
1924.

Published in the United States by
WEYBRIGHT AND TALLEY, INC.
3 East 54th Street,
New York, New York 10022

Published simultaneously in Canada by
CLARKE, IRWIN & COMPANY, LIMITED, TORONTO AND VANCOUVER

Library of Congress Catalog No. 69-10602

PRINTED IN THE UNITED STATES OF AMERICA

Contents

———◆———

v

Law of the Jungle

———— ✦•••✦ ————

*Once upon a time there was a poor farm
boy who dreamed of being rich . . . .*

———— ✦•••✦ ————

JASON GOULD stood in the middle of the cornfield leaning on the
long, sweat-worn handle of his hoe, thinking. This very ordinary
cornfield was located quite near a big white farmhouse and not far
from the exact center of the village of Roxbury in Delaware
County, New York. Few people had then heard of Delaware
County, with good reason. The year was 1850, and Delaware
County was still next-to-frontierland. Delhi, the county seat, was a
village itself. Roxbury was simply a way point in the road that ran
from the Pennsylvania state line to Delhi, a mudtrack in winter,
and a dustpatch in summer.

Jason Gould thought of the mud and how much he hated

hoeing corn. He thought of how much he hated plowing, planting and slopping the hogs, how much he detested milking the cows and shoveling manure. Jason's father was out of sight, and so the boy leaned languidly on the hoe and considered the misspent first fourteen years of his life. Jason's mood was particularly pensive because of an incident the day before. He had gotten up in his room in the loft of the big house and slapped his face with cold water from the pitcher, and decided not to go to school. It was enough to have to get up at dawn and go find the cows, count all twenty of them to see that they had not strayed, and then bring them to the barn. It was not fair that he should have to help his sisters with the milking, for he had to get up earlier than they did and he had to walk barefoot through the thistle field, both ways. Then carrying slops—girls' work too—he just was not going to do it any more.

So after the cows were found and led lowing home, and when he had come into the big kitchen at the back of the house for breakfast, Jason Gould had tensed the muscles of his thin frame and screwed up the courage in his sallow, narrow face, and announced to his father that he was never going back to Beechwood Seminary, the local school. The schoolmaster, Jason said, had taught him everything he knew about mathematics and geography and business, and had no more to offer.

There was an argument at the round breakfast table, and Jason's father seized him roughly and hustled him out of the room. The wife and five girls sat numbly, not daring to ask the husband what he was doing to the son. John Gould came back to the table alone, panting slightly as after some exertion, sat down, picked up his mug, and finished his breakfast without a word. John Gould was small and slender and blackbearded, and gave promise of what his son would someday become. His cold temper and cold tongue kept anyone at the table from uttering a word until the meal was finished. Then John Gould silently rose and went about his farmer's chores, while his wife and daughters busied themselves with the breakfast dishes and then moved into the other rooms to begin the day's regular work of "straightening" and washing, ironing, scrubbing, separating cream, churning the day's butter for the market, and preparing for the next meal.

Young Jason had been forgotten until evening when it came time to bring in the cows. His sisters had gone to the barn, ready for the milking, but Jason had not appeared. They had sought their father, who at first grew angry with the boy for another failure to do his duty. Then, with a startled look of recollection, their father suddenly rushed out of the barn toward the house. Later, Jason came to the barnyard and started his trek through the thistle field; over the milking, he told the girls that he had been confined in the cellar all day long by their forgetful father.

The forced incarceration had given Jason a chance to think, and he had taken it. On this following day, he reviewed his conclusions and found them sound. Whistling happily for the first time in many days, Jason went back to the corn and dug at the weeds. He was going to get off the farm and out into the world. He was going to make his fortune in business. At the moment, he waited only for the proper time.

In the evening, when the chores were done and supper dishes put away, the boy spoke to his father. He wanted to go away. The father listened and said nothing.

The Goulds of Delaware County were in no way strange for upstate New York farmers of the 1850s. They differed from their fellows only in their slightly elevated station. The Gould life centered around the big old white saltbox house with the dark shutters. The Goulds had come from Connecticut, and they had come to Connecticut from England in 1647. The name had been Gold in those days, and although some said the family was Jewish, that was not true: many who worked with, or whose fathers had worked with, gold bore that name. In two hundred years the Golds had become the Goulds, and intermarriage with other Puritan families had so mingled many strains that the Goulds could be called nothing but eleventh or twelfth generation Americans. In Delaware County they attended the Baptist meeting house. The taciturn John Burr Gould, who now listened to his son's plea for release from the farm, realized full well what had been asked. So did the boy. Practice was to divide the land among sons and daughters, with the sons taking the lion's share, and the daughters who married well taking nothing, perhaps, save the small goods of the household—keepsakes, quilts, pewter, silver, and the like. But the implied bargain between father and son compelled the son to give his labor on the land until released, either with lands of his own, or with permission to go out into the world. Jason Gould was asking to break with the family, to give up his share of the 150-acre farm, with its barn, its sheds, its farmhouse, and its cider mill.

John Gould was not necessarily opposed to Jason's leaving. Jason's little half brother, Abraham, was small still, but he could do Jason's chores, and the girls could work harder. Jason wasn't worth much at home, and that was a fact. The boy proposed to go off to the select school in Hobart. If he went, he would have to pay his way. The elder Gould sat on his front stoop and considered the request as the spring evening lowered.

Chores finished, Jason had gone walking lightheartedly down the road to spend the last hours of daylight with his friend John Burroughs. It was enough for the moment that he had asked. He discussed his forthcoming adventure—no question of what the answer would be existed in his mind—and then he and the younger Burroughs began feinting at each other, dropping into a wrestling stance. The heavier Burroughs seized Jason tightly in a strong hold. To break it Jason took a choke hold that made his opponent cry "uncle." Then there were recriminations, Burroughs claiming loudly that Jason was cheating. The older boy had heard *that* complaint before.

"I'm on top, ain't I?" he said.

Jason Gould was a very pragmatic boy.

2

Honesty Is the Best Policy

———◆••◆———

Pragmatic—yes—but this young farm boy knew that "honesty was the best policy," because his father, his mother, his step-mother, his five big sisters, his aunts, uncles, and cousins, the pastor and the schoolmaster all said so.

———◆••◆———

"HONESTY Is the Best Policy," Jason Gould had written slowly and carefully in a fine hand at the top of the page. "Composition. Jason Gould. Beechwood Seminary. April 9th, 1850."

"By this proposition, we mean that to be honest, to think honest, and to have all our actions honestly performed is the best way, and most accords with the precepts of reason. Honesty is of a self-denying nature; to become honest it requires self-denial; it requires that we should not acquaint ourselves too much with the world; that we should not associate with those of vulgar habits; also that we should obey the warnings of conscience . . . ."

Reconciliations between meaning well and the practical necessi-

ties of American life have never been easy, and they were no more
so for Jason Gould. As it does so often, pragmatism won in the end.
The right rules were learned but not always followed.

Jason studied hard because he knew that one way out of the
farm trap was to become a surveyor. Therefore he went beyond
the simple mathematics taught at Beechwood Seminary—he borrowed books and studied calculus and trigonometry, which could
help him get such a job. (He could never bear literature and
poetry which had to be learned by heart.) Shortly after the
schoolmaster's praise for his "Honesty Is the Best Policy" composition, Jason's dream suddenly materialized. His father agreed to
release him, the masters at Hobart Academy agreed to take him
on, and he found a friendly blacksmith in nearby Hobart who
would give him board and room in return for keeping the blacksmith's books.

So Jason entered the Academy at fourteen. "Queer boy," said
the gentry of Delaware County. The neighbors had always noticed
his quirks: staying inside, studying books, when he could be out
skating or tossing pebbles. Now all this talk about education convinced them that the village would be better off without him.

One fine summer morning Jason Gould came downstairs in his
best clothes, a rolled-up pair of spare trousers under one arm and
fifty cents in his pocket. He ate breakfast with the family. There
were tearful farewells from his five sisters but no visible display of
emotion by anyone else. Then he was on his way. He walked the
eleven miles to Hobart that morning, and took up residence with
the blacksmith. His duties amounted to far more than he had
imagined, he discovered: the blacksmith also kept the general
store, and the job of "keeping the books" ended up as "keeping the
store." Jay—as he now styled himself to the outside world—
handled the odd jobs as well.

He lasted only six months at Hobart Academy, in spite of the
headmaster's interest in him. The decision to leave was all his. He
knew as much mathematics and "business" as was being taught,
and he had no interest in the rest of the curriculum. Jay had only

one ambition, a very normal ambition for a young American in the 1850s—he wanted to get rich quick.

Wealth always represents security, but in the 1850s, far more than half the people of the United States were "poor," a handful of capitalists were extremely rich, and the middle class was relatively unpopulated. Jay could easily see that "owning property" was not enough: his father owned property and was not a poor man. But Jay's father drudged from morning till night every day of every year and there was no end to it, nor would there be until death ended it for him. No, one needed a great deal of capital, Jay saw clearly, enough capital to earn money in its own right. His fortune, then, would not be dependent on his own efforts.

How could all this be accomplished by a boy with no money and no prospects? Jay did not know the answer—but he did believe that one day he would find it.

Jay was prepared to do anything necessary to increase his own knowledge of how to make money. He left the school, believing it a waste of time, and began to work sixteen hours a day for the blacksmith. He rose at three in the morning and studied for three hours—surveying and engineering—before going down to build the fires, tidy up the counters, and prepare the store for business. All day he clerked and replenished the shelves, after hours he swept up and closed the store, then did the bookkeeping, finally retiring at ten, only to begin the routine again at three.

Such diligence in the store may have been rewarded. According to a later story of Gould's, the blacksmith offered him a half interest in the store, which he held for a year before turning it over to his father, who had sold his farm.

Meanwhile, however, Jay believed that escape from village life lay in becoming a surveyor. He borrowed a compass and went out into the fields, taking other boys with him as chain bearers and flag holders. He surveyed one piece of land after another for practice until he felt proficient enough to handle any surveying job given him. The young capitalist was eventually offered a job with a promise of $20 a month and board to help an engineer. (This was a good wage for a young boy, but nothing at all to someone who owned half a store. Thus the tale of Jay Gould's immediate success in merchandising probably represents someone's stretched imagination. The confusion is caused in part by the Algerean adoration of biographers Murat Halstead and Henry Davenport Northrop and by the less than admiring testimony of scores of writers over the years, but the known facts indicate that Gould pursued a planned course and waited for his opportunity in surveying.)

In answering the knock of opportunity, Jay learned. His first lesson had involved breaking the home ties. The second lesson began as he set out for Ulster County to meet his new employer.

When I came to start I questioned whether I should take any of my own scant supply of money with me or not. I could have had it, but I thought it was better to break down the bridge behind me; so I took only enough to pay my fare. . . . I met a gentleman (the engineer) and he started me out to make these surveys. The map he was making was one on which all the roads and the residences are located—a map showing the general topography of the country. They are useful for reference.

When this man came to start me out he gave me a small passbook and said, "As you go along you will get trusted for your little bills, what you will eat, and so on, and I will come around afterward and pay the bills." I thought this was all right. I think it was on my second or third day out that I met a man who took a different view.

I had stayed at his house overnight. They charged in that part of the country at that time a shilling for supper, sixpence for lodging, and a shilling for breakfast, making two shillings and sixpence (eight shillings to the dollar) in all. I took out my little book and said, "I will enter that." The man turned on me with an oath and said (referring to my employer), "Why you don't know this man! He has failed three times. He owes everybody in the county, and you have got money and I know it and I want the bill paid." There I was. I hadn't a cent in my pocket, so I just pulled my pockets out and said to him, "You can see that I tell the truth. There are my pockets." So finally he said he would trust me. "I'll trust you," said he, "but I won't trust that man." This incident had such an effect on me that it seemed to me as though the world had come to an end. This was in the morning, and I could not have the heart after that to ask anybody to give me a dinner; so along about three o'clock in the afternoon I got faint and sat down for a few minutes.

After this rebuff I was naturally timid. It had a great effect upon me and I debated with myself whether I should give up and go home or whether I should go ahead. I came to a piece of woods where nobody could see me, and I had a good cry. Finally I thought I would try my sister's remedy—a prayer. So I got down and prayed, and felt better after it, and then I made up my mind to go ahead . . . ." *

This was Jay Gould's second lesson: he could expect that every man was out to fleece him—nothing personal, of course, simply a matter of business. Jay cried and prayed, and hardened his heart. From this point on he knew that the harsh world around him required harsher dealings.

* Murat Halstead.

3

Or Is Honesty the Best Policy?

———◆◆◆◆———

After this second lesson, the young businessman sat down and considered his affairs. His first slogan, "Honesty Is the Best Policy," had been seriously in error. But, with the confidence of youth, he was sure that a new slogan would come along, and in the meantime, all he need do was mind his business and not let anyone else take advantage of him.

———◆◆◆◆———

THE Ulster County map job was good, despite all its defects. Jay Gould saw that clearly. His employer owed everyone in the county and had failed three times. Here was a chance for superior brains to improve the situation for his own profit. But first, he had to support himself.

The young surveyor found the key to self-support almost immediately. When he stopped at a farmhouse for food, the farmer asked him to make a *noon mark*—a line that ran north and south, through a window of the house, placed so that at high noon the sun crossed the mark, providing the farmer with a way of regulating his household clocks. The going rate for noon marks was one dollar. At this first house, he paid a shilling for his dinner, made the mark, collected seven shillings from the farmer, and went off, pockets jingling.

In this fashion, the summer of 1852 went by very quickly for the sixteen-year-old boy. Living off his noon-mark profits, he had supported himself while, with two other youngsters, he had mapped the entire county for their employer. Meanwhile, the chief engineer and manager of the project had gone broke again, so there was no money for publication of the survey. Fortunately, however, one of the boys was Oliver J. Tillson, the son of a well-to-do Ulster squire, and the other boy, Peter H. Brink, was from an equally prosperous home. The two Ulster boys wanted their names on the map, and even more, they wanted control of the project. Jay Gould saw his chance and took it: he offered to sell his interest in the entire survey for $500. It was agreed and done, the parents of the Ulster boys took over, and Jay Gould retired with three times as much money as he would have earned in wages.

Trouble followed—there was always to be trouble in Jay Gould's financial dealings for somehow *others* got the impression that Jay Gould was cheating or dealing sharply with them. In the survey case, the engineer who had failed maintained the strange impression that he still held an interest in the survey, and he brought suit against Gould, Tillson, and Brink. Jay Gould stayed very calm for a teen-ager. He immediately hired a lawyer, T. R. Westbrook, to fight the case, and the suit was dismissed in time.

The summer's work had given Jay Gould a fair understanding of the surveying process and mapmaking. If Ulster County men would buy a map of their county, then Albany County and Delaware County men would buy similar maps. In this belief, Jay Gould went to Albany. But a bigger scheme quickly developed. A promoter named John Delafield suggested that he and young Gould persuade the Legislature to back them in making a survey of the entire state of New York. Delafield would provide the brains and Jay would provide the work. Jay agreed. The idea was under consideration when Delafield suddenly died. With considerable perspicacity, Jay Gould realized that no one would pay attention to a seventeen-year-old boy, and he shrewdly abandoned the grandiose scheme to return to his county surveys.

Three boys had done the survey of Ulster County in 1852. In the summer of 1853, Jay Gould surveyed Albany County alone. That same summer he took time off to survey and map the village of Cohoes for the Cohoes Manufacturing Company—a job which paid him an additional $600—and he surveyed at least part of the Albany and Muscayuna Plank Road. During the winter, Jay Gould prepared the map, then supervised the printing and the sales.

In 1854 Jay Gould moved to spread out his resources using the tried and true method he had learned—getting others to do his work so he could undertake more of it. He sent surveyors into Delaware County and into two counties of Ohio and two counties of Michigan. He had hopes of becoming the surveyor king of America, and perhaps its principal mapmaker. As for himself, he supervised the drafting department from a little office in Delaware County, surveyed part of a railroad route from Newbury to Syracuse, and undertook part of the Delaware County engineering.

Turning for the moment to letters, he also wrote a history of Delaware County, published it himself, and sold it through printing houses and local stores. That project occupied part of two years. In addition, he went on to promote new surveys, farming them out to others. But most notably, he got involved in the promotion of a new and better mousetrap invented by his maternal grandfather, Alexander Moore. It was the summer of 1853, and New York was holding a World's Fair at the new Crystal Palace. Jay Gould decided that this was just the time and New York was just the place to peddle the better mousetrap. To impress prospective manufacturers, Gould brought the mousetrap in an expensive mahogany case, a case so magnificent that it attracted the attention of one of the thieves who then, as now, ply their trade on the New York public transportation system. The young man from upstate was sitting aboard a Sixth Avenue horsecar with his case under his arm one moment; the next, the case was securely in the hands of a large man pelting down the avenue away from him.

Jay ran after the thief and caught him, much to his own surprise. With Jay's finger wedged in a buttonhole of his coat, the man could not move far. Nevertheless, he loomed large and threatening. Fortunately a policeman came up. The thief predictably claimed the box was his and that Jay was trying to rob *him,* and off they went to the police station. There Jay identified the contents—the other could not—but he was totally disgusted when he learned that he had stolen a mousetrap.

Newspapermen soon heard of the case of the man with a better mousetrap. They interviewed Jay, and the story was given as much as half a column in the New York *Herald*. A New York manufacturer offered to take on the better mousetrap and to pay royalties to Jay's grandfather. Jay had discovered publicity.

Having learned of the uses of the press, Jay Gould sought to manipulate the press. He befriended the editor of the Delaware County *Mirror* with small amounts of cash for advertising, and then demanded editorials in favor of his maps. He got the editorials. Soon, he was one of the busiest young men in all Delaware County, promoting maps, selling histories, and looking for new ideas.

But it was too much. Overtired, Gould fell victim to the typhoid fever that was endemic in the countryside. He had no sooner recovered when he was again laid low by an "inflammation of the lungs"—perhaps a serious case of pleurisy—which left him partly invalided for the rest of his life.

The life he had built for himself was out. At seventeen, his career seemed finished.

4

The Taking of Zadoc Pratt

———◆◆◆———

*The young businessman had learned early
in life the dangers of spreading oneself too
thin. Furthermore, in several years in business he had acquired a new maxim. "Take
them before they take you" became his
new philosophy.*

———◆◆◆———

IN THE COURSE of his surveys, engineer Jay Gould had come across
a sharp old gentleman, Zadoc Pratt, who lived in Greene County
bordering Delaware on the east. Zadoc Pratt, a semiretired businessman, had served ten years in Congress. He lived in Prattsville, which was named after his family. Gould, who was never
given to encomiums, described Pratt's estate as "a beautiful place."
The kindly old businessman owned half a dozen tanneries in the
East, and although his affairs were in such condition that he need
not even supervise the tanneries, he was always on the lookout for
a good thing or a bright face. Squire Pratt respected shrewdness,
and when the seventeen-year-old proprietor of a surveying firm

14

had proposed to him participation in a Greene County survey, with a special drawing of Prattsville and a "view" of his fine residence, provided Pratt came through with "proper remuneration"—the offer suggested to the old entrepreneur that here was a fine boy just fit for business. Pratt refused to pay up, but he marked Jay Gould down for future reference.

Squire Pratt need not have worried about keeping track of Jay Gould—the young man had already added the old Squire to his list of hidden assets. When Gould felt that he had gone about as far as he could go in the survey business without a complete reorganization, and when, in addition, he was too ill to do anything about it, Pratt offered the young man a new opportunity. During a visit to the master of Prattsville, Gould mentioned that in his surveying he had discovered that the Delaware, Lackawanna, and Western Railroad had some large tracts of hemlock timber for sale. Hemlock contains tannates, a commodity vital to Squire Pratt's business, and the squire was very much interested. Young Gould offered to put up capital of $5,000, cancel out his surveying business and other enterprises, give the mousetrap back to his grandfather, and go into the tannery business full time if the squire would make him a partner.

The squire was not "born yesterday," as his neighbors were fond of saying, and he gave only conditional approval to the plan. But in a remarkably short time, Jay Gould went to Pennsylvania, made conditional contracts for the purchase of some land and more timber rights, and hired sixty men to cut timber, to build a tannery and vats, and to work permanently in the woods. He returned, the arrangement was formalized for one year, and Jay Gould rushed back to Pennsylvania to cut the first tree.

Zadoc Pratt retired to his 365-acre model farm, kept up his correspondence with his old friends in Washington, watched over his interests in Prattsville and Tannersville, and let the twenty-year-old Gould run the tannery in the mountain country not far from Stroudsburg, just across the Pennsylvania border from home. The Delaware, Lackawanna, and Western was so delighted to acquire a new customer on the New York to Scranton line that it gave cut rates for freight. The future seemed very bright. The firm was capitalized at $120,000. The investment was far less, of course, but since Gould and Pratt might want to sell stock or make loans, they jumped their capitalization to the limit, as was the fashion at that time.

First, Jay Gould put up the sawmill and the blacksmith's shop and slept on a bed made of hemlock bark in the shop while the other tannery buildings were finished and quarters were constructed for the men. The tannery completed, it formed a community that needed a name. Since Squire Pratt already had a town, this community was named Gouldsboro. A village named for a twenty-year-old—but that was the way of America in 1856. Luck and pluck could take a man about as far as he wanted to go.

Jay Gould wanted to go just as far as he could. He supervised every aspect of the business until the tannery was in full operation and the hides were coming in from the New York and Pennsylvania farm country. Seeking markets for the tanned leather, Gould went to the major marketplace, the "swamp" which bordered what had been the old meadow land of the east side of Manhattan Island in New York. Each year the swamp grew smaller as the growing land values in New York forced more and higher building. Yet, in 1856, the swamp area of Manhattan was still the tannery section of the city, holding also a few glue factories and some other noxious businesses which added to the unpleasant odors on the east side of town. Jay Gould came here to learn the New York market.

Young Gould learned quickly, and he was soon filled with zest for the big city and its opportunities. His pulse raced when he came into New York, and he knew, suddenly, that this was the place for him. As with the survey, the book, the mousetrap, the "doing" of things interested him, and once a business was started and the difficulties conquered, he found the details of operation irksome. He knew the necessities of business, but neither his will nor his temperament would allow Jay Gould to stop with the tannery business, relax, and settle down in the foggy hills of Pennsylvania to prosper and grow fat. He began preparing for the future.

The first step was to establish a capital reserve. Old Zadoc Pratt would have applauded so wise a gesture, but not quite the manner in which Jay Gould went about it. Gould took the company profits as they came in and established a private investment bank, Jay Gould and Co., in Stroudsburg. Theoretically, the company owned the bank, but the books were so doctored that old Zadoc did not even know the bank existed, nor would he have approved of it, since through the bank, Jay Gould was using tannery money to speculate in the markets of New York City.

Second, Jay Gould began to cultivate money men in New York. One of the first such men he met, and one with whom he quickly became friendly, was Charles M. Leupp, reportedly a millionaire and an investor and leather merchant, who owned a handsome mansion at Twenty-fifth Street and Madison Avenue. White-haired and grave, Leupp was one of the most astute and most honorable of the New York merchants. His word was his bond. He had never been known to cheat a business acquaintance.

Toward the end of 1856, Zadoc Pratt became concerned, and then irritated. He knew the tannery business. He had access to the company's reports. He learned how many hides were taken in, how many men were employed in tanning them, and how many sheets of leather were sold—but cash returns did not add up to the sales. Pratt demanded some explanations from Jay Gould.

Jay Gould, in the "swamp" of New York, had been talking long and earnestly with Charles Leupp about the wastefulness of the leather business. With Leupp's connections in the marketplace and Gould's tannery, to say nothing of his abilities, could they not make a fortune by combining forces? Leupp quickly saw that the elimination of buying and selling expenses would increase net profits on a producer-to-consumer basis, and he was interested. Would he be willing to put up the money to buy Pratt out—and go into business with Gould? After much consultation between the two, David W. Lee, Leupp's brother-in-law and attorney, entered the picture. The discussions continued.

Back in Prattsville, Zadoc Pratt grew daily more upset about the stories and rumors that were reaching him from Gouldsboro. Back in Gouldsboro, Jay Gould sized up the situation, then travelled to Stroudsburg on his own business, and went on to New York. Attorney Lee, a very conservative man, was not impressed with Gould's answers to all of Leupp's questions, but Leupp convinced him that this young man knew the tannery business and *knew business.* Just how well they did not yet know.

One day in January, Pratt learned that Jay Gould was involved in some outside dealings in Pennsylvania business affairs. Presumably, Zadoc Pratt knew that the investments belonged to the tannery, but no record of them appeared in the reports Pratt received. When the squire could wait no longer, he took the train down to Gouldsboro and hired a hack to run him over the plank road that led across the swampy land to the tannery.

Gould was in New York, and Zadoc Pratt had the books and the bookkeeper to himself. Pratt investigated, discovered that the books were falsified, set out for Stroudsburg, learned of the existence and of some of the operations of the Gould bank, and settled down to wait for the return of his junior associate.

Jay Gould returned the next day, January 27, 1857, to face Pratt who furiously accused him of "cooking" the books and swindling the firm out of his money. Gould tried to quiet him, but the old man was obdurate. The firm owned the Gould bank, he said, and he was simply concealing the operations from outsiders. Pratt would not believe *that* tale. Protestations of innocence were useless. Pratt could always bring back the same charge: misusing the company funds. So Gould said nothing at all.

Calming down, Pratt demanded that Gould either buy or sell, he did not care which. (Pratt did not, probably, think that Gould could buy.) Gould offered to buy Pratt out and the deal was made.

In his biography of Jay Gould,* Richard O'Connor indicates

* *Gould's Millions.*

that Zadoc Pratt took a loss of $60,000 just to get rid of Gould. This seems most unlikely for there was probably no need for the old man to take any loss at all. The sum of $60,000 would buy a great deal of tannery in 1856 and 1857. The $60,000 settlement simply represented half the capitalized value of the firm, not what Zadoc Pratt had invested, which must have been far less.

Given business practices, the story that bears the ring of truth is the one offered by Trumbull White in his book *The Wizard of Wall Street.*

White says Pratt offered first to close down the tannery and Gould pleaded with him not to ruin him. A loss of a few thousand dollars would have meant little to Pratt. Pratt then offered the "buy or sell" proposal. Gould could either take $10,000 for his interest and get out, or pay $40,000 to Pratt and the old man would get out. Gould then had ten days in which to make up his mind and raise the money.

The timing is far more interesting. Jay Gould allegedly either knew or suspected the moment that Pratt would descend on him. The situation has the marks of an annual meeting, in which Pratt came to the tannery to make a decision about the future, did not like what he saw, and got out, while Gould, who had suspected that this would be the case, was already prepared with new financial backing that would allow him to pay off Zadoc Pratt and start anew as a partner of Charles Leupp.

Jay Gould seemed to have pulled his first grand coup. He had taken $5,000 and the trust of an associate, with his own energies and abilities he had run up a going concern, and he had forced his old associate out. His half of the firm was worth at least $60,000, plus whatever he had put away in investments in Stroudsburg. Furthermore, by disassociating himself from the old tanner and associating with the established New York leather merchant, Jay Gould earned a foothold in the biggest marketplace in America. It was a grand year's work. Old Zadoc Pratt returned to Prattsville, mourning his loss of faith in another specimen of mankind. Young Jay Gould, meanwhile, prepared himself to call on his new friends and cement their partnership.

5

Who Killed Charles Leupp?

———◆•◆•◆———

The young businessman soon established a new philosophy to guide his actions, although he had not put it into words. He was too busy in the marketplace, buying and selling, trading and dealing, shuffling and holding his hole cards. "Play them tight to the vest" was what he was doing.

———◆•◆•◆———

WHEN it came right down to it, Leupp and Lee drove a hard bargain. It was one thing for Jay to promise old Zadoc Pratt that he would buy him out; it was quite another to do so once the cat was out of the bag and Leupp and Lee learned that Gould really needed the money. The New Yorkers put up the $60,000 to pay off Squire Pratt and prevent him from foreclosing on the property. But they demanded their businessman's due: they took a two-thirds interest in the tannery.

Early in 1857, Jay Gould began making more and longer trips to New York, ostensibly to confer with his partners about business affairs. Actually, through the Stroudsburg bank which was again

20

"investing" the profits of the tannery, he was hip-deep in speculations in the various markets of Manhattan. Besides, Gould was using company money to attempt to build up a "corner" of the hide market and hides futures. All spring and summer Gould speculated on a rising market. Leupp and Lee, who never speculated, did not even suspect that he was doing so. Then came August 23, 1857, and the collapse of the New York City branch of the Ohio Life Insurance Company. When that firm was unable to pay its obligations, other houses began falling like flies, and soon the secret of Jay Gould's speculations was out. He had been buying futures on margin, and suddenly the brokers, who needed the money, demanded more cash from Gould. Since he did not have it, he began drawing on every account in sight, and Charles Leupp shortly discovered that Gould had been using his position as partner in the tannery to inculpate Leupp in other tradings. On the day that the market failed, Gould, Leupp, and Lee owned all the hides on hand—on paper—and every hide that would be delivered to the New York market within the next six months—also on paper.

But when Jay Gould failed to meet the calls for more cash to bolster his margin accounts, the paper became worthless. Gould awoke on the morning of August 23 a millionaire, and went to bed that night a pauper again.

Had Jay Gould gazed in the mirror, unflinchingly, on that evening, he would have seen a twenty-one-year-old man with hair already inching back from his forehead. To appear older, he had also adopted a full beard, and since his whiskers grew black and fast, the transformation had been complete. Jay Gould looked at least ten years older than he was. He was about five and a half feet tall, and what could be seen of his face was pale and pasty. His black, deepset eyes, set beneath bristling black eyebrows, bored out like gimlets. His mouth and his facial expressions were nearly invisible, giving the impression of total coldness. A good poker face, it matched his new habit of playing the cards close to his vest.

In his travels, Jay Gould had learned how to dress—no one could find fault with his tailoring. He wore the broad-bottomed, baggy trousers of his day, high button shoes, a double-breasted long jacket with big lapels. His collar and tie were seldom visible under the beard. He wore a tall beaver hat with a silk ribbon and carried a stick. In winter, he wore a heavy, coarse overcoat of a blanket-like material, made more stylish by the addition of a velvet collar at the back.

Retreating to his tannery at Gouldsboro, he was confronted by Charles Leupp, who had come to ascertain the cause of the sudden flurry of paper demands made on his hitherto-solvent leather business. In the general absence of state and federal regulation of business, a great deal of business was conducted on simple faith. For example, a man might walk into a brokerage house, buy stocks, and pay for them by drawing a "bill"—what later would be called a check; the check would not be payable through a bank, but would be drawn directly against the house in question, as it was when Gould walked into a brokerage house, bought a thousand hides, and gave a bill on the Gouldsboro tannery—or on Leupp's own firm. Bills of credit sat until the merchant or broker involved needed money; then he took them around to the firm and collected cash, gold, silver, or paper money, depending on the mood of the market. Since everybody in the swamp knew that Gould and Leupp were partners, Gould, in effect, turned Leupp's credit into Gould's credit.

Suddenly, on August 24, a flood of bills began to descend on Charles Leupp and his credit was seriously threatened. Thus came the Leupp trip to Gouldsboro.

Clutching a sheaf of these bills and other papers, Leupp confronted Jay Gould, who admitted that, "in both their interests," he had been playing the hide market and pledging every asset in sight. Young Gould was not particularly contrite about his actions. It was all in the rules of the game, he said. The thing to do was to go out and do it again, but avoid being "suckered" as old Commodore Vanderbilt would have put it. If only that insurance company had not collapsed, he said—but then there was always next time.

A businessman and not a speculator, Charles Leupp declared that Gould had forced the firm, both firms, into bankruptcy. Gould admitted that technically this was true; if Leupp would keep a stiff upper lip, however, it would all come out right. The whole of Wall Street was in the same condition, and they had at least producing businesses that supplied necessities.

Unconvinced, Leupp declared that Gould had betrayed him. In this tragic mood, the senior partner returned to New York by train, brooding all the way. He had been unable to make Jay Gould comprehend honor, good name, the trust of employees and customers, the goodwill of fellow businessmen. Charles Leupp felt these assets were irrevocably lost—destroyed by the actions of his young partner. On leaving the train, Charles Leupp took a cab to his Madison Avenue mansion, walked in the door, marched into his library, locked the panelled doors behind him, picked a revolver out of the desk drawer, put the barrel in his mouth, and pulled the trigger, sending a bullet through his brain.

All this happened in the summer of 1857 when Charles Leupp gave himself to history as the first notable ruined on Wall Street to choose death by his own hand rather than public dishonor—an honored, if unpleasant, custom to be developed in the American business community.

At the time, the business world was shocked. Up and down the street it was said—although not loudly—that Leupp's association with that young man from Pennsylvania had been the cause of his death. The charge might have been made openly had Jay Gould and his theories been well known on Wall Street. One might even say that Jay Gould was still in the process of developing these methods, and so far, only two men had fallen his victims. But he also had hundreds of satisfied customers, and business being business, men were not quick to complain about another man's methods if they were not personally affected.

From Gould's vantage point at Gouldsboro, all these events seemed far away. Jay Gould was protected by his bank in Strouds-burg from the worst effects of the panic. He was solvent, even if his work had left Charles Leupp insolvent. The Gould search for fortune went on.

From the beginning of the partnership, Gould had sensed that he must be careful of David Lee, Leupp's lawyer and brother-in-law. Now Lee undertook to drive Gould to the wall, to take the Gouldsboro tannery from him, and to force him to repay to the Leupp family all that had been lost. But Gould, in Pennsylvania, was not subject to all the New York laws covering debts and agreements. For the next three years, Gould managed the tannery, played the markets in Wall Street, and fought off Lee, who repre-sented the widow and orphaned daughters of Charles Leupp. Lee demanded the return of the $60,000 that the partners had put up for the firm, and eventually, after nearly three years of stalling, Gould prepared papers for an agreement, stipulating that the money would be repaid over six years, at $10,000 a year. But when the papers were finally drawn and ready for signing, the lawyer discovered that no provision for interest had been made. At nor-mal 6 per cent rates, the interest would amount to $12,600, not an inconsiderable sum, and Lee demanded it. Gould refused to pay. The agreement collapsed. Jay Gould apparently believed that he could stall his way out of paying the interest.

But Lee was a businessman as well as an attorney, and wearing that hat he went to Scranton and recruited a force of some fifteen men to seize the tannery—Gouldsboro's single greatest asset. In 1860, the town consisted of the tannery, the station of the Dela-ware, Lackawanna, and Western Railroad, a handful of rude shops built of native lumber, Jay Gould's cottage, a few other houses, and the wooden hotel, which also doubled as the village center and restaurant. The population was about three hundred people.

On the afternoon of March 13, Lee's men came in "on the cars," got off the train, marched in a body to the tannery, which had ceased operations for the day, and took possession. Although they held the position all night, practically no one in Gouldsboro knew they were there. Next morning, Jay Gould came from his quarters in Gouldsboro to the tannery to begin business as usual, and found himself looking down the barrel of a musket. He tugged at his beard for a moment, turned about, and walked to the hotel. From there, Gould sent his men out to round up the townspeople. He called a meeting at the hotel and waited. Nearly everyone in town was on the payroll of the tannery and almost the entire population of Gouldsboro jammed into the hotel lobby to discover what was the matter. Jay Gould rose, told them that Lee was a city slicker from New York who had hired a gang of Scranton toughs to take the tannery away from them all, and, he said, if Lee succeeded, everyone within hearing would lose his job if not his shirt. Jay Gould's listeners appreciated the truthful elements in these remarks, and soon Gould had enlisted a force of about one hundred and fifty men. Fortunately for Gould's plan, most of the men owned guns or fowling pieces. While they assembled their arms, Gould went to the hotel and ordered the management to open up several barrels of oysters and prepare a banquet. The one hundred and fifty men assembled and ate oysters and drank whiskey until they were full and happy. Then Jay Gould jumped up on an improvised stand and made a short speech urging them on to take the tannery without using unnecessary force. The qualification carefully exempted him from the charge of inciting to riot.

"The Battle of Gouldsboro" began at about 10:30 the next morning. The Gould men, generously fortified with whiskey, surrounded the Scranton men in the tannery, broke down the wooden gates, and swarmed inside just after noon. They outnumbered the Scranton men so heavily that it was really no contest. The Scranton men had begun firing when the gate was attacked, and the Gould men fired back. There was violence, and there was bloodshed.

Gould said he had selected fifty men as assault troops and kept the rest in reserve. He divided his men into two companies, one of which went to the upper end of the building and pried loose the boards while Gould headed for the front door.

> "I burst open the door and sprang in," he said. "I was immediately saluted with a shower of balls, forcing my men to retire, and I brought them up a second and a third time and pressed them into the building, and by this time the company at the other end of the tannery had succeeded in effecting an entrance and the firing now became general on all sides and the bullets were whistling in every direction." *

The battle was over. Four of the defenders were wounded and the rest either beaten or routed from the premises. The authorities arrived, and some arrests were made, but the arrested men were released on bail, and the tannery was returned to Jay Gould's hands.

In spite of this apparent victory, Jay Gould was beaten, the victim of his own foolish refusal to pay interest on the investment of the Leupps and Lee. Lee undertook an intensive campaign of legal harassment which interfered with production and prevented Gould from selling finished leather. As a result, the tannery grew unprofitable, and later that same year Jay Gould closed it down. Thus everyone lost, especially Gouldsboro, which faded away to a ghost town.

* Murat Halsted.

6

The First Million

———◆•••◆———

*The young businessman was rapidly
learning the ways of business. Few other
men of twenty-four could say they had put
two careers behind them (three, if you
count his brief literary career). He had
learned to trust no man out of his sight;
he had learned that exploitation of natural resources brought fortune; that every
man was jealous of his own prerogatives,
and partners were not desirable. He had
learned to take every advantage offered
him, and to worry about the legal consequences later. He was, in brief, prepared
to enter the business community of New
York City.*

———◆•••◆———

THE New York to which Jay Gould returned in 1860 was a fasci-
nating city finally acquiring an air of permanence, enhanced by
such buildings as Trinity Church and the far newer Greek-
columned customs house which was to live on as the sub-Treasury
building. A fire had destroyed the Crystal Palace in 1858, but new

auditoriums and exposition grounds were being built. The Cooper
Union building had just gone up at Fourth Avenue and Seventh
Street, and Abraham Lincoln would soon make a famous speech
there. The year that Jay Gould arrived, the huge British steamer
Great Eastern also came on its maiden voyage across the Atlantic,
proving at last that the ocean was no more than a lake. Also
established that year was a newspaper, *The World,* which was to
be important to Jay Gould's future. New York was indisputedly
the great city of the western hemisphere, with a population of
813,000.

The Wall Street which lured Jay Gould was dominated by the
figures of Daniel Drew, George Law, Commodore Vanderbilt,
and a dozen others whose names are now half-forgotten. Vanderbilt, Law, and Drew were then constantly shaking the financial
world of Wall Street with raids on each other and on lesser figures. No quarter was asked or given here. Jay Gould had already
discovered that honesty and the golden rule were irrelevant to
business. The motto on Wall Street was "get it while you can"—by
bull buying, by bear raids, and by cornering markets in specific
goods and even services. The stock exchanges existed and were
cheap enough—a seat on the New York Exchange cost only $460.
Speculators there traded heavily in all kinds of securities, but as
investments, railroads, toll roads, canals, and other public utilities
were becoming increasingly popular. These men were virtually
unfettered. They made up the rules as they went along, and almost
all aspects of business were unregulated. The sky was the limit,
and if a man thought he could corner the wheat market, for
example, the invitation was open. Although stealth and trickery
were all-important, a cornering was more honored by Wall Street
than any other triumph. It won both actual fortune and the respect
of the men on the street. To corner a commodity, a businessman
had to bring every device to bear, and it made no difference that
trickery was chief among these.

The financial community had been unable to keep up with the
rapid westward expansion of the nation in the 1840s and 1850s.

Most of the money for expansion came from Europe, from bankers in France, Germany, and England who put up capital and actually owned huge chunks of American industry in the form of stocks and first mortgage bonds. Expansion or room for expansion was present in nearly every field of endeavor, from clothing manufacturing to cartage. In this bursting economy everything imaginable was needed, and more and more, the country turned to the largest city for financial support. If they wanted to build a railroad, they came to New York to sell bonds and stocks. If they wanted to sell cotton, they came to New York to find the English markets or the American middlemen. If they wanted to float a company and begin to manufacture a new product, they came to New York for promotion and finance.

The year 1860, when Jay Gould began operations in New York, has been characterized as the Year of the Robber Barons, but that is not entirely the case. For twenty years, Vanderbilt and Law and Drew had been squabbling and knifing one another in the steamboat trade, blowing up and burning up passengers by the score. The atmosphere of eat-or-be-eaten was established long before Jay Gould's advent, and even the acquisition and mismanagement of railroads for quick personal gain was part of the daily life of Wall Street. Still, the fifteen years that began in 1860 were the roaringest, harshest, and widest-open of any yet seen in America, and more fortunes were made and lost more quickly than in any other decade. There were two reasons for this development. First, the Civil War offered unlimited opportunities for speculation in anything and everything, from eggs to army blankets, from gold to railroad stocks. Second, before the war, the expansion of the nation as a whole had been tremendous; immediately afterward, the expansion of the North, still financed by foreign capital, redoubled as the South tried to lick its wounds. So for ten years, the atmosphere in New York was redolent with the heady perfume of quick profit. Even in the seventies the musk was almost as strong, relieved only occasionally by newspaper outcries. The 1880s would bring some demands and some regulation, particularly when "Four-Square"

Grover Cleveland took office. The 1890s would see stronger regulation of business and revulsion against the past, but only the twentieth century would bring a virtual end to the old abuses upon which many of the greatest American fortunes were founded.

So Jay Gould came to New York and set up offices at 39 Spruce Street as a leather merchant. He knew the field, his substantial nest egg had been taken out of the profits of the tanneries and converted in the bank at Stroudsburg, and he was ready to move where opportunity offered. Personally he was a modest man, he dressed quietly, if carefully, he neither drank nor smoked nor gambled (except in business), he was of quiet mien, almost mousy, and never made a scene. He lived at the Everett House, uptown at Fourth Avenue and Seventeenth Street, a very decent address for a bachelor—one of his fellow guests was James Gordon Bennett, proprietor of the New York *Herald*. But Jay had little to do with the other guests at the fashionable hotel; he was totally occupied with business.

Jay Gould had once had romance on his mind. In the Delaware County days, he had become engaged to a cousin of his, Maria Burhans. He had built a house at Gouldsboro especially for her, and they had planned to be married in 1856 or 1857. But Maria's mother fell ill, and on her deathbed she persuaded Maria to promise to look after her father. The father opposed the marriage because the two were first cousins, and he persuaded Maria to break the engagement. When her father married again, Maria did not get in touch with Jay, nor he with her. The marriage was off, and romance was eliminated from Jay Gould's life for the time.

In his early New York days it was just as well. Jay Gould was busy learning the ways of Wall Street. Railroads were the thing. There was talk even then about a transcontinental railroad, but that was the least of it. The railroads to be considered were the dozens, scores, hundreds of lines being built up to interconnect all the new markets as the country moved west and towns arose to fill in the gaps on the map. Industries brought more people to towns, and both industries and people needed railroads. So while Gould played with hides, he lost his heart to the railroads—and to Wall Street speculation.

On Seventeenth Street, not far from the Everett House, lived Daniel G. Miller, a solid, conservative merchant, they said—but still a speculator in railroad securities. Gould often passed the Miller house, and one day he saw the merchant's young daughter Helen in the window. He saw her there again, and again, and finally managed an introduction to the father—not too difficult an accomplishment given their shared interest in securities. Jay Gould began courting Helen Miller.

Meanwhile, down in Spruce Street, he continued seeking new ways to make money. He did little else but make money. Nearly friendless, if he had had an inclination to befriend others in the street, he was quickly disabused of it. Henry Clews tells this tale of an abortive excursion into business friendship:

The wealthy Cruger family of New York and the Hudson River Valley tried to befriend the hard-working young man in the summer of 1860. They invited him on a yachting weekend. Jay Gould went to the family estate at Cruger-on-Hudson for the party. On the afternoon before he was to go back to New York, the Crugers took the party sailing on the river. Gould went along. But as time passed, he began to worry about missing his train and kept pulling out his watch and looking at it ostentatiously. Finally, the skipper, annoyed with this sour-faced one, announced that he would make his train. Gould was not sure. The sailboat sailed on, racing against time as far as Gould was concerned—until it approached the shore that the railroad ran by. The train was in the station. Gould became agitated. The Crugers then went running in toward shore with the centerboard down, instead of pulling it up, and the sailboat grounded in the shallow water offshore. Jay would have to swim for it, they said. Determined not to miss that train, Gould stripped down to his underwear (violent scarlet, Clews reported) and, holding his dry clothes and shoes over his head, waded through the water to the shore while the men laughed and the women hid shyly (but not too shyly) behind their parasols. Then, when Jay was inshore, the Crugers pulled up the centerboard and sailed in alongside, jeering at him.

Jay Gould did not forget that for a long time. As affairs turned out, of course, neither did anybody else in Wall Street. But it was not completely unpredictable that Jay became the coldest man in the business community.

Yet this aspect of Jay's character, his whole public character, was not at all apparent to his family, to his old friends from upstate New York, or to the handsome young Miss Miller he courted. Gould's biographers say that Mr. Miller was not enchanted with the prospect of having Jay for a son-in-law. That might well be true, not because Jay Gould had a bad reputation, but because he was a nobody—bright, promising, but still a nobody—and Miller was in a position to expect, perhaps, a marriage upward in the New York community for his daughter.

Yet Jay tried to get around the old man. Miller came to be impressed with the youth's abilities and his energetic pursuit of the dollar. Some months after arrival in New York, Jay Gould became associated with one of the more important Wall Street firms, which was operated by Henry N. Smith. When the name became Smith, Gould & Martin, Jay bought a seat on the New York Exchange.

Even with so advantageous a connection, Jay did not persuade Mr. Miller that he was the ideal son-in-law. He did persuade Miss Miller that he was the ideal husband. What a contretemps! The young lovers pined for one another, indulging in secret clutches in doorways and lingering glances through the plate glass windows of the house at 33 East Seventeenth Street. Unable to stand it any longer, they made an engagement to go walking one afternoon, walked to a nearby minister's house, and were married without fanfare. Back at the house, they informed Mr. Miller that his bird had flown. The old man took the surprise rather well, and Jay moved in with the family. Father-in-law and new son began to discuss the importance of railroads and what might be done to make them profitable to the household.

Jay had already been toying with various railroad investments.

Using moneys that began with the tannery funds, he had steadily been buying up the first mortgage bonds of the Rutland and Washington Railroad, a 62-mile line that ran from Troy, New York, to Rutland, a little industrial town and marketplace in central Vermont. With backing from his father-in-law, Jay Gould now bought control of the railroad, and then became chief operating officer. He was president, secretary, treasurer, and superintendent. He went to Troy and set up shop, then studied the line, made the necessary changes to make this monopoly show big profits, and settled back to wait. The country was packed with such shortline railroads in these days before state control. Anyone who had the money could build a railroad to anywhere, and many people did. But when it came to operations, the railroad men soon discovered that the more miles of track they controlled and the more markets for freight and passenger traffic, the greater the economy of operation and the higher the profits. So it was not long before the Rensselaer and Saratoga Railroad, which ran from Troy and Albany and Schenectady to Saratoga, began showing interest in the Washington and Rutland. Here would be a line that would give them access to Vermont farm products and such industrial goods as were made there. It would also work the other way, supplying Vermonters with goods from New York State, and the world, by way of the Hudson River Railroad and the Hudson River steamboat trade. By itself, the Washington and Rutland was showing profits. Combined with the Rensselaer and Saratoga, the operators could envision huge profits.

So Jay Gould, who controlled the Washington and Rutland, did well to sit tight. He sat and talked, and talked and sat, while the proprietors of the other road squirmed and urged action. Finally the others got action: the line was sold, and Mr. Miller and Mr. Gould reaped the profits. Jay Gould suddenly became a wealthy man. It was said he was worth $750,000 after that consolidation.

7

The Fox Makes Ready

———◄••••►———

*The young businessman knew where he
was going. Railroads represented the challenge of his time, and there were so many
of them, so badly managed, that almost
anywhere he might turn he could find
opportunity. European investors in the
1860s regarded America as the source of
two kinds of investments, government
bonds and railroad securities. Everyone
with money was eager to invest in profitable railroads because the future was so
obvious. Here was the young man's future, all mapped out for him by the time
he was twenty-seven years old.*

———◄••••►———

IN HIS successful assault on Wall Street, Jay Gould was the creature of circumstances, his own shyness, and a totally undeveloped
sense of public relations. Other men did as he was doing and were
admired, if not totally loved, by the penny press, because they had
a way of pleasing the reporters and giving them "a story" which
would satisfy the editors. Not so Gould. He never had anything to

say to newspaper men, treating them so curtly that they soon turned against him.

Knowing that they would not get their story from Gould, they sought out any and every other source connected with him. So the stories that were written about Jay Gould were wild, irresponsible, and nearly always negative. Commodore Vanderbilt could corner the stock of the Hudson River Railroad, as he did, sell short, and nearly ruin Daniel Drew in one great venture, as he did, and in the meantime drag down scores of innocent investors, as he did—and still come out of the mess he had created smiling like a sphinx, roaring to the press like a lion, and receiving worship for it all. When Jay Gould worked out the consolidation of the Washington and Rutland Railroad with the Rensselaer and Saratoga, the move was all for the betterment of stockholders, bondholders, customers of the railroad, and even the cause of the Union in the war. But instead of lionizing Gould, the press indicated that he was more jackal than hunter. He was a strange young man, walking alone through Wall Street, his eyes always fixed straight ahead of him. Too young not to serve in the Union Army without leaving questions as to his patriotism, he was too proud to tell anyone that his lungs were such that he could not pass the physical examination even if he wanted to. That would have been excuse enough, because the Union war was not a Wall Street war. New York, by and large, agreed with prewar Mayor Fernando Wood that the war was an evil matter, and hundreds of otherwise eligible young men walked in Wall Street seeking their fortunes while their brothers shed their blood for North and South in the battlefields.

Three previous studies of "robber baron" families * have shown that the men in each case have behaved in about the same way. By the standards of the twentieth century, the practices of these men —and of all men in Wall Street—were illegal. Their own century did not deem such activity illegal. And how much morality pre-

* *The Vanderbilts and Their Fortunes, The House of Morgan,* and *The Guggenheims and the American Dream.*

vails in the business world in the twentieth century? At any rate as to the Jay Gould who was emerging in the 1860s, Julius Grodinsky found that Gould was a "master in the field of corporate expansion." *

"Operating in his twin fields, corporate relationships and security manipulations, Gould displayed a streak of objectivity, of cold bloodedness, of lack of emotion. Personal scruples seem to have been lacking in him. If a thing had to be done, it was done. There were legislators and judges to be bribed and bought. Gould outbid Vanderbilt."

Gould was simply high bidder in his field. Was he, then, more guilty than the others?

Grodinsky continues:

"To his loyal followers, however, he was a man of his word. He never flinched from carrying out a promise. Even at the cost of heavy personal sacrifice he would do this." And Grodinsky cites statements by General G. M. Dodge, the railroad builder, W. E. Connor, the stockbroker, Russell Sage, Sidney Dillon, and other Wall Streeters to make his case.

The point, not accepted by many historians, is that the system encouraged dealings that are evil by modern, more humane standards and that these men, Gould, Vanderbilt, Morgan, and the Guggenheims did not regard themselves as anything more than shrewd businessmen who had the good of the nation at heart. The rapid building of the railroads, essential to the expansion of the country, would have been impossible without these men. The ruin of the railroads was caused later by the bankers. A balance is hard to strike, but although Gould was not as good a man as his family and friends believed, he was not as bad a man as the press painted. And in the end, he served a useful purpose in the building of railroads and the American telegraph system.

But in the beginning, Gould was a speculator through and

* *Jay Gould, 1867–1892*, Julius Grodinsky, University of Pennsylvania Press, Philadelphia, 1957.

through. He speculated in gold in the Gold Room at Broad Street and Exchange Place, as did hundreds of his contemporaries including J. Pierpont Morgan. "Gold speculation" is as old as money in the world, and continued elsewhere long after it was outlawed, and thus made immoral, by American fiat. We might consider it immoral in the 1960s for speculators and even allied governments to drive down the value of the American dollar by buying and hoarding gold—but they continue to do it in precisely the same manner that Jay Gould and Pierpont Morgan bet on the price of gold during the Civil War. It has been said that the Gold Room speculations were carried on at the expense of the Union government and thus of the American people, and this charge is true, but it is based on public morality which does not find its way into business unless brought in by law and strict control. Fortunes are not made except by exploitation, and exploitation is a violation only of twentieth-century codes of morality as the old businessmen would be shocked to learn. But critics ought to remember that had there been no great land grants of the sixteenth and seventeenth centuries, no adventurous exploiters of a hundred varieties, there might be no United States of America.

During the war, Jay Gould was not well known to the newspapers; the Vanderbilt and Drew names were still dominant in Wall Street. Gould was simply another bright young broker who sometimes crashed into the pages of the papers with one coup or another, such as the purchase of control of the Cleveland and Pittsburgh, a short-line railroad in financial difficulties because of poor management. Of course, "poor management" was relative—the line was in trouble because short-line railroads did not have a solid place in the scheme of American expansion. Jay bought the line from another speculator when the stock stood at $40 a share. By buying and selling, creating a market and a flurry, Gould managed to run up the price of the railroad to $120 per share. The Pennsylvania Railroad was expanding west, and needed either to take over the Cleveland and Pittsburgh or build a competing line. It was cheaper to buy control at a high price such as $120 a share than to build and then compete, and that is what the Pennsylvania did. Jay Gould, having had the prescience to buy at the right time, sold for three times his investment, and made a fat profit; his name made the papers. Gould also became known, or at least he aroused suspicion, for his apparent access to confidential information about the war. Perhaps he had bribed a subordinate in the War Department. Perhaps he had his agents in the military telegraph offices. In any event, Gould seemed to know more about the affairs of the Union armies, and more quickly, than any other broker or speculator in Wall Street. Early in the war, he began speculating on the rise and fall in the market on battle days, having several hours advance knowledge of the turn of the battle—thus he could "predict" an upturn in the market if a Union victory was announced or a drop if the Confederates had won. This ability to acquire inside information brought Gould much admiration, and by war's end he was regarded as one of the "insiders" among the manipulators and was sometimes asked into the pools that conducted a bull corner or a bear raid.

Thus Jay Gould became involved in the affairs of the Erie Railroad, which brought him very much to the public eye. It came about in 1867.

Commodore Vanderbilt had succeeded in taking control of three lines that served New York City from the north and west: the New York Central, the New York and Harlem, and the Hudson River Railroad. If he could secure control of the Erie, he would have a monopoly of all the traffic coming into New York from those north and west directions, and could fix rates as he pleased. So at the end of the Civil War, he bought heavily in the stock of the Erie and tried to take control.

Daniel Drew, the old Methodist Episcopal skinflint of Wall Street, and the leonine Commodore's principal opponent in those years, was also intensely interested in the Erie. Drew had been treasurer of the line since 1854, and he held, personally, huge chattel mortgages on the line's equipment. In 1859, he had sought to take it over as receiver when the road was in trouble, but the building of a line through the rich Pennsylvania oil fields solved the railroad's problems for a while. Yet by 1866, the Erie owed old Daniel Drew two million dollars. A year later, when it came time for the annual election of officers, Vanderbilt and Drew both sought control, and a brisk market developed in Erie stock. Jay Gould watched this development and decided to get into it, and he secured control of enough shares of Erie to get himself elected to the board of directors in October of 1867. Daniel Drew was again on the board, and Commodore Vanderbilt seemed to have gained control. Everyone believed that Vanderbilt had a majority of the stock.

But actually three factions were involved, the third led by John S. Eldridge, a Boston financier, who wanted to merge the Erie with a line from New England. Everyone seemed to think Eldridge had allied himself with Vanderbilt; in fact, he had made a deal with Jay Gould, and he, in turn, had made a deal with Daniel Drew and his young ally Jim Fisk, Jr., a Vermonter two years older than Gould, a champagne swigging, womanizing, roistering fellow whose porcine appearance disguised a sharp mind.

What followed was this: Vanderbilt decided to run the Erie as part of his empire and combine rates and pool earnings with the three roads he controlled. But at that moment, the Commodore discovered that he did not have control of the Erie board.

From Commodore Vanderbilt's point of view, the way to remedy that failing was to secure control by going back into the market and buying more stock, and he did just that. Then Daniel Drew unveiled his secret weapon. In handling the affairs of the Erie as treasurer, Drew had made it possible for certain bonds to be sold and then to have the value of stock. Convertibility it was called, and it was done when a company was in dire straits and needed to give every enticement to investors. Now the convertibility of some 50,000 shares of Erie bonds became an issue. Drew put them on the market. Vanderbilt secured an injunction from his pet judge, Judge George G. Barnard of the New York State Supreme Court. Vanderbilt then ordered his brokers to buy Erie—every share they could get.

All this action was aimed at Daniel Drew, Gould's partner.

Vanderbilt did not at the moment know or care about that because the Commodore knew Gould as a relatively small stock speculator and he did not consider him a factor in the situation. But all this while, Gould and Drew were partners in one stock-trading joint account. Gould was also close to Eldridge; it was even believed that he had made Eldridge president of the line by throwing proxies to the Boston man during the election.

Vanderbilt began buying Erie in November, 1867, with the price at about $80 a share. After he discovered the existence of the bonds and got the court order to stop their trading, he thought he was safe. But Drew, Fisk, and Gould continued to sell the bonds as stock, and Gould used power he had as a member of the Executive Committee to authorize issuance of another $5,000,000 in bonds worth 50,000 shares of stock.

The battle continued. In March, 1868, Judge Barnard enjoined the sale of the second 50,000 shares. Now 100,000 *new* shares of stock floated illegally on the market. The Commodore was buying furiously, but even he paused for a moment—at the going rates, this addition meant a new investment of at least 4.1 million dollars just to control the new stock, or 8 million dollars if he wanted to buy all of it. This was a lot of money even for Vanderbilt. He hesitated. As he did so, the price of Erie dropped to 67½ and threatened Vanderbilt's whole investment. No one knows precisely how much he had invested in Erie, but it was many millions. To keep the price from dropping he had to buy, and he did, again. Meanwhile, he persuaded Judge Barnard to issue contempt of court orders against Drew, Fisk, and Gould for selling stock when they had been ordered not to do so.

On March 11, the three conspirators were in the Erie offices in New York City. There Gould began tying up money in bundles and throwing it into trunks, while carrying on a meeting of the Executive Committee of the railroad. He learned that morning that Commodore Vanderbilt had secured the contempt orders, and he moved fast. The Executive Committee, which had this power, voted to move the operations of the Erie to Jersey City, across the

Hudson River and out of the jurisdiction of Vanderbilt's pet judge. They packed money, stocks, and papers into trunks and told the Erie's employees to move across to the railroad's terminal. That would be the new office.

Old and tired, Daniel Drew did not want to leave New York because he was afraid that he would never again be able to return. But Gould insisted, so Drew went ahead with the trunks while Gould and Fisk stayed behind to finish up business for the day. Judge Barnard fulminated in his chambers and told reporters that he would hold the conspirators for $500,000 each if he could catch them. Gould went home to say goodbye to his wife and two baby sons, and Fisk went off to spend an hour with his ladylove, Josie Mansfield, an actress who did not act and who gave the profession a new black eye by her open dalliance with Fisk.

That evening the two, Gould and Fisk, met at Delmonico's Restaurant at the corner of Fourteenth Street and Fifth Avenue, and there Fisk quaffed champagne and ate steak while Gould toyed with crackers and milk—all the excitement had brought on one of his attacks of dyspepsia. Before Fisk was finished, someone came to warn them that the constables knew they were at Del's, so they signed the bill and fled to the Canal Street dock. There they hired a pair of deckhands from a steamer to row them over to Jersey City. It was a dark foggy night, the ice still clogging the river, and the crossing was a dangerous one. The oarsmen got lost, and rowed around and around in the river, in constant danger of being run down by steamers and ferry boats, and it was midnight before the skinny, shaking Gould and his fat companion were landed on the Jersey shore, soaking wet from the backwash of two ferries which had come that close.

So the Triumvirate—as the newspapers dubbed them—took a whole floor of rooms at Taylor's Hotel and converted it into a rump extension of Wall Street.

Soon it was rumored that Vanderbilt was planning to lead an assault force of fifty or more men who would cross the Hudson, kidnap the Executive Committee of the Erie and bring its members back to New York to face his judge. Jim Fisk—who was sometimes called the Admiral because he liked to play with steamboats —was chosen to defend. Fisk secured assignment of fifteen policemen to the hotel. The Hudson County Artillery furnished three 12-pound guns to be mounted on the shore and sink any Vanderbilt fleet. Four lifeboats were manned by armed Erie employees, who patrolled day and night with rifles loaded. Jim Fisk paraded daily up and down the waterfront talking to reporters who flocked from New York to report on the greatest story of the day.

Soon Vanderbilt had invested some $10,000,000 in Erie stock to protect his original purchases, and he kept on buying, keeping the price above 70. The danger was great. He was using stock as collateral to get money to buy stock, and had the public lost confidence in his ability to pay, the whole house of cards could have collapsed.

But the conspirators over in Jersey City were also in danger. Jay Gould was in torment being kept away from home. He had taken a house of his own to care better for the needs of his growing family: a son, George Jay Gould, had been born in the Miller house in 1864, and another son, Edwin, had been born in 1866. Jay Gould was as sentimental and kind to his wife and babies as he was objective and cold to his business associates. He was associated with Drew and Fisk, and yet neither man knew Jay Gould well enough to know the names of his children.

Much headshaking took place in Jersey City. The Triumvirate's trouble involved incorporation and the law. The Erie did business in New Jersey, but its headquarters had been New York and it was a New York corporation. Gould had to rush to the New Jersey legislature and persuade those lawmakers to make the Erie a New Jersey corporation so the railroad could do business, in spite of being in violation of the laws of New York.

Yet Gould and company could *never* go home, as long as Vanderbilt's judge held those contempt citations against them. They must deal with Vanderbilt, Gould saw that, and he began to work.

First, he went to Albany with a bag full of greenbacks to pass out among the New York State legislators. The object was to secure passage of a law legalizing, *ex post facto,* the sale of the convertible bonds so that he and his friends would not go to jail. While in Albany, handing out money, Gould was arrested and taken down to New York. He appeared before Judge Barnard, got out on bail, and rushed back to Albany. In time he was successful, and the bill he wanted was passed. How much had it cost? someone asked him years later. Gould knitted his brows: "You might as well go back and ask me how many cars of freight were moved on a particular day," he said. The cost of buying the legislature was unimportant—it was important only that the legislature was bought, at some price between $300,000 and $1,000,00. Jay Gould did not talk well in public, but he knew the symbols that appealed to New York's legislators—$$$. The bill to legalize the sale passed, and further, made it illegal for Vanderbilt to create an interlocking directorate of any of the lines that he owned with the Erie. Here was a new note. It made the Erie useless to Vanderbilt. Too, as the struggle continued, Daniel Drew lost his nerve. Some of Drew's fortune was tied up in New York, some in New Jersey, and he was afraid of losing all of it.

Vanderbilt was also sick of the fight. He recognized Drew as the weak one of the Triumvirate—and Vanderbilt sent an agent to tell Drew to come and see him to settle the whole business. So one Sunday, Daniel Drew slipped over to Manhattan without telling Gould or Fisk. Obviously Drew intended to doublecross his associates, because at the same time, secretly, he moved the Erie treasury back to New York. Gould discovered this action, and attached Drew's personal fortune, which was still in Jersey City. When Drew brought the Erie treasury back to New Jersey, his money was freed.

All then seemed serene—if not perfect. But Jay Gould was not serene. He no longer had any use for Daniel Drew, and he intended to break with him as soon as he could. He and Fisk went over to see the Commodore. They made their own arrangements, leaving Daniel Drew quite out of it. Vanderbilt recouped $4.75 million from the Erie itself and was in a position to sell his other Erie stock without loss, and Gould and Fisk cemented control of the Executive Committee of the Erie.

So Gould had the Erie, with Fisk as his mouthpiece, and Commodore Vanderbilt paid Jay Gould the ultimate compliment: he was, the old man said, the smartest man in America.

As for Daniel Drew, he retired from the Erie with his personal fortune intact, but on July 2, 1868, the day Gould was elected president of the Erie, Daniel Drew was removed from the board of directors. Elected to the board was William Marcy Tweed, Grand Sachem of Tammany Hall and boss of New York City, whom Gould had come to admire during the fight in Albany. That admiration alone, however, would not have brought Tweed to the board of Erie: Tweed owned Judge Albert Cardozo, Judge John H. McCunn, and as much of Judge Barnard as did the Commodore. The three jurists were now the willing slaves of Erie.

Gould then adopted a trick he had learned from Commodore Vanderbilt: he increased the capitalization of Erie from $34,000,000 to $54,000,000, creating a fortune of $20,000,000, on the spot, most of which went into his pockets, with some for Fisk, his front man. But Gould's planning went beyond simple greed: he was out to punish Daniel Drew for betraying him, and at the same time, to make another fortune. With all this stock in pocket, Gould and Fisk began a bear raid, selling and forcing the price of Erie down until it went from 70 to 35, the low point coming in November, 1868. Daniel Drew was the wiliest bear on Wall Street, and he gladly joined the raid, selling short thousands of shares of Erie—which meant he promised to deliver at a future date these shares of stock. Usually a bear raid kept the price going down and down, but this time suddenly the price began going up, and rose to 62. Secretly, Fisk and Gould had begun buying Erie stock, while Drew was selling. Before the maneuver was over, Gould had punished Daniel Drew and had ruined his position on Wall Street. He no longer had the means to control any corporation, and although he continued in Wall Street until 1875 when he went bankrupt, he was never again an important factor.

Commodore Vanderbilt, still irked at being outfoxed, now began a rate war against Erie, hoping to drive that overcapitalized and underfed railroad to the wall. In the war, Vanderbilt dropped the rate for cattle cartage on the New York Central from $125 a car (Buffalo to New York) to $1. Gould went with him all the way, then suddenly jumped the Erie rate back to $125 a car, meaning the end of the rate war. But just before he did so, Gould managed to buy up every head of cattle available west of Buffalo— and shipped the huge herd to New York, *via the New York Central system*. When Vanderbilt learned what Gould was doing he was flabbergasted for one of the few times in his career and publicly stated that he would never again wage an attack on Jay Gould. (Actually, he said that he would have nothing to do with Gould except to defend himself.) Thus was born the long feud between the Vanderbilts and the Goulds which was to keep Jay and his descendents for many years out of the sacred realm of the Four Hundred which Astors and Vanderbilts vied to dominate in the years just after the Commodore's death. Jay Gould, in the late 1860s, was not concerned with high society, and he never would be concerned. Business was his whole concern, and suddenly in 1868, this relatively unknown Wall Street speculator, at thirty-two, had become president of one of the nation's mightiest railroads and a mighty power in American corporate finance.

8

How to Get Gold
Without Actually Stealing It

*The complex young businessman, now
thirty-two years old, was setting out to
build up the railroad he had acquired and
he meant to do it. But he could not ig-
nore the world around him. He was
sorely tempted, and he failed to resist the
temptation.*

THE period of Reconstruction after the Civil War was notable for
every abuse on the bodies politic, social, and economic. Such a note
must open any discussion of the Great Gold Scandal of September,
1869. To understand what Jay Gould and Jim Fisk set out to do,
and why they thought they could do it, one must remember that
the United States had in March of that year installed in office the
most corrupt administration that was to lead the country in all of
its history, that the extent of the corruption was suspected months
before President Ulysses Simpson Grant came to office, but that

actual corruption immediately outraced the wildest fears. Through the Whiskey Ring, the Washington Ring, and personal corruption of the highest federal authorities, fortunes were made in Wall Street and elsewhere, and what Jim Fisk and Jay Gould planned was simply to extend a normal Wall Street operation just a little bit further than usual. Perhaps it *was* more than that. The boy wonder of 1857 had set out to corner the American hide market: the Wall Street wonder of 1869 set out to secure a corner on *all the gold in the United States.*

For a contemporary American without gold to understand the economic theories involved and the reasons for the actions taken, some background is necessary. Gold was both a commodity and a medium of exchange—it was bought and sold on the market much as pearls or diamonds might be sold today, and for the same reason—as an investment by the very conservative who did not believe in the stability of any government. The price of gold on the market fluctuated in terms of supply and national welfare. The United States government did not dictate the price and had no way of controlling price except by buying or selling gold on its own account, which would increase or decrease the supply on the market.

In the summer of 1869, the United States was enjoying a year of bumper crops for a certainty. The United States was primarily an agricultural nation, and the best way to get full value for these crops was to sell them abroad. So various bankers and merchants asked the Grant administration to allow the gold market to soar, thus making crops more valuable than paper money (and raising prices in terms of paper), and encouraging people in European countries to buy American wheat, corn, and cotton.

Under the Lincoln and Johnson administrations, Secretary Hugh McCulloch of the Treasury Department had looked with strong disfavor on speculators in gold, and he let it be known that if anyone tried to corner the market, he would step in and wreck the foray with sales of government gold. But when the new administration came to office, Secretary George Boutwell announced his distaste for McCulloch's propensity for interfering in the normal laws of supply and demand—and it was indicated that he would not step into the marketplace except in case of national calamity. When Jay Gould learned this piece of apparently academic information, his ears pricked up.

Jay Gould's ingenious mind began to work. In the interest of the Erie railroad, Jay Gould had to cooperate with the bankers. Since London was the financial capital of the Western world, the price of grain in New York was regulated by what American grain would bring in London. Were the price of gold raised, the price of grain would go up, the farmers would find it advantageous to ship their grain east, and the Erie railroad, along with the Vanderbilt lines, would profit. But there was another angle to it.

When Jay Gould learned, furthermore, that the treasury had agreed to let the price of gold rise, Gould saw an opportunity to make a killing on the market. He would buy *all* the gold available, and do it so quietly that he would have a corner on the market. Then, in that brief period before panic set in—when there was no gold available except his gold, before government could sell gold or foreign agents could enter the market with gold shipped from Europe—he could raise the price as he willed and make a fortune.

This plan depended on two foundations. First, its initiator must have huge resources behind him, resources quickly available and quickly convertible. In 1869, Jay Gould had these: the Erie railroad treasury was his basic strength, and he and Fisk had also acquired control of the Tenth National Bank of New York. Gould already owned $7,000,000 worth of the $15,000,000 in gold that was actually in circulation in the United States, so he would have to buy perhaps only $8,000,000 more.

Second, he must have strong reason to believe the federal administration would back the agricultural policy Gould favored. If the government could not be persuaded to keep the price of gold high, and if it began selling some of its $100,000,000 worth of gold, the Gould plan would quickly collapse. Two methods of persuasion suggested themselves: convince the administration or give the administrators a personal interest. Jay Gould set out to pursue both courses, not by outright bribe, as has been suggested, but by letting new friends in on a good thing. It had been done before and it has been done since: for example, twentieth-century presidents have accepted huge gifts from Texas millionaires, ranging from cattle for their farms to investments made in their behalf (and thus the United States still has the oil depletion allowance for Texas millionaires).

If Jay Gould had one grave fault as a businessman, it was probably the absolute lack of any sense of public relations that we have already noted. He made a bad impression and he did not much care. He labored in a pit where the devil took the hindmost. Some of his peers tried to perfume the atmosphere with honeyed words, but Gould was not the type: everyone knew the rules of the game and he played by those rules and did not try to seem better than he was. Gould's ways became clearly apparent in the Gold Corner maneuver.

In the first place, when he began buying gold in the spring, Gould had invited Fisk to enter the venture with him as a partner. Afraid, Fisk backed off. Only in summer, when Gould had driven the price of gold from 131 to 140, and then let it fall back to 136 by temporary inactivity, did Fisk ask to come in. Gould let him.

Gould began trumpeting the value of his economic theory (that is, high prices for gold) and secured considerable support for the ideas. But the government still had to keep out of the gold market or the plan would fail.

Jay Gould made the acquaintance of A. R. Corbin, the brother-in-law of President Grant, a New Yorker who boasted that he was the power behind the administration. To hear Corbin tell it, Grant did nearly nothing without consulting Corbin and never crossed him. Apparently Gould believed this, and one reason seems to have been that when Grant came to New York and Gould sought an appointment with Grant, Corbin arranged it with no trouble at all. Gould spent the time elaborating on his high-price-for-gold theory. Grant was noncommittal, but when the appointment ended, the President berated his secretary for letting Gould in without telling the President what he wanted. He did not like Gould around, he said. Gould was too aggressive. "He is always trying to get something out of me."

Gould, in turn worriedly went back to Corbin after this interview fingering his beard. The President seemed not to believe in the Gould theory of crop and gold management, and if the President did not believe, the gold corner scheme ought to be abandoned right then and there.

"I am right behind the throne," said Corbin reassuringly. "Give yourself no uneasiness. All is right."

President Grant was on his way to attend a Peace Jubilee in Boston, and since Jim Fisk owned the Fall River steamship line, Gould suggested that the Presidential party be the guests of himself and Fisk and that they make a social affair of the trip. The President, never loath to accept a gift or a favor, agreed, even though he still purported to dislike Gould. Cases of champagne were loaded aboard the steamer *Providence* and every other delicacy available was brought aboard before Fisk and Gould took the Presidential party up to Boston one evening in June. The trip began with a champagne supper and was followed by cigars, brandy, and talk. While a great bibber, the President was not interested in Gould's and Fisk's ideas, and the talk thus failed.

The party went on. Gould went to the Peace Jubilee in the Boston Coliseum, and then back to New York where, on June 19, the Goulds and Fisk and the Corbins joined Grant and his wife and daughter in Fisk's box at the Fifth Avenue Theater for a performance of *La Périchole*.

The maneuvering continued, but Grant remained untouchable. He returned to Washington knowing only that he disliked Jay Gould because the financier was always probing at him—and not really knowing why Gould was probing, or what danger he had been in.

Corbin, an old lobbyist and political hanger-on, eagerly assured Gould that the deal was safe enough without Grant, and, knowing the feeling of the Secretary of the Treasury and how much Grant disliked interference in economic affairs, Gould was inclined to agree.

Corbin, of course, was eager to protect the deal, for Gould, in the fashion to be so honored by time, had made an investment in Corbin's behalf. He had bought a million and a half dollars in gold in Corbin's name, using Gould capital. Gould would retain the capital, but the increment was all to be for Corbin. Thus, every time the price of gold went up a dollar, Corbin made $15,000 without turning a finger. Gould was also persuaded to make an investment of $500,000 in Mrs. Grant's name, and he did so. Every time the price of gold went up a dollar, Mrs. Grant then earned $5,000, although apparently this was to be Corbin's little gift to his sister and she did not even know about it.

Gould's investment of this money in people was very shrewd and very simple. He would buy the gold anyhow; he simply let them know that the account was in their name and they would have the profits. He also bought a million dollars worth more and put it in the name of General Daniel Butterworth, the Assistant Treasurer and head of the subtreasury in New York, and another half million dollars worth in the name of General Porter, secretary to Grant (the latter gentleman, however, refused the honor).

Using checks drawn against the Tenth National Bank Gould bought heavily in July and August, and at the end of the period, he owned, in theory, some thirty million dollars worth of gold or gold contracts, which meant that gold must be delivered to him at the price of that summer. The price rose until it reached 141, which meant a hundred dollars in gold was worth $141 in paper money.

With the price that high, others in Wall Street realized that more than the normal market was at work, and bears began selling short. Bulls began showing signs of panic, as speculators very easily do. They were further panicked when Gould persuaded Corbin to write an economic article for the New York *Times* and persuaded the *Times* to run it, for the article declared flatly that

President Grant would not sell gold to support the gold market. (To be fair to the *Times,* it must be said the government had so indicated.) Referring to the article he had planted, Gould then wrote Secretary Boutwell to smoke him out on the subject, but Boutwell's reply was guarded.

So the tension grew. Gould sat impassively in his office, tearing paper into shreds—at day's end, he walked out through a sea of torn bits. He walked home but was such a poor companion that at dinner with the family on this night as on some others Jay Gould spoke not one single word.

Early in September, President Grant came through New York on his way to Saratoga, and from Corbin's house, informed Secretary Boutwell that he should not sell much if any government gold while the crops were moving to market. (Gould's theory was taking hold after all.) Corbin informed Gould of the move, and Gould continued to buy gold. On September 10, Grant came back to New York, and used the Erie directors' private car to return to Washington, giving rise to further rumors that Gould had Grant in his pocket. On September 12, with the bulls and the bears all clamoring for government help (action or inaction), Grant advised Boutwell against action. On September 13, Fisk decided to join the gold boom and threw $8,000,000 of his own into the market. Fisk swore later that Gould had said President Grant was in the plot—a charge which Gould denied.

Anyhow, Jim Fisk was a big noisy fellow who liked to talk about what he was doing, and soon the whole of Wall Street knew that he had joined Gould in buying gold.

Gold hit 141 on September 22. At about that time, with pressure from all sides, President Grant apparently learned of Corbin's speculations and Gould's offer to purchase a margin account for General Porter. Mrs. Grant sent Mrs. Corbin a letter saying the President was distressed because of Corbin's speculations. Corbin panicked, showed the letter to Gould, demanded to be taken out of the market with the $100,000 he had helped to earn on the million and a half account Gould had established in Corbin's name. Gould persuaded Corbin to keep the letter secret to give him a few hours to unload gold. Otherwise, he said, "I am a ruined man."

Gould's prime interest was in unloading the $50,000,000 he had purchased in futures and gold, and he did not tell Jim Fisk what he had learned. On September 23, Gould went to the Gold Room and made ostentatious purchases of gold while secretly selling a great deal more than he purchased. Grant's preparations to break the market remained a secret. That day gold rose another three points, and Gould alone in the marketplace knew that President Grant was giving his brother-in-law a chance to get out before dropping a bomb in the market.

September 24 was a Friday, a clear, sunny day of the kind that makes New York the most pleasant city in the world in early autumn. Usually, Jay Gould began his day's work by going to the Grand Opera House at Twenty-third Street and Eighth Avenue, which he had purchased as offices for the Erie, at Fisk's urging. The offices occupied the three floors above the opera house where Jim Fisk played impresario. But today Gould went to the offices of the Heath and Company brokerage house on Broadway, and not long after his arrival, Fisk showed up too. Fisk, with a bevy of actresses and other companions, sat in one corner, Gould sat in another, writing notes and tearing up paper. It was not really odd that they were not together. Jay Gould was then and always a lone wolf. Nor, common talk and common knowledge to the contrary, was Jim Fisk a particularly close friend of Gould's. Gould still did not have friends in the street, and, with his own high sense of personal morality, he was disgusted by Fisk's pursuit of wine, women, and song. So Gould sat alone, nursing his knowledge that the market must break, and Fisk stayed happy in his fool's paradise, issuing loud orders for his brokers to buy, buy, buy. The price rose from 140 to 144. Secretly, Gould's brokers were selling every minute, being careful not to sell to Fisk.

At 10:00 a.m. gold reached 150. Stocks began falling as business firms felt the pinch. Some were forced into bankruptcy because paper money was dropping fast in relation to gold and then to buying power. General Butterfield, who was a member of the "conspiracy," became so frightened that he telegraphed the Treasury to sell gold in the national interest. On the White House lawn, an unsuspecting Grant played croquet, while business empires tumbled in New York.

At 11:00 a.m. gold hit 160, and a jovial Jim Fisk offered to bet $50,000 that it would hit 200 before the day was over. Following the precedent established by Charles Leupp years earlier, a ruined broker went home and shot himself, and the Gold Room was a mass of confusion and despair. Just after 11, the price went to 164.

Jay Gould was playing his own game. His brokers were selling or getting ready to sell. He had no sympathy for Fisk and neither gave Fisk any advice nor sought any that day—nor did Fisk seek his counsel. Gould always believed it was every man for himself in the marketplace. His brokers were selling, and in that, at least, they were keeping the price from rising. But their selling alone was not enough to counteract the buying of Fisk and others who were still bulling it on gold.

The break came just before noon when General Butterfield came to the Gold Room to announce President Grant's order to sell immediately $5,000,000 in federal gold, and to imply clearly that the President would sell whatever was necessary to bring down the price.

Gold dropped. From 164 it went immediately to 160, to 155, to 150, down into the 140s, and quickly to 133. The hot-tempered speculators of the Gold Room lost far more than they made. Albert Speyer, one of Fisk's brokers, quite lost his senses and was led away mumbling and raving to his friends that he would buy gold at 160—an hour after the bottom had dropped out of the bull market.

Some of the beaten crowd decided to revenge themselves on Jay Gould and Jim Fisk who had created the bull market in gold. But the quarry had flown to the safety of the Opera House office building, where thick marble walls and their personal police force were strong enough to protect them. Playing the market was indeed a dangerous game in the 1860s.

The day after the failure of the market, Jay Gould's old partner, Henry N. Smith, encountered the financier in the street and, according to author Trumbull White in *The Wizard of Wall Street,* Smith shook his finger in Gould's face.

"I'll live to see the day, sir," Smith shouted, "when you have to earn a living by going around this street with a hand organ and a monkey."

"Maybe you will, Henry, maybe you will," Jay Gould said soothingly—it was axiomatic in Wall Street that he never lost his temper. "And when I want a monkey, Henry, I'll send for you."

In the end, it was said that Jim Fisk did not lose nearly so much as he feared because he simply refused to honor his contracts to buy gold at 160, and two of the tame judges the Erie had purchased issued injunctions which prevented the sellers from collecting. And as for Jay Gould, they say he made $11,000,000 in the Gold Room in the bull market and the bear market. Herein was the essence of Jay Gould's success in American business—he could adapt himself so quickly to changing circumstances that he could turn a profit even when his plan was wrecked. Also, Gould always expected that at some point he might be forestalled by government interference, and he planned for it.

9

The Mephistopheles of Wall Street

———◆◆◆———

*So the young businessman had created a
legend. The day of the Gold Raid, September 24, 1869, was called Black Friday,
and it lived on in infamy. But the young
businessman felt ill used, too. He testified before Congress that his sale of gold
long before the government came on the
scene caused the break in the market. But
he really knew it was a question of confidence, and that his sale would not affect the price as much as the government's
tardy announcement that it would guar-
antee an orderly market. He had made
enemies of the press and the businessmen
of Wall Street. How could he possibly
fare well in the future?*

———◆◆◆———

FOR another quarter of a century, Jay Gould remained in business
in New York and in railroads, and what he did in business has
been largely misrepresented, either glorified in its results or calum-

niated in its effects on the public weal. Jay Gould was a "business-man," a very shrewd one to be sure, and he operated in the business field just as many others did. If he enjoyed the reputation for brilliance that he secured in the Erie deal, he certainly did not enjoy the reputation for cold-heartedness that followed the Black Friday affair. Neither reputation was totally deserved. In his study of Gould, Julius Grodinsky reached this conclusion:

> Gould was, and still remains, a business type. He had his virtues and he had his faults. His defects have been exaggerated beyond their true significance. Gould possessed a coldblooded unscrupulousness which enabled him to take full advantage of the primitive nature of the art of corporate finance and the status of corporate law, and to adapt to his purposes the low state of political morals prevailing at the time.

As to his personal morality, Jay Gould was accused of ruining Jim Fisk, or very nearly so. Yet after Fisk was shot by Edward Stokes on the staircase of the Grand Central Hotel, and as he lay dying of his wounds, Jay Gould came to visit him. He turned into the corner to sob visibly and audibly, even though Fisk was not really a friend of his. Jay Gould came to the widow's rescue too. Had it not been for Gould alone, she said, she might have been in serious trouble. The hard-hearted financier did have his soft spots.

The story of Jay Gould, businessman, has been told so thoroughly by Grodinsky, and the story of Jay Gould's adventures has been told with such verve by Richard O'Connor in *Gould's Millions,* that it would be little more than repetitious to go into the manner in which Jay Gould made his money. He made it with nearly everything he touched. There were occasional setbacks, largely in wild speculations, but where Gould took a property, examined it, invested in it heavily, and worked on it, he managed to milk the property successfully, although many times he also built it up. That was simply the fashion of the day.

Gould remained in control of Erie until 1872 when a stockholders' uprising forced him out of the presidency. He had thrown $53,000,000 in new stock issues into the market in the first year and a half of his control and although some of this money (estimated at 10 per cent) was used for building the road, still the vast majority of the money went into Gould's bank account. The stock paid no dividends, although the road was supposed to be profitable, and the profits seemed to be relegated entirely to the benefits of management.

After Jay Gould fell out with his old brokerage partner, Smith, the latter brought evidence to the Erie's new management that Gould had transferred $3,000,000 from Erie to his own account by fiat. Then the legal fireworks really began. Gould was arrested and freed only when he produced bond for *a million dollars*. He settled with the stockholders for a chunk of real estate which he said was worth $6,000,000 but which a stockholders' committee later valued at only $200,000. By that time, however, the agreement to settle had been reached and the criminal and civil suits against Jay Gould had been withdrawn.

Such was Gould's life. Almost continually between 1860 and his death, the cycle of control, milking, and suit was repeated in the Union Pacific and the Western Railroads. In these early Erie days, Gould and Fisk had employed a gang leader named Tommy Lynch, who headed up an organization of tough young men who had grown up in Hell's Kitchen. Ever after the Gold Corner affair, Jay Gould kept guards at easy call, and scarcely a week went by when he was not threatened with death or bodily harm by someone who fancied that Gould had done him wrong, or could prove it, or simply hated bloated capitalists. Who would not keep guards?

Gould remained vitally and primarily interested in railroads. There was a certain massive dignity to having been forced out of the Erie at the age of thirty-six, and Gould might have retired then with a fortune of perhaps $30,000,000, but he felt too young to retire. Not a petty gambler, Gould was not interested in anything less than the great gamble: the lure of staking his millions on his brains in business ventures.

His next venture was the Pacific Mail Steamship Company,

Wall Street, 1864. (Museum of the City of New York)

*Jay Gould and his friend
Edward Burhans, about
1855. (Lyndhurst, copy
photo by J. Halpin)*

Helen Miller, shortly be-
fore her marriage to Jay
Gould. (Lyndhurst)

Jay Gould's library, 579
Fifth Ave. (Wide
World)

Furlough Retreat. (Lynd-
hurst)

The Atalanta. (*courtesy New York Yacht Club*)

Jay Gould in his last years. (Lyndhurst)

LEFT: *The greenhouse during Gould ownership.* (*Lyndhurst*) BELOW: *Lyndhurst and grounds, showing the greenhouse.* (*Lyndhurst*)

Jay Gould's children. (Lyndhurst, copy photos by J. Halpin) TOP LEFT: *Helen and Anna.* ABOVE: *Howard and Helen.* LEFT: *Frank in 1889.*

Helen, Edwin, Howard, and Frank with (seated) a friend and a cousin.

George, Howard, Helen, Anna, and Edwin, about 1877. (Lyndhurst)

ABOVE LEFT: *George Gould, about 1884. (Lyndhurst, copy photo by J. Halpin)* ABOVE RIGHT: *Edith Kingdon, about 1884. (Lyndhurst, copy photo by J. Halpin)*

George and Edith Kingdon Gould, 1908. (Lyndhurst, copy photo by J. Halpin.)

*Georgian Court, the Mansion.
(courtesy Georgian Court College)*

*Georgian Court, the stables. (photo
by G. J. Gould, courtesy Georgian
Court College)*

*Georgian Court, Casino in-
terior. (courtesy Georgian
Court College)*

ABOVE: *George Gould's children in 1908. Edith, George, Vivien, Marjorie, Jay and Kingdon. (Lyndhurst)* LEFT: *George Gould with his second wife (Guinevere Sinclair), 1923. (Wide World)*

RIGHT: *Edwin Gould with his wife Sarah, about 1892. (Lyndhurst, copy photo by J. Halpin)* BELOW: *Edwin in his Rhinecliff, N.Y. home. (Museum of the City of New York)*

Helen Gould (far right) and companions on a railroad tour, 1912. (Lyndhurst)

FAR RIGHT: *Helen's husband, Finley Shepard. (Wide World)* RIGHT: *The Gould mansion, 579 Fifth Avenue, 1918. (Museum of the City of New York)*

RIGHT: *Howard Gould in Scotland, 1937. (Wide World)* BELOW LEFT: *Odette Tyler, about 1895. (Museum of the City of New York)* BELOW RIGHT: *Howard's first wife, Kathrine Viola Clemmons. (Museum of the City of New York)*

Anna (Gould) de Castellane with her sons Boniface and George.
(Lyndhurst, copy photo by J. Halpin)

ABOVE LEFT: *Frank Gould's third wife, Florence LaCaze, 1934. (Wide World)* ABOVE RIGHT: *Frank Gould in France, about 1934. (Wide World)* LEFT: *Frank's first wife, Helen Kelly. (Lyndhurst)*

Frank's second wife, Edith Kelly. (Wide World)

*Portrait of Mrs. King-
don Gould, the former
Signorina Annunziata
Lucci. (courtesy King-
don Gould, Jr.)*

*Kingdon Gould with his son
Kingdon, Jr., 1935. (Wide
World)*

which had been created to carry passengers from New York to Panama and then from Panama to San Francisco, and had been given a mail franchise by the government as a subsidy. This line had been milked thoroughly by George Law and Commodore Vanderbilt in the 1850s and it seemed hardly worth exploring. Its stock might be worth $40 or $50 in 1872, but it was certainly worth nothing like $100 a share. Yet the stock was selling at just that price that season because the bulls were manipulating the market in Pacific Mail. About the time that Gould was being bedeviled by the Erie stockholders, he watched Pacific Mail being driven down by the market men who turned overnight from bulls to bears and sold short in great quantity; that was what was done when a stock was inflated. Thus the sellers, who did not own any stock, guaranteed the buyers that they would deliver the stock at $100 at some future date. The buyers thought the stock would keep on going up in specified price. The short sellers had ways of producing rumors and letting the world know that they were selling short, which almost invariably dropped the price back. So Pacific Mail was victimized by a raid, and then along came Jay Gould.

But Jay Gould never *joined* on a raid in these later days, and that is what made him different from the general run of Wall Street brokers and other speculators of his day. He *created* raids. Like the other really important Wall Street men, Gould knew that the way to make money out of a company was to control it and then milk it, not try to work from the outside. In this case, Jay Gould bought heavily in stock that had been forced down to half its "value" of a few days earlier. Another financier was also buying heavily, he found, a man named Russell Sage, who had been a wealthy merchant, served a term in Congress, and was already a multimillionaire from his speculations. Sage was twenty years older than Gould, but the two became fast and real friends. The Sages were to be closer to the Goulds than any other people in New York. At this point, Gould and Sage bought heavily enough to become members of the Board of Directors of the Pacific Mail line. Then, from the inside, they manipulated the stock up and down so that they profited and other speculators lost.

To milk the company, Gould first forced out its president, A. B. Stockwell, who had gained fame on Wall Street by running up the fortune of his heiress wife (Elias Howe sewing machines). As soon as Gould was in, Stockwell disappeared from the pages of American finance with a rueful commentary on the Wall Street of 1873.

> When I first came to Wall Street I had $10,000, and the brokers called me "Stockwell." I scooped some profits and it was "Mr. Stockwell." I got to dealing in a thousand shares at a time, and they hailed me as "Captain Stockwell." I went heavily into Pacific Mail, and folks lifted their hats to "Commodore Stockwell."
>
> Then one day Jay Gould came along, smash went Pacific Mail, and I went with it. They did not call me Commodore Stockwell after that. Then it was: "That red-headed son of a bitch from Ohio."

The uptown crowd was heavily bullish on Pacific Mail—the same crowd also known as The Fifth Avenue Hotel Party by the wiseacres of Wall Street, and the crowd being led by that gentlemanly conservative, Leonard Jerome, who was to become known to history as Winston Churchill's grandfather. Jerome was invested in Pacific Mail by many hundreds of thousands of dollars, during the summer of 1873, while Jay Gould was manipulating. Then came the Panic of 1873 and, along with a hundred other companies, Pacific Mail went down the drain. To assuage his pains, Leonard Jerome went abroad that winter, and in the course of his travels he came to the famous Temple of Karnak in Egypt.

"There, Mr. Jerome," said a companion, "are the most remarkable ruins in the world."

"No. Oh, no, don't tell me that," said Leonard Jerome with great feeling. "You ought to have seen Pacific Mail last summer."

But if the Panic of '73 put an end to Jay Gould's game of bulls and bears with Pacific Mail, by this time he really did not care. It is said that Gould took $5,000,000 out of the line (Richard O'Connor confirmed it), and he turned in the days of the Panic to the purchase of large blocks of the stock of the Union Pacific Railroad.

This road had been the vehicle for the most remarkable railroad swindle *ever* worked on the American people and their government. The incorporators of the Union Pacific had also established the *Crédit Mobilier,* a financing organization, through which they drained off capital as profits. They bribed Congressmen, Senators, and the Vice President of the United States, and ruined the financial condition of the railroad. Oddly enough the incorporators of *Crédit Mobilier* have come down through history with their reputations scarcely scratched. They have certainly never been condemned by the public in the manner that Jay Gould has been condemned although their thievery was unmistakable and their corruption odorous. One of the major incorporators was Levi P. Morton, later honored for his machinations in Wall Street by being elected Vice President of the United States. No one curses the memory of Thomas Durant, but he was the instigator of the whole program. So successful were these infamous financiers at their grisly profit-taking that by the time the Panic of 1873 rolled in, little was left of the Union Pacific except for its bare bones.

The Union Pacific's stock went down to $15 a share, and during this period, Jay Gould purchased a controlling interest in the line. One might pause and ask what kind of investment it was—a look at the map indicated that its condition aside, the Union Pacific was the central part of the *single link* between East and West coasts. Obviously it was vital.

"I was always a bull on America," Jay Gould would say later— and the investment in Union Pacific at this particular time indicated his peculiar genius for finding depressed property that had basic intrinsic value far beyond the dreams of the avaricious Wall Street speculators, and then working this discarded property. True, Jay Cooke and his successors were pushing the Northern Pacific, but even when complete, that road would not seriously affect the profits of the Union Pacific line, nor would lines that might be built through the South and Southwest.

So Jay Gould went into Union Pacific. The stock was soon back up to $75 dollars a share, and Gould had recouped his investment and now controlled another railroad which could be milked. Soon Gould owned 200,000 shares of Union Pacific and his own man, Sidney Dillon, was president of the company.

Keeping control of what was left of Pacific Mail, and taking control of Union Pacific, Jay Gould ran up western freight rates. The railroad began making profits so high that in 1874, Congress felt impelled to legislate a stop to rate discrimination against western shippers and receivers.

Jay Gould also set out to control the competing Kansas Pacific line which drained much of the same territory as the Union Pacific and threatened his road from the south. This line ran from Kansas City to Denver, with a spur line to Cheyenne. The Union Pacific ran from Ogden, Utah, to Cheyenne, to Omaha. Shippers might use the Kansas Pacific as far as Kansas City, and then take another road east, rather than use the Union Pacific to Omaha. Guarding against this circumvention occasioned Gould's original interest in the Kansas Pacific. But, also, Gould could buy up the Kansas Pacific cheap—or so he thought until he ran into another Wall Streeter who owned a big chunk of it, Henry Villard. Gould fought Villard for several years, the latter representing the interests of the original Kansas Pacific investors. During those years, the Jay Gould juggernaut slowed considerably.

Gould's attempt to move to the West Coast began in 1873. Four years later, Jay Gould was well on his way to outright ownership of the Union Pacific Railroad. He was speculating idly in other matters, usually on a dip-in–dip-out basis, but he was making a career at that time of the Union Pacific, gaining more capital investment in it. In 1873, Gould bought 10 million dollars worth of the stock, had it bound in a book, and put it in a safe at home.

Home then was one of a succession of houses on or near Fifth

Avenue, New York City's street of millionaires. Jay Gould's houses were not particularly impressive showplaces, because Jay Gould was not spreading himself, but they had to be ever larger for his growing family. George and Edwin had become big boys. Their sister Helen was born in 1870, Howard in 1871, Anna in 1875, and the last child, Frank, in 1877.

The year of Frank's birth was a year of decision for Jay Gould in many matters. In that year, he decided to use the Kansas Pacific to create another transcontinental railroad system. He was also dipping his fingers into the Western Union Telegraph Company.

Jay Gould's original interest in Western Union was purely financial. He joined a California miner–millionaire named James R. Keene in a bulls and bears game with the stock of the line. The two were introduced by a Wall Street promoter. He was Major A. A. Selover, a big blond six-foot Californian who had known Keene in the old mining days. Gould and Keene and Selover went into business together to wreck a little bit, and come out with pocketsful of money. But the trouble with dealing with Jay Gould in any given enterprise was that no one ever knew what other schemes he might have in mind at the moment. It was conceivable for Gould to be playing both bears and bulls with a given stock at a given time—and making money at it, simply because he could take a short-term profit by "bearing," and achieve long-term control by "bulling." He avoided losses in the current market by simply holding on to the stock—since he knew he would eventually control it and run the price back up. Thinking like this was beyond most Wall Streeters whose interests were transient, but it was a key to Gould's success.

Something of the above sort went on with the stock of Western Union and Atlantic and Pacific Telegraph, a competing firm, when Gould and Keene were involved in the bear raid, and somehow Keene and Selover discovered that they were "doublecrossed" by Jay Gould, who was playing both bull and bear. Gould and Keene met in Russell Sage's office. Keene brandished a pistol in Gould's face before Sage could calm him down. Gould left the office, annoyed. Although by this time he was usually guarded, he was alone.

Heading out of Sage's office, Gould walked toward Broadway. His small, slight figure was unnoticed by passersby—he looked like no one so much as the clerk next door. He turned into Exchange Place and made his way toward Beldon & Co., his brokerage house, at 80 Broadway. Not far from the entrance to 65 Exchange Place, Gould was accosted by Major Selover, a very big and angry man, shaking with rage at the manner in which he said Gould had led Keene and himself on in the telegraph stock deal. Gould and Selover exchanged words, and Selover suddenly struck Jay Gould in the face. Before Gould could recover, Selover seized him and dumped him off the sidewalk into an areaway in front of a barber's shop seven feet below the surface, then walked off.

Gould picked himself up and, with the assistance of a passerby, made his way into the Belden office around the corner. Unhurt, in a few moments he was transacting business as usual.

It caused a sensation next day in the press. Selover had given every newspaper the story.

"I attacked him on my own account alone," said Selover virtuously, "and regardless of the fact that he had played Jim Keene the same trick. He is notoriously treacherous, and this is not the first time he has been punished for the same offense."

Gould said nothing. The papers did not defend him. Most of the newspapers disliked Gould because he never gave them a "break," and so the attack was publicly called a display of "moral courage," in spite of the great disparity in the sizes of the two men.

Jay Gould still said nothing. (From that point on, however, he was seldom seen without G. P. Morosini, his confidential clerk, a big man who also became his personal bodyguard.) Selover never again prospered and eventually drifted away.

Black Friday, Erie, the Pacific Mail, the Union Pacific— together they identified Jay Gould to the public as the trickiest of all the tricksters in Wall Street. Soon it was said that Gould was the most unpopular man in the United States. Quite possibly it was true.

True or false, how did Gould react? Here is one of his rare statements to the press:

> I never notice what is said about me. I am credited for things I have never done, and abused for them. It would be idle to attempt to contradict newspaper talk and street rumors. As to enemies, any man in my position is likely to have them. With me the bitterest enemies have always proved to be men to whom I had rendered services. As a general thing, I do my best to be on good terms with everybody I come in contact with. I am not of a quarrelsome disposition. But, on the other hand, I have the disadvantage of not being sociable. Wall Street men are fond of company and sport. A man makes $100,000 there and immediately buys a yacht, begins to drive fast horses, and becomes a sport generally. My tastes lie in a different direction. When business hours are over I go home and spend the remainder of the day with my wife, my children and books of my library. Every man has natural inclinations of his own. Mine are domestic. They are not calculated to make me particularly popular on Wall Street, and I cannot help that.

Morosini, Gould's factotum, illustrated how the rumors went and how Gould reacted to them in his description of some transactions in Pacific Mail, with which Gould liked to speculate even after '73.

One time Gould was selling short on Pacific Mail over a period, and he bought and sold for some weeks until the commissions paid to brokers amounted to $36,000. Then he tired of it and went out of the market. When he asked that the account be brought up to date, he discovered that he had earned precisely $.14 net profit in all these weeks of speculation.

Meanwhile, a rumor swept the street that Gould had made a fortune on Pacific Mail in his maneuverings, and one afternoon when Gould was at home in his library, William Henry Vanderbilt, who had come by on some other business, mentioned something about the fortune that Gould had just made in Pacific Mail.

Jay Gould looked up from his book. He turned to Morosini.

"Morosini," he said, "how much have we made on that deal in Pacific Mail?"

"$140,000," said Morosini.

"What?" Jay Gould said, leaning forward in his chair with a startled look.

Morosini looked back, blandly. Gould, who never wore his heart on his sleeve, said no more.

After Vanderbilt had left, Gould turned to Morosini.

"Why did you say we had made $140,000?"

"Did we want to disgrace ourselves by saying fourteen cents?" Morosini said, in a plaintive voice.

Jay Gould laughed.

Gould never bothered to correct this wrong impression. Neither did he discuss his home life. Few people knew that Jay Gould's personal interests were catholic and surprisingly intellectual. He began in these years to assemble a library which would eventually be catalogued in a book of some 250 pages—thousands and thousands of volumes. It was not a "collector's" library either, but that of a reader, one devoted largely to books meant to be read, on economics, politics, geography, travel. In it were such disparate items as a study of the geography of "Hindoostan," and a five-volume study of nymphomania.

Gould read everything and anything. Most remarkable about the library was the *absence* of huge leather-bound, presentation sets of popular authors, books which rested, pages uncut, in the libraries of Jay's contemporaries such as William Henry Vanderbilt. Gould did not have much education, but reading was his relaxation, his escape from the workaday world, and he seized on books the way other men seized the ratlines of their yachts.

His personal unpopularity was undeniable. For one thing, he never said anything he did not mean, and usually said nothing at all to the public. For another, he did lead fellow businessmen on to destruction. But if, as was sometimes said of Jay Gould by his contemporaries in Wall Street, he could not be trusted, why did so many of them continue to go along with him for so many years?

In 1877, when the railroad workers of the nation began to strike, Jay Gould gave force to the utterance of William Henry Vanderbilt whose "the public be damned" is a matter of history. The railroads cut pay, the strikers struck, they began to destroy railroad property, and yet Gould, seeing the signs of the times, rescinded the pay cut on his railroads. For this action he was damned by the workers for not paying enough and damned by the owners for breaking the employer front. As usual, Jay Gould went on playing his own game.

Part of Jay's problem with the world was illustrated during this strike, at a point when he and other millionaire railroad owners went out on the Hudson aboard one of the gentlemen's yachts for a conference that could be both relaxing and private. They came back to the west side pier at Twenty-third Street and went ashore in small boats, two or three millionaires at a time.

Jay happened to be riding into the dock with Chauncey Depew, the lawyer who had been brought down from Albany years before by Commodore Vanderbilt to be chief operating officer of the New York Central System.

There was considerable contrast between the two men, including nearly a foot in height. Depew was big and open-faced with no more than sideburns to hide his expression. Jay secreted himself behind his black face-muff, and nobody could tell precisely what was going on in there—with the possible exception of Mrs. Gould.

As the gig moved inshore, down came the reporters to the stair, quick and hungry as a flock of vultures. Their editors were pressing for news, news meant stories, and they meant to have a story out of this boatload of millionaires.

"Any news, Mr. Depew?" asked one of the hawks.

Depew smiled broadly as he grasped the rail and hoisted himself onto the stair. He reached into his breast pocket.

"Not a thing, boy. Here, have a cigar."

And the president of the New York Central clapped the reporter on the back and began handing out cigars all around.

"Come and see me at the office," he said. "I'll see if we can't dig up a story for you."

In a moment, he was through the crowd and striding jauntily toward Grand Central Station.

Behind, the reporters clustered about the tiny figure in the baggy pants and stovepipe hat who climbed out of the boat next.

"What happened out there, Mr. Gould?" one said.

Jay said nothing.

"Come on, Mr. Gould. We've got to have a story for our editors. Tell us something."

Impassively, Jay Gould brushed his way through the crowd and headed for the office on Broadway.

Two years after this strike, Jay Gould settled with the Kansas Pacific bond holders and secured undisputed control of that railroad, and that same year, he began buying up control of other lines in this region that could be as troublesome to the Union Pacific. He bought the Denver Pacific, the Missouri Pacific, and the Texas and Pacific. Now why was he buying? He could have been protecting his interest in Union Pacific by keeping away possible competition. He could have been planning to wreck Union Pacific by establishing these lines and then using their strength to pull bear raids in the market. He did frequently pull such raids, but was possession the cause of the raids or a sideline? That question only Gould could answer, although the world concluded that he wrecked for the sake of wrecking. Actually, he was working to create his own transcontinental railroad.

Jay Gould was in the habit, in these years, of taking long trips across the country to look over his railroads. He would board his private car, the *Convoy* (later the *Atalanta*), and it would be attached to a locomotive, a coal car, and a baggage car. This special train would cross the countryside travelling at top speed while Gould looked out the window and dictated to a male secretary. Gould went everywhere, observing the growth of the West. He decided to cast his lot with western railroads, and began the purchase of the roads mentioned.

It was not an easy job to put together a system paralleling the Union Pacific. The maneuver involved a trip to Europe because the Denver Pacific had fallen into the hands of Dutch investors. Gould went to Amsterdam and bought 2 million dollars worth of Denver Pacific bonds at $.74 on the dollar. But then he was held up by C. K. Garrison and the owners of the Missouri Pacific which ran from St. Louis to Kansas City and paid a huge premium for stock in a railroad that was worth very little at the time. Finally, he had his line, which ran from St. Louis to Kansas City, then to Denver, and up to Cheyenne, plus two branch railroads, the Kansas Central and the Central Branch, which drained the rich stock and grain country of Kansas.

Wrecker or prophet? Could Jay Gould have seen the need for a road to drain the Colorado plateau and serve the Southwest? Or did he simply want to use the line as he did that year: to present to his Union Pacific fellow directors a proposition to buy the Kansas Pacific system on an even exchange, when the former was earning 6 per cent and the latter was earning nothing? The directors scoffed, but when Gould threatened to extend the Missouri Pacific–Kansas Pacific system west to meet the Central Pacific and reach the coast, they capitulated, and Gould ended up making more millions—at least $40,000,000, according to biographer O'Connor. Dastard or brilliant businessman? It depends on the point of view.

This period in which Jay Gould took over the Missouri Pacific and made it a vital part of the Gould empire was a busy time. He was also beginning in 1877 to move in on Western Union, the telegraph system whose lines ran conveniently alongside the railroad tracks in most places. The important figures in Western Union were William Henry Vanderbilt and William Astor, whose families had long since declared war on the Goulds in business and social affairs. An Astor, a Vanderbilt, or one of their friends had undoubtedly blackballed Jay Gould at the New York Yacht Club when his name was put up for membership. They knew not what they did, perhaps. For Gould would never again attempt to gain admission to that club, and he would never give quarter to men who had embarrassed him. He was a quiet man but the best hater on Wall Street.

IO

The Devil at Play

———◆•◆•◆———

The young businessman was young no longer. His gentle wife had found her entire life disrupted and changed by her marriage to this volcanic man of action. This gentle but iron-willed man never raised his voice in the house, but somehow continued to be the most hated man in New York. His wife's girlhood friends fell away as their husbands became fearful or disenchanted, and she was snubbed in her simple attempts to continue the place of her family in the social world. The lady retreated within the household and became virtually a recluse. This was her private tragedy, the inability of great fortune to bring popularity and contentment.

———◆•◆•◆———

PERHAPS it was natural that Wall Street needed one villain on whom to blame all the ills of the business community. If so, Jay Gould, with his secretive nature, his black beard, and his air of mystery, was born to the part. The leaders of New York society let it be known that his forbears were Jews (which happened not to be true) while concealing or failing to discover that Gould came from a family in which one line claimed passage on the Mayflower and all lines went back to the early days of American colonization.

Jay was not particularly interested in parties or high life. He did not drink. He did not smoke. He did not sail small boats or shoot billiards. His passions were moneymaking, reading, walking, and the enjoyment of nature. As a boy he had spent his days out of doors, as a youth he had trundled his surveyor's odometer across fields and through woods, and as a man he liked to walk. Strolling released Jay Gould's nervous energy and made humdrum life bearable. He asked very little for himself.

But as a husband and father, Jay saw with concern and irritation that his family was snubbed simply for being Goulds. Husband and wife were attractive, the girls of the family pleasant looking, the boys positively handsome. The children were raised by governesses and well-trained servants. Their manners were excellent and they were kind and generous to one another and to outsiders. But they bore the hated name of *Gould*. To compensate, in a way, Jay Gould determined to give his family the finest life that money could buy. Money or not, the children had the father's affection and the mother's complete attention, and the family was happy. Jay was a fair, considerate man at home. Every night at dinner the children recounted their activities. Every night at bedtime they trouped down to the library to kiss their father goodnight before going off to bed.

Near the turn of the decade that began the Eighties, Jay considered the happiness of his children in relation to the outside world (George was in his teens) and decided then to expand the young Goulds' horizons. The family was living on Fifth Avenue, on the west side of the street, between Forty-seventh and Forty-eighth Streets. Jay purchased a larger house at the northeast corner of

Forty-seventh Street and Fifth Avenue—579 Fifth. No expense was spared on decorators or furnishings to create a handsome Victorian home.

Mother and children customarily escaped the humid atmosphere and heat of New York in the summer by going upstate or to some resort, and after trying many places, in the summer of 1878, Jay had settled on a rented estate, Lyndhurst, located at Irvington-on-Hudson. A New York merchant named George Merritt had bought it from the Paulding family, for which the house was built by Alexander J. Davis, beginning in 1838. In the Gothic revival style, the house was called Paulding's Folly after General William Paulding, one-time mayor of New York, who had asked the architect to build him a country seat. The architect, given unbounded latitude, had let his fancy wander, and the result was a cruciform house of Sing Sing marble, with huge entrance porch, central hallway, large drawing room on the left, and dining room on the right. From the outside it was a swallow's paradise, with its turrets, bays, buttresses, trefoils, filials, traceries of stone, and crenellated roofs. The windows were filled with diamond-lighted sash and edged with bits of colored glass. Inside, the house was dark as sin, but it contained all the billiard parlors, guest rooms, and luxurious living space a gentleman's family might require.

When George Merritt bought the estate in 1865, he had added his own mark, again using architect Davis. With increased gusto, Davis improved on his Gothic creation—the house looked so much like a medieval castle that at least one writer described it as "the culmination of the Gothic Revival, a glorious crescendo and finale, though basically *retardataire.*" *

To finish his Gothic masterpiece, Davis added a wing to the north, a dozen rooms, and a huge tower, making Lyndhurst a real river castle as seen from the Hudson River. He added to the new

---

* *Historic Preservation, The Magazine of the National Trust for Historic Preservation,* March–April, 1965, pp. 50.

wing more vaulted ceilings and the *trompe l'oeil* technique, matching wood and marble, even indicating third dimensions where none existed. Davis also designed some of the furniture, made of ornate, carved, heavy wood.

After he began living in the house, Merritt had added a carriage entrance, had drained the swamp below the house, and had laid out 20 acres in lawns, an acre and a half for a grape arbor, stables, sheds, and a huge greenhouse topped by a Saracenic cupola. (It was, in fact, the largest private greenhouse in the world.) Off to one side of the greenhouse lay the billiard room, gymnasium, and bowling alley.

So the Gould family came to their own palace on the quiet reaches of the Hudson, far from the irritations of Wall Street and the snubs of Fifth Avenue. Here the children were princes and princesses of a woodland kingdom. From here in summer, Jay rode William Henry Vanderbilt's Hudson River division of the New York Central into New York to work. Here in Lyndhurst, Gould spent happy hours pottering in the greenhouse, raising camellias, ferns, rubber plants, and especially orchids, which he came to fancy. After two summers of renting, Jay and the family became so fond of the estate that he bought it for a quarter of a million dollars. In came a new army of decorators and workmen to do the Goulds' bidding, but most of the furnishings, the collection of sculpture, and above all, the books of the Merritts were kept. Jay hired Ferdinand Mangold, the Merritt gardener, put him to work in the orchid rooms, and gave him his head. Before autumn, Mangold had developed the finest palm garden in the Western hemisphere, with two hundred and fifty varieties of palms, ranging in cost from $20 to $500, brought from Africa, Samoa, South America, Hawaii, and India. Soon Jay Gould was wandering happily through his garden, mumbling about *Viridifolium, Hyophorbe Americanlis,* and *Plectocomica Assamica* with the sure knowledge of a collector.

Every morning after breakfast Jay would go to the greenhouse. After a day in the city, Gould returned to spend another hour in the long summer evenings strolling through the conservatory, with his family or alone. In one room, he kept nothing but roses: pink, white, burgundy, speckled, yellow; Guelders, Austrians, and dozens of other varieties in a tangle of color. Other flowers had their own rooms. Soon the orchids came to number nearly 8,000 plants in one hundred and fifty varieties. In one room were 2,000 azaleas. A special fernery held six hundred varieties of ferns in pots and huge bins. Merritt had spent perhaps $1,250,000 to improve the place; now Gould undertook the expenditure of another $1,500,000 to finish the job. He added to the land until he had 500 acres, woodland, farm, and lawns. In the barns, he kept fifty cows, twenty-five horses, a span of oxen, three bulls, and over a thousand chickens, ducks, pigeons, and even deer. He filled in 120 acres of swampland to eliminate malaria. His farmhands raised 250 tons of hay on the place, while the greenhouse men, some twenty of them, were also responsible for the truck garden that supplied vegetables in the summertime.

The barns also housed some fifteen different types of carriages, so many that some of them were not used once a year. The vehicles were the result of an early Gould enthusiasm, one like the art collection, and both of which predated the interest in the gardens and flower growing. The art collection was scattered throughout the big house, but with special emphasis on the second floor gallery which opened off Jay Gould's master bedroom. Earlier this room had been the billiard parlor and upstairs reception room, but Gould made it into his gallery. Here hung more than thirty paintings, some of them, by the more professional general standards of the twentieth century, remarkably good ones—certainly they represented a more cultivated taste than that of Vanderbilts or Astors, who sniffed so audibly at the mention of the name Gould. There were Courbets, Daubignys, Bouguereaus, Baugniets, Casanovas, Duprés, Rousseaus, and one Corot.* (Another group of paintings hung in the house on Fifth Avenue, including a Rosa Bonheur which Gould had bought from the estate of the ruined James

* The Corot was later valued at $80,000.

Keene.) The house was loaded with works of art of the period, paintings and much statuary, including fierce Berbers, languid Roman maidens, and lifesize Greek goddesses in marble.

The big stone house with its gently sloping hills and dales and the froth of greenery captured the heart of this strange, lonely man, and he made 935 Broadway—that was its unpretentious address—the real home of the Gould family. A house in New York City was necessary, but every hour that could be snatched was spent at Lyndhurst. Gould's only other social interest was the opera, and during the season he was often seen in the family box.

But above all these pleasures, Jay Gould's overwhelming interest remained making money.

In the 1870s, Gould had hired away from Western Union its most expert technicians and had cagily persuaded Thomas Alva Edison, inventor of a high-speed telegraphic sending process, that Gould could and would pay more money for patents than the Vanderbilts and their allies in Western Union. Edison and others had come over to Gould's rival Atlantic & Pacific Telegraph Company. Immediately, Western Union filed a suit against Gould for patent-right violation. But suits took time, and Gould had what he wanted. With his new strength, he quickly swallowed up the Franklin Telegraph Company and sold out to Western Union for just under a million dollars plus 12½ per cent of Western Union's stock. Gould asked to be put on the board of Western Union, Vanderbilt refused, and Gould started still another telegraph company, called American Union. In a year, the company built 50,000 miles of wire and acquired 2,000 branch offices.

At about this time Gould entered a venture in journalism. He had acquired the New York *World* when he bought the Texas and Pacific Railroad from Thomas Scott. He always said he did not particularly want the newspaper, that it was more or less forced on him as part of the deal for the railroad he did want, but once he had it, Gould used the *World* with his usual thoroughness for his own purposes. He was later to sell the *World* to St. Louis

publisher Joseph Pulitzer, but in those years under Gould ownership, the *World* became a key in the Gould fight against Vanderbilt and for control of Western Union. The *World* was instructed
to go after Western Union. The *World* soon called that telegraph
company the "most vicious" of all American monopolies. Along
with the effects of Gould's play of bulls and bears on the market,
the bad publicity began to hurt, and in 1880, Western Union stock
dropped from 113 to under 100.

The reason for the fall in price was good enough: Gould's
competing telegraph line reached the Pacific, and Gould was cutting rates for messages everywhere that he and Western Union
competed. So apparent was it that he was working to force a
merger that legislators in New York State tried to pass a law
prohibiting such a merger in the public interest, but the majority
of legislators in 1880 and 1881 were still welcoming bribes, and
Gould had no trouble in preventing the passage of the law.

In all this maneuvering, Gould was playing the business game
as a master plays chess, using one piece to back up another. He
had the *World* and it trumpeted loudly against the "monopoly" he
hated for the moment. He gave the *World* a louder voice by
buying new office space and modern presses, thus improving its
efficiency, and its income. He also used the Union Pacific Railroad
to force the removal of the Western Union wires and change over
to American Union. Knowing that word of these activities would
soon reach Wall Street, Gould sold short once more, selling 30,000
shares of Western Union, which had climbed back to 106. On
receipt of the word of the changeover, Western Union began to
fall. When it hit 88, Jay Gould picked up 30,000 shares of stock on
the market and delivered it to those who had agreed to buy from
him at the price of 106. He made $840,000 on this transaction
alone!

Western Union continued to lie dormant. Then one day in
January, 1881, William Henry Vanderbilt summoned Jay Gould to
his house, and they sat down to talk in the library of Vanderbilt's
sumptuous mansion at the corner of Fifty-first Street and Fifth

Avenue. When the word got out that the two giants had met, Western Union jumped—first to 103½ and then to 114½ a day later.

The result of these meetings was merger, an increase in capitalization from $41,000,000 to $80,000,000, and declaration of, stock dividend of 38.5 per cent, or more than $15,000,000. Naturally it was discovered that Gould held a heavy interest in the company, and soon Jay Gould, his friend Russell Sage, his friend and employee Sidney Dillon, and his employee Thomas Eckert were on the Board of Directors. General Eckert became the vice president, general manager, and chief operating officer. In a few months, Jay Gould *owned* control of the company. Realizing that in Western Union he held a major communications monopoly worth an emperor's fortune, he made it his parent company and moved his offices to the Western Union building at 195 Broadway.

Gould was to make one more grand coup—in New York elevated railroads. Along with Russell Sage and another friend, Cyrus W. Field, he was going for control of the Manhattan Railway Company, using the *World* first to trumpet the wrongs done the public by the railroads, which, indeed, were badly run. Field and Gould fell out, but Gould and Sage did not. The story of earlier bull and bear raids repeated itself, Field was ruined and saved from outright failure only by Gould's intervention as one of his rare gestures of public relations. Field retired to eke out his existence, having tried to brave the Wolf of Wall Street, and Gould retired, or very nearly that, with more money than ever.

Retired is almost the word. It might not seem so if one consults the Wall Street references to Gould in the years after 1882, but compared to his earlier forays, his later work simply consolidated his gains of the early years. By the time Jay Gould was 45 years old, he was slowing down perceptibly.

Gould's lungs had never recuperated from earlier illnesses. (In later years he used to say that there had been so many holes in the roof of the house at Roxbury above his loft room that he spent every winter sleeping in the rain.) Whatever the reason, in middle age Jay Gould contracted tuberculosis. Had he been willing to give up all business activity and travel west to the mountains, he might have been cured. Had he been willing to quit and enjoy himself in the hothouse at Lyndhurst, there could have been hope. But Jay Gould would not quit, would not give up his business activity. He could only be persuaded to slow down a bit.

The first sign of this change came in 1881 when Jay Gould commissioned the building of the most modern steam yacht in America. Cost, as usual with Gould in these years, was not a consideration. The contract was let in October, and the eminently respectable firm of William Cramp and Sons in Philadelphia won it. They were ordered to build an iron steam yacht with every luxury and every modern wrinkle, suitable for royalty.

So she was built on the banks of the Delaware. The builders laid her out big and strong: from knightshead to taffrail she was 230 feet 3 inches long, on deck, she was 225 feet long, with a beam of 26 feet 4 inches, and she drew 13 feet of water.

The yacht's upper deck was flush—that is to say it was unbroken except for the masts and a deck house 80 feet long in which were located the steam capstan that raised the anchors, the companionways that led below, the skylights that lit up the living quarters, the galley (so odors would blow away), an upper saloon and lounge for passengers, a wheel house in the front of the deck house, and an office for the captain in the back.

The yacht carried boats as large as some other yachts: the launch was a six-oared cutter 32 feet long, hung from davits on the starboard side. Immediately behind this boat was located the whale boat, 38 feet long, of United States pattern carrying five oars. This latter boat was the one to be used by the owner as a gig, or small boat for landing and visiting other ships. To port, forward of the mainmast hung the 32-foot steam launch, and behind her, an 18-foot dinghy which was the crew's work boat. The steam launch, the builders said, actually cost as much as did some of the other yachts they built.

In shape and function, the ship was a steam-powered three-

masted schooner with standing gaffs and lug sails, plus a square
sail yard on the foremast, a short bowsprit, and a jib boom. Her
decks and skin were made of half-inch iron plating, and her two
boilers, the Cramps said, could turn her propeller at 100 revolu-
tions per minute. She was going to be a fast craft.

She was also safe. Below, the yacht was divided into seven
watertight compartments, and the engine room was carefully cut
off from all others so that even if she struck some submerged
object (icebergs were much in the public mind just then), she
would not sink, nor would her power plant be affected by striking
at bow or stern. She had plenty of stowage room below, huge
fresh-water tanks, and a condensing unit to make her own water.
She had an ice room and an ice machine so she could carry fresh
provisions for a long voyage. She could carry 170 tons of coal.

Altogether she was a sound ship, built for strength and power.
She even boasted a basic system using the new Edison patent
electric lights, and nothing was more modern than that system
afloat or ashore.

The yacht, over a year in the building, was launched on April
7, 1883. Jay Gould's employees ordered up a special train from
Jersey City, and the financier and his crowd boarded the cars at ten
o'clock in the morning. The crowd included Mrs. Gould, George,
Edwin, Howard, Frank, Helen, and Anna, for this was a major
family event. Jay Gould might be unacceptable to the New York
Yacht Club, but that did not prevent Commodore J. D. Smith of
the club and others from coming down to see the new yacht.
Gould had grandly issued invitations to General Grant, then in
business in Wall Street, and to President Porfirio Diaz, the dictator
of Mexico, who was visiting the United States, but neither of them
could make the trip. Still, the party aboard the private car *Convoy*
was eager, excited, and dressed in their best—Gould in tophat,
frock coat, and baggy trousers as was his style, the others dressed
more modishly, the ladies with parasols and hoop skirts and lace
showing handsomely. *Convoy* was hitched to a Pullman palace car
carrying railroad officials, Wall Street acquaintances, and lesser

dignitaries whom Jay Gould wished to honor but could not accommodate in his private car. All cars were hitched to the Pennsylvania Railroad's engine No. 274. With a blast of the whistle, the train set out at ten o'clock sharp. The track was clear, and the engineer had his orders—to make a speed run to show Jay Gould how the Pennsy could operate.

In one hour and fifty minutes—exactly—they arrived dockside where the yacht was sitting in the ways, alongside the steamer *Alameda* which was being built to carry the mails to New Zealand. The Gould party was met, as befitted the most powerful man in Wall Street, by Mayor Samuel King of Philadelphia, a handful of generals and admirals, the Superintendent of the United States Mint, the president and most of the vice presidents of the Pennsy, and assorted others, all in stovepipe hats and stiff collars. And 5,000 assorted Philadelphians had come out to see the fun and enjoy the bunting and the breezes.

The *Alameda* was on hand to serve as the viewing stand for the guests and spectators. First there was lunch aboard the *Alameda*. A stand had been run up alongside the yacht, and Gould, Commodore Smith, and daughter Helen (Nellie to the crowds) stepped down to this point, where Helen firmly grasped a bottle of champagne suspended by a cord from the bow of the ship and waited while Commodore Smith said a few words about the lines of the ship. Then, at a signal, fifty workmen on each side of the yacht began hammering at the wedges that held her in the ways. It was one o'clock by the superintendent's silver watch. The hull began to quiver, Helen looked at Commodore Smith, expert in such matters. He nodded, and, with a wild swing, Helen smashed the bottle at the iron prow, struck home, and the champagne bubbled over her arm and down into the water as the whistles and cheers of the crowd rose up behind her.

"I christen thee *Atalanta,*" Helen piped bravely.

"Three cheers for the yacht and her owner Mr. Gould," shouted Commodore Smith, waving his hat.

The yacht rolled down the ways and out into the Delaware,

sending up a froth of her own and wavelets along her sides. The crowd cheered again and again and shouted for a speech from Jay Gould, the owner.

Genially, Jay Gould turned, smiled, and lifted his hat.

"I give you the health of Commodore Smith," he said, bowed, and clapped his hat back on his head. It was as long a speech as he had made in many a year.

Then E. S. Jaffray stepped forward to do the honors. He spoke for several minutes about Gould—"among the greatest benefactors of his age," he said. Jay Gould, the Wolf of Wall Street? The man who was blackballed from the New York Yacht Club? So lauded by the senior captain of steam yachts of the club? The newspapers had record of it, and so did Jay Gould in a special account hand-printed and framed for his house at Lyndhurst.

William Henry Hurlburt of the New York *World* (Jay Gould's tame editor), then spoke in behalf of yachts in general and the new *Atalanta* in particular. Suddenly Gould looked at his watch. It was three o'clock, time to head back to New York in time to put an orderly close to the day at the office before going home to Fifth Avenue.

The party boarded the special train again, while the workmen warped the yacht hull alongside the dock for her fitting out, and the train sped back to New York, 86 miles from the Philadelphia Junction to Jersey City, in 94 minutes. President Thomson of the Pennsy came up with Jay Gould and clocked it himself.

Gould went back to the workaday world for a few weeks while the Cramps finished their job. Since they were not furnishers, they turned over to others the task of doing the regal interior of the yacht. The job was taken by W. W. Smith, the same outfitter who had done *Corsair* for J. Pierpont Morgan. Smith was a cocky little man, having now outfitted the ships of several lions of the street, and he had invented a name for his style: *American Renaissance*. It was only more of the same Victorian splendor that the million-aires had in their palatial mansions, brought to waterside, although splendor perhaps enhanced by Mr. Smith's absolute disregard for money when cultural renaissance was in the wind—and when it was somebody else's money.

For example, the floors of the yacht throughout the passenger decks were covered by parqueted floors of hardwood. But Smith was not content with simply parqueting hardwood floors in oak, or any other material that an ordinary builder would use in rich apartments. No, the decks of the yacht were parqueted in squares of maple, alternating with butternut, cedar, California laurel, and sycamore.

And Jay Gould's cabin, the owner's cabin, as they called it, had to be just *so*. Nine and a half feet by 13½ feet, not very large as such things go, it had an extra alcove 4½ by 7 feet forward into which were stuffed the twin beds. The bulkheads were concealed by mahogany panelling as was the ceiling. The whole deck (parqueted too) was concealed by a wall-to-wall India rug. The decor was fashionably repetitive: drapes, the hangings of the bed, and all the furniture was covered with the same silk gold-and-silver tapestry cloth, woven in a design invented especially for this room and set aside by the clothmaker for no other use than this yacht owner's stateroom.

The cold sweaty bulkheads of iron were all panelled in rare woods. The deckhouse and smoking room forward under the bridge were both panelled in mahogany. Even the armory was panelled. Its complement of cutlasses, rifles, fowling pieces, revolvers, flares, and even two Krupp rapid-firing guns (for real emergencies) was displayed for the most part in locked cases.

Smith quite outdid himself with the main saloon of the *Atalanta,* with its huge dining table for thirty-two people, four sofas, six easy chairs, one dozen side chairs, and leaf carvings everywhere. The most impressive of the carvings was a series of three panels in the middle of one side of the room. The middle panel displayed the Gould monogram (all American millionaires had monograms) surrounded by panels depicting various tropical fruits. There was a player piano and a Tiffany clock. China cases held rarities, each piece locked in place against the weather, and the cases themselves set in gimbals on the deck.

Each of the eight staterooms for passengers was decorated throughout in pink, maroon, green, orange, red, or blue. The toilet sets were made of triplated silver by A. Ledig and Son of Philadelphia. Forward on each side of the main passageway were toilets and baths for general use. The owner had a magnificent sunken bath of his own. In the 1880s plumbing with running water was so rare that neither builders nor decorators thought of a bath for every room—that would have been *de trop*. It was almost *de trop* the way Jay Gould treated his crewmen whose quarters were behind the forward bulkhead. It was said that the fifty-two crewmen, including captain, steward, three cooks, and six waiters, of the *Atalanta* lived as well as the *passengers* of other yachts. Their quarters even had electric lights, more than some millionaires had ashore. (Altogether there were 150 electric lights in the ship's Edison system, making it one of the electrical marvels of the age, with even an electric bell signalling system throughout the ship.)

On June 8, the *Atalanta* was finally pronounced outfitted and Captain John Shackford was ready to take her out for trials. The captain was an old salt; Gould had stolen him away from the American line where Shackford had last been in command of the steamship *Illinois* on the Atlantic run. He knew the Atlantic like the back of his hand and was ready to take the *Atalanta* across.

Such eagerness was unusual only to those who did not understand the pleasure ships and habits of the wealthy. Their yachts were usually constructed strictly for coastal travel. When J. Pierpont Morgan wanted to cross the Atlantic, for example, he did not steam over in *Corsair*. Rather he took a steamship across and the *Corsair* went over seeking the best possible weather, and met him on the other side. On June 8, Captain Shackford and the Cramps were ready to certify that Jay Gould's yacht was as he wanted it. Gould was notified and next day he came down from New York. Shackford took Gould and a small family party down the Delaware and, while the Captain tended to his duties, one of the two mates took the family around the ship to examine the $15,000 in furnishings and the $50,000 in other fittings that had been installed since they were last aboard.

Then they went to Chester where the steamer *Shadyside* lay with steam up. She was just about the size of the yacht—perhaps a touch longer—and it would seem that a race between them ought to be stirring. Like a shot she sped out from her berth, and the smoke pouring out of her stack was all the challenge needed, the blasts from her impudent whistle were quite unnecessary. But it never developed into a race. Captain Shackford telegraphed the engine room of the yacht for full speed, meaning, of course, that the chief engineer was to let her out all he could within reason, and soon *Atalanta* was making 125 rpm and 16 knots. She passed the *Shadyside* as though the steamer's captain had changed his mind, and five minutes later, the steamer was out of sight astern while *Atalanta's* journal boxes were not even hot.

Down river, they reached a point below Newcastle where they hit 17 knots. Then, fully satisfied, Captain Shackford reported to Gould, who was wandering about, fingering this fixture and that one, admiring his grand new ice machine with its half-ton daily capacity (a prototype that had been somehow shanghaied from the Navy), and staring into his sunken bath. Gould was happy and satisfied, and the captain turned the ship around and came back up river under a heavy head of steam, past the *Shadyside* which lay sulking bow in at her berth. At four o'clock that afternoon, the yacht was off the Market Street station. A tug had been laid on to pick up the busy New York businessman and his party. Gould disembarked and took the salute of his fifty-two crewmen standing at attention in uniforms by Wanamaker, blue and white uniforms with gilt buttons ("guaranteed not to tarnish") stamped with a coil of rope around the edge, the name *Atalanta* and an anchor above. The New Yorkers boarded their special train and were home within an hour and a half.

The final test run was held on June 23. A few details were

taken care of: Gould took over the $100,000 insurance policy against fire and was informed that Lloyd's registered his yacht as A No. 1, 20 years, 3-3-3—the highest rating a steam yacht could get. His ship, the broker informed him, was the only private steam yacht in the United States of America so rated. This pleased Gould, as well it should, for she had cost him a quarter of a million dollars, and she would cost him an estimated $30,000 a year to operate, or, as a Gould henchman put it, "more income than nine-tenths of the big presidents of the banks ever dream of possessing." Up to this point, Gould had been genial enough with the press, allowing them access to the launching and the trials (although, of course, not aboard the yacht). Now he wanted the privacy he hoped to have bought with his expenditure. The second son Edwin was the only one of the family who could get away for an overnight trip, so with a few associates and Edwin, the financier set out at four o'clock on the afternoon of June 23 for a brief voyage. Next morning, the ship was seen just outside the Delaware capes by the steamer *British Crown* and the news reported to the press. Then *Atalanta* headed north. When next heard of, she was anchored in the Hudson off Lyndhurst.

The Gould party disembarked with a grand sense of contentment. No more jostling and rushing by carriage to the railroad station. No more hustling through public places. Jay Gould could hereafter commute from office to summer home in style and comfort. Never had the financier been happier than when he could enjoy his beloved Lyndhurst without facing the madding crowd.

The Bankruptcy Scheme

━━◆◆◆◆━━

The world of millionaires is a fairy world which exists mostly in the eyes of the beholders. Long ago, perhaps with the first newspapers, the proprietors of the press learned this fact and began feeding the public on a diet of the doings of the rich—and so the rich became objects of admiration and even hatred, neither of which they entirely deserved. Now that he was rich as Croesus, the middle-aged businessman suddenly discovered all these complications.

━━◆◆◆◆━━

FROM the day of the Selover attack in 1877, when a bruised Jay Gould had been dropped down into the areaway in the financial district to land like a sack of flour on the steps of a basement barber ship, the millionaire had never gone out without a body-guard. He literally maintained an army to protect him, an army of servants and guards who never left his railroad car, Lyndhurst, 579 Fifth Avenue, or the yacht when he or the family were aboard. Continually threatened by anarchists, he was high on their list of those marked for extinction simply because he was rich and powerful. He was threatened by men like Colonel J. Howard Wells, a ruined speculator (not by Gould) who wanted money and market information. The threats caused the Goulds to retreat more and more behind their bars of privacy, and even Helen, Jay's wife, gave up most of her Murray Hill friendships and seldom went out of the family circle. Jay developed insomnia in middle age, and would walk up and down in front of 579 Fifth Avenue on the nights he was in residence, sometimes pacing for hours at a time, always with a pair of bodyguards at his elbow. During the 1880s when in fact the Gould activities were greatly curtailed, he became the most hated man in America, and the most often attacked in the newspapers. In response, he became nervous and worried and that, in turn, affected his health.

It was no more than he deserved, sneered the newspapers. Croesus was reaping his just reward.

"No Bed of Roses For The Cold-Blooded Stock Jobber" said the New York *Times.** The occasion for this editorial sneer was the presence aboard Jay's yacht during a trip to Charleston, S. C., of a private detective along with the whole family. This detective, said the *Times,* was the employee of a New York agency entirely supported by meeting Jay Gould's protection needs. The remainder of the report was an amalgam of fact, speculation, and downright libel, or at least open insult.

> Gould, it is said, began to employ private detectives extensively a half dozen years ago, when by some means he discovered a plot that had been made by dissatisfied spirits on the line of the Wabash Railroad to wreck a special train on which he was preparing to make an inspection trip with Russell Sage. A man who knows Gould well says that his detectives cost him more than all the clerks in his New York offices. He never makes a journey, even the shortest, nowadays, without sending first his scouts on ahead to discover if any obstacles are likely to be encountered. . . .

* January 26, 1886.

In the same story the *Times* writer stated flatly that Gould was afraid to travel over his southern and southwestern lines, that twice within a year he had planned trips and then fearfully abandoned them, that people in the North "who have been startled and angered at his open and notorious purchase of Legislature and courts of justice" were vowing vengeance.

The *Times* story might well have been cause for action under other circumstances, for it even tended to incite: "It isn't idle talk," continued the writer, "to say that the wickedest deed against even the life of Gould would be excused and even justified, by multitudes who see in him only a sordid and cruel taskmaster, hounding armies of men to death for his own gain."

Threats against him never ended, and Gould and his family learned constantly to live with the fear of death. One night at Lyndhurst, for example, the whole family was roused on Jay's orders and brought down to the drawing room for comfort and safety. A prowler had gotten past the gates, and until he was found, none of the family was allowed out of Jay's sight. The life of a multimillionaire was obviously not all champagne and caviar, no matter how large the fortune.

The height of Jay Gould's fortune, on paper at least, was probably reached some time in the boom year of 1881. He then owned huge chunks of stock and bonds worth millions of dollars at face value, most of it in railroads. But, as Richard O'Connor traced the story, in the mid-1880s even Jay Gould was forced to retrench. This period marked the fall of the railroads and the rise of the bankers, such as J. Pierpont Morgan, who were capable of recapitalizing failing roads and restoring the financial viability of the transportation system. Family members indicated that just before the fall in the railroad market, Jay Gould's fortune was worth a billion dollars. Perhaps it was worth a quarter as much. It did not remain that way, but from 1881 to 1884, Jay Gould may well have been the richest man in the United States, as Commodore Vanderbilt had been in 1877. Gould controlled the Missouri Pacific system, the Texas and Pacific, the New York and New England Railroad, the Wabash system, and Manhattan Elevated, and he had huge holdings in Union Pacific and in Western Union.

In the spring of 1884, however, Gould fell on evil times. He was the outright target of a number of bear raids staged by men who simply felt that Gould was or should be vulnerable because of the spread of his holdings. If he could be forced to the wall, they thought, they could enrich themselves in the old-fashioned Wall Street way. It was a case of slickers outslickering the slicker.

In Washington at this time, vast public outcries against the railroads had brought on a series of investigations. Reform was in the air. James G. Blaine was seeking the presidential nomination of 1884, and his enemies were talking about the Crédit Mobilier scandal. In the Democratic party, the name of Grover Cleveland, a Reform mayor of Buffalo, was suddenly heard.

In the United States Senate, as the move for reform brought about investigations of railroads in which Gould held interests, he was forced out of the Union Pacific, at least out of its control. That government attack signalled a stronger Wall Street attack— bear raids. In April and May of 1884, Jay Gould's properties were forced down, down, down in the quotations. The bears were helped by a natural shift—a break in wheat futures based on the announcement of a bumper crop expected in the fall. The whole stock market began to dive, and soon Jay Gould's major companies were down so far that had he been speculator and not investor, he would have been bankrupt. As it was, he held properties such as Missouri Pacific, which at one time was selling at $85 a share. Perhaps he had borrowed heavily on this stock (as he must have borrowed on some), and suddenly the stock was worth $65 a share. At such a point a bank is likely to come forward and demand more security for its loans, and that is precisely what happened to Jay Gould in the spring of 1884.

Gould's enemies in this affair were his old partner Henry N. Smith, his old associate James Keene, and a pair of bears named Addison Cammack and Charles Woerishoffer. Their cabal drove prices further down, concentrating always on the Gould holdings. The panic grew severe on May 13, and banks began to fail. General Grant's brokerage house went down that week. Several of Gould's properties failed. Still, he bought Western Union, in particular, to save it from the bears. They continued to sell faster than he could buy, however, and the price continued to go down.

By the beginning of the last week of May, all eyes in Wall Street were focussed on Jay Gould. The plot was known on the street. Newspapers watched Gould, speculating publicly as to whether or not he could stand up under the strain. (Such speculation alone would be enough to force most men into bankruptcy because, with speculation, they would suddenly find that they had no new credit and their creditors were closing in on them.) In this period, as always, Jay Gould was a lone Wolf of Wall Street. His only possible assistance could come from Russell Sage—and Russell Sage alive was anything but an elemosynary institution.

So the situation worsened daily, until the last Sunday in May.

On that day, the conspirators were known to be sunning themselves at the fashionable resort of Long Branch, New Jersey. There came Jay Gould's yacht the *Atalanta,* and Captain Shackford ordered the anchor dropped in the harbor. Gould then sent ashore one of his assistants in the owner's gig. The man bore a document —the draft of an assignment of property to his family. This meant that Lyndhurst, 579 Fifth Avenue, the yacht, and the unencumbered holdings of Jay Gould would all be turned over to other members of his family. Thus the encumbered holdings would all have to bear the total weight of the Gould misfortunes. He was ready for bankruptcy, but if he took it thus, holding out perhaps a third of the fortune for family, such companies as Western Union would certainly also go bankrupt immediately, and the stock dealers, bears that they might be, would lose outright all that they had guaranteed to sell and would be unable to deliver the stocks. They would therefore be ruined and forced out of Wall Street. Further, if Jay Gould declared bankruptcy in the spring of 1884, his influence in so many corners of Wall Street was such that the panic brought on by Jay Cooke's default in 1873 would be repeated—or so the bears believed.

Gould himself went ashore later in the day in his five-oared gig, conferred with Woerishoffer and his group, and made an agreement with them. He received $2.5 million in much-needed cash against 50,000 shares of Western Union stock. He used this money the next week to bail out Missouri Pacific and to bring Western Union back up to the 80s. In a month, Gould's fortune was again secure, but he had learned something. Earlier, in dealing with Jay Gould, Commodore Vanderbilt had put it in his own forceful if uncouth way. "Never kick a skunk," he had said when Gould and Fisk had engineered the Erie coup. Whatever the ways of saying it, they added up to this: *Once you've made your pile, never speculate.* The point was that men like Woerishoffer had little or nothing to lose—maybe a few millions, as Gould once had himself. But Gould, having acquired Lyndhurst and the yacht, and with a family used to wealth, was no longer a speculator or just a businessman. He had acquired new characteristics, the character of the very rich, and the institution of wealth weighed heavily on him. Too many people depended on him: his wife, six children, dozens of sisters, brothers-in-law, nieces, nephews, and lesser relatives, and, if one counted the employees at 579 Fifth Avenue, Lyndhurst, the office, the yacht, and the shooting lodge in the Catskills, they amounted to perhaps two hundred people. The responsibility was a heavy one.

Most directly, Jay Gould felt responsibility for his children. He loved them and they him. Since the earliest days, he had managed to spend an evening hour with them. As they grew older, he also began to confide in them. George was twenty years old, a handsome young man with the curling mustaches of a dashing British officer, Edwin was eighteen and equally handsome, and Helen, Jay's first-born daughter, was fourteen, and the apple of his eye. When it was possible, Jay took one or more of his children on his frequent trips across country, but after 1884, the elder boys stayed home more and more. George would not go to college but had entered his father's office after studying rather haphazardly under a series of tutors and at Dr. Cromwell's school. Edwin did go on to Columbia University and received a bachelor's degree in 1888.

So, in about the summer of 1884, Helen Gould became her father's favorite travelling companion.

They took a trip that summer to Chattanooga (among other places). It was sometimes said that Jay Gould ran his special trains at breakneck speed, but on this particular occasion, at least, he gave orders that the train was not to run faster than 25 miles an hour—slow enough to make an old lady happy and to infuriate nearly everyone else on board.

The Chattanooga *Times* welcomed the party with a long, illustrated article about Gould and his empire. This millionaire twenty times over, said the *Times,* was "the railroad king of the world, the principal owner of the Western Union Telegraph Company and probably the richest man on earth."

The entertainment committee from Chattanooga included most of the first citizens, from Adolph Ochs to Mayor I. B. Merriam, and President Tomlinson Fort of the Chamber of Commerce. There were judges and generals and retired city officials. The special train carried Jay Gould; Helen and a young girl friend; Sidney Dillon of the Union Pacific; General Sam Thomas of the East Tennessee Virginia and Georgia; S. M. Felton of the same line; Senator Calvin S. Brice of Ohio; Governor Bullock, President of the Atlanta Chamber of Commerce; Nat Baxter, President of the Southern Iron Company; Dr. Munn, the Gould family physician; and half a dozen other notables. The party went to see the principal sight, Lookout Mountain. They lunched at the Lookout Inn and then visited the Southern Iron Company's steel works. The public was invited to meet Jay Gould and friends between 8 and 10 p.m. at the Chamber of Commerce.

The same issue of the Chattanooga *Times* that carried the article about the visit carried a reprint of a New York *Herald* article in which Pennsylvania Railroad officials expressed consternation because, they said, Jay Gould was down South making special deals with the Baltimore and Ohio, the Pennsy competitor, to freeze the Pennsy out of Missouri Pacific freights. Whenever Jay Gould moved, it seemed, the fur began to fly. Actually, it was

an inspection tour to talk over the problems of the lines in which
Jay Gould had financial interests and to look over steel plants
which produced rails. But who in New York would believe that
anything in which Jay Gould could be involved would be so simple?

How George Broke his Mother's Heart

*The grandest dreams of the middle-aged
businessman had been realized. He had
become a hundred times a millionaire,
he owned a castle on the Hudson, a palace on Fifth Avenue, and a yacht that
would vie with any other for luxury. His
wife was loving and loyal, his children
were fond and obedient. And yet, life was
not happy. He had lost his health. He had
kept his wife's respect, but the dark ha-
treds borne him by so many reflected dimly
on this pure woman and blighted her life.
And there were other problems.*

YOUNG GEORGE GOULD grew restless. He was twenty, nearly twenty-
one. He owned carriages of his own, horses, a sailing yacht called
the *Atalanta* after his father's steam yacht, and nearly every luxury
known to man. For two years he had been laboring in Wall Street,
and, frankly, he had discovered that the workaday business world
which so fascinated his father bored him. He liked girls and they

returned the feeling—he was lavish with gifts, took them to the
finest restaurants and places of amusement, laughed readily and
talked well, and was as handsome as a matinee idol. George had
curly mustaches, he stood as erect as Napoleon, and he was slender, well-formed, and broad enough of shoulder to compensate
for his diminutive size. He was taller than his father, just a little
below the then-average height of 5 feet 8 inches, but women were
shorter then, too, and the man of fashion of the day was the slim
dandy, not the Hercules.

The difference between generations could hardly have been
more visible. Jay continued to wear his full beard even though hir-
sute fashions were beginning to change. To passersby he looked
like a cross between an Old Testament prophet and one of the
Smith Brothers. He wore his old frock coats and baggy breeches
and dull black shoes every day. His peculiar bent-over walk was
easy to burlesque, and he was often imitated by young bloods and
his sneering enemies in the street. When the nattiest young man
imaginable strolled at the side of this seeming ragpicker, only
those familiar with the precincts of lower Broadway knew that
they were father and son, and that the brilliant, immensely
wealthy father was teaching this fashion plate the investment
business.

Jay Gould's business was "investments" by the middle of the
1880s. After the debacle that nearly cost him his fortune in 1884, he
had sworn to lay off stock speculating. Jay Gould never played the
market again in his old way. George had no thrill of the corner to
tempt him but only the solid management of a communications
empire that would extend from coast to coast—if Jay's plans materialized. Meanwhile, there was more time for relaxation.

Obviously plenty of amusements existed to attract George, and
Jay supplied some of them himself. Having been refused entrance
into the exclusive New York Yacht Club, Jay took George, his
heir-apparent, gathered together a coterie of other come-latelys who
could not get into the New York Yacht Club, joined the Eastern

Yacht Club and the Larchmont Club, and formed the American Yacht Club at Larchmont, with a New York clubhouse at 80 Madison Avenue. The other incorporators included Thomas C. Platt (known as Mousy Platt), a leading Republican politician, proprietor of a political club at the Fifth Avenue Hotel bar, and sometime United States Senator from New York. The list also included Jesse R. Grant, scion of the Presidential family, and businessmen George S. Scott, Cornelius F. Timpson, Washington E. Connor, William P. Dowd, and Alfred de Cordova.

The American Yacht Club clubhouse was pleasant enough but a bit far downtown. So, a few months after its opening in 1884, Jay had it moved up to 574 Fifth Avenue, right across the street from the house—a much more convenient spot. That summer he also took the family on the yacht club's first official outing, which went from the Larchmont anchorage up to the flagstaff of Fort Trumbull in New London, and then back again.

Thus began George's interest in clubmanship. One time, young George and a friend went down to Florida with his father on a combined business and pleasure trip. Their destination was Palatka. When they arrived at this tourist center, they found everything arranged as it should be with a suite of rooms at Orvis' Hotel for *every* member of the party. Hearing this announcement, Jay looked around the lobby. The room was jammed with people who could not get sleeping rooms because Orvis' Hotel had been turned over to the Goulds.

"See here," said Jay to the hotel manager, who was bowing and smiling before the capitalist. "Why give me all these rooms?"

"But . . ," said the manager, intending to refer to the great Jay Gould's eminence.

"That's all right," said Jay Gould. "I know all about that. These people need rooms and should have them, and if there are not enough here for the ladies, just send those boys of mine over to the barn."

So the dandy George and his equally impressive young friend

slept in the Orvis Hotel barn that night. The boys were not totally spoiled, but perhaps only because their father was so practical a man.

George developed a considerable interest in the popular theater. The family maintained a box at Augustin Daly's Theater. Daly's was one of New York's successful theaters and brought the fashionable plays of the day to the city. Jay sometimes attended opening nights, but the box was kept largely for the younger generation, especially twenty-year-old George, eighteen-year-old Edwin, and their youthful companions.

On November 26, 1884, Daly brought to New York a new comedy called *Love on Crutches,* starring the inimitable John Drew and the indestructible Ada Rehan. The comedy also introduced an ingenue named Edith Kingdon, whose previous experience in the theater had largely been confined to amateur theatricals in Brooklyn. But she stole the show with her dark beauty, long brown hair, and hourglass figure. Miss Kingdon was new, different, gorgeous to behold, and she quite warmed the hearts of all who saw her, including George Gould.

In the 1880s, actresses were usually "no better than they ought to be," a cliché which meant they were inclined to snuggle under the covers with anyone who had the price of a champagne dinner at Del's, or so, at least, the respectable matrons of New York believed. George apparently believed so, too. At the end of the performance that November night, the last huzzahs still reverberating in the theater, the footlights still glowing, George Gould descended from the family's proscenium box to the lobby, collared John Duff, the business manager of the theater, and demanded an immediate introduction to the new girl.

Duff explained that there were problems. Miss Kingdon was not, he said, an ordinary actress but a lady down on her luck. She had been raised in gentle if impoverished circumstances in Brooklyn. Only after her father died and taking in boarders had not solved her mother's financial problems had Edith agreed to cash in on her amateur theatrical experience and go on the public stage. But she was not ready to risk her virtue, even for Gould.

These protestations apparently whetted George's interest, and soon he was first among the stage-door Johnnies, bearing flowers and candy and sending Western Union telegrams to Miss Kingdon. Jay encouraged the suit. For some time, George's interest was kept from Mrs. Gould's attention. Meanwhile, George grew ever more serious about Edith.

When Helen Miller Gould learned that George was in love with an actress, she fell ill with fear and loathing before she ever met the girl. It made no difference how sweet and virginal the beautiful Edith might be. She was an actress, and Mrs. Gould was a daughter of a genteel old New York family. People brought up on Murray Hill simply did not marry actresses, under *any* conditions. It did no good for Dr. John Munn, the family physician, to prescribe smelling salts and attempt gently to persuade the lady that times were changing. Helen Gould could not be reconciled.

Jay finally settled the matter. To all his wife's protestations he turned a deaf ear and acceded to George's wish to wed the girl. The "proper people" of the glittering society around him had already snubbed Jay Gould to the limit, and if George wanted an actress, he would have one.

So, one wintry day in 1884, the family assembled in the great drawing room at Lyndhurst with its statuary and marble-topped tables and leaded French windows for what was to Helen Miller Gould an unutterably grim occasion. Jay sat smiling. Helen was pale and silent. The younger children were subdued as adolescents often are at a family crisis—and everyone knew it was a crisis. George and Edith Kingdon were there, but not even Edith's mother was in attendance, nor was there a friend or a witness from outside the family.

Soon a carriage drove up, and out of it stepped the Reverend Mr. Choate, pastor of the Presbyterian Church in Irvington-on-Hudson. The minister's carriage drove on down the hill to the stables behind the house, and the Reverend Mr. Choate came nervously into the great entrance hall, turned left, and walked into the drawing room behind the butler.

Jay then rang for the servants, brought them in, and told them they were to witness a wedding.

"George is to be married," he announced to Miss Terry, the housekeeper, when she came down the stairs.

The self-conscious minister took his place before a great marble statue on one end of the room, and fingered his prayer book. George and Edith Kingdon stood in front of him, she dressed in a simple everyday costume and he in a dark business suit. Jay stood at his son's side. The pitiful little ceremony began, Helen Miller Gould standing tragically behind them all, stifling her sobs at the horrid prospect of her son's *mésalliance*. The servants said that Mrs. Gould looked for all the world as though the vengeance of God had at last descended on the family.

The service finally came to an end. Edith, who had struggled bravely to keep a happy face in spite of her mother-in-law-to-be's disapproval, collapsed in tears on George's shoulder. Mrs. Gould stood back, red-eyed but unwavering, the opposition of all Murray Hill burning in her eyes.

Jay stepped forward and awkwardly patted his son on the shoulder. He kissed Edith on the cheek with a few fatherly words. He stood by George as the minister prepared the wedding book and Miss Terry and other servants signed as witnesses that God's will had been done.

At a signal, the butler disappeared, and soon two vehicles appeared in the carriage-way of the Gothic castle. George supported the clinging Edith to one carriage, Jay clucking along comfortingly behind them. The Reverend Mr. Choate shook hands all around—except with Helen still nearly sick with grief—then slid briskly into his carriage and departed. Mrs. Gould staggered upstairs to bed, accompanied by her maid. The children moved mutely about the house. Below stairs the house was abuzz. Imagine, Master George marrying an actress! Miss Terry, the housekeeper, said that although it was unfortunate, George could hardly be blamed. He was young and full of high spirits, and Mrs. Gould had never had the knack of bringing young people into the house—especially young ladies of the proper class.

While the servants gossiped, George and Edith boarded the *Atalanta* and steamed down river toward New York where they spent a few days at 579 Fifth Avenue. Helen Gould remained at Lyndhurst, nursing her grief. Many days later, when niece Alice Northrop came to visit, she was still nearly prostrate and confined to her room for most of the day. She sat writing at her desk that morning while Alice chatted idly of household and family matters. Suddenly, Helen arose and began to pace the floor, intense, distracted, and seemingly unaware that her niece was in the room. Suddenly she spoke.

"Oh, Alice," she said, "Why has this happened? Just to think of it, George married to an actress! What next? How do we know that Helen won't fall in love with a coachman?"

And she collapsed in tears.

"Why, Aunt Helen," said Alice, "Please stop worrying. Of course she wouldn't do anything like that."

But Helen Miller Gould could not listen. She desperately feared that the evil alliance contracted by her eldest son would encourage the other five children into similar or even worse mistakes. And in 1884, that fear was not entirely groundless. A few months before George's "great mistake," the daughter of G. P. Morosini, Jay's assistant and bodyguard (and almost a member of the family), had run off with her father's coachman. Elsewhere, coachmen were very much in favor with well-to-do young ladies. Nearly every day one read in the penny press scandalous stories such as the tale of Miss Josie Barnard, described as an "heiress" of an illustrious family of Fall River, Mass.

An orphan, Josie was living with her grandmother when she became attracted to Philip Scully, her grandmother's coachman. She read in the newspapers about other heiresses marrying coachmen. After a whirlwind honeymoon, the family usually set the groom up in business. So Josie encouraged the handsome Philip. Eventually they were married, although it was kept secret at first. When the other servants somehow got wind of it, however, the guilty pair fled. The furious grandmother wanted Philip jailed. They went to Providence, confident that Philip would find work there, but he did not. They went to Pawtucket, where chances seemed better. Still no job. They went to Lowell, arriving with two trunks and seventy-five cents in cash, and even in bustling Lowell Philip could not find work.

So Josie made a hard decision: she had to go home to grandmother to convince the old lady that all was for the best. But how to get home? There was no money, and no apparent way of earning any money. Josie chose the practical way out. She went to the Lowell town hall and applied to the Overseer of the Poor for enough money to return alone to Fall River.

Such scandals fascinated Helen Miller Gould during the days after George married the actress. She cried and cried for days, and finally washed the tragedy of Murray Hill out of her system. But her heart was broken. She was never the same again.

13

Mephistopheles Takes a Trip

*No one, not even a middle-aged busi-
nessman millionaire, is safe from family
tragedy, and in the years after 1884, it became quite clear to Jay Gould where one
of his major tragedies would lie.*

GEORGE and Edith Gould did all in their power to reconcile the
mother to their marriage. They moved to a house at 1 East Forty-
seventh Street, just around the corner from the mansion on Fifth
Avenue. Jay built a passageway connecting the two houses. Edith
offered to do anything and everything for her mother-in-law, but
Helen was not interested in making the relationship either personal or pleasant. She was willing to abide the presence of the
actress at her table, but she would not stir herself to make friends
with her daughter-in-law.

Part of the reason for this obduracy—or perhaps it was the
result—was Helen Miller Gould's suddenly deteriorating health.

Mrs. Gould began to suffer from high blood pressure, whether from physical or emotional causes no one was prepared to say. Within six months after the marriage, the elder Mrs. Gould's decline was so noticeable that everyone in the family commented on it. She gave up social life entirely. Weak and listless, she often remained in her room for many days at a time.

In Mrs. Gould's stable on West Forty-fourth Street, between the Berkeley School and Fifth Avenue, Coachman James Downs waited all day long to serve her with three and sometimes four or more pairs of fine horses at the ready. As for carriages, there was a brougham, a landau, a victoria, and a gaudy yellow and black hunting wagon that was just the thing for a sporty jaunt to Central Park. But the dark green livery of the Goulds was not seen in the park during these days, nor were coachman Downs or the footmen. Jay seldom used the carriages. Now neither did Helen.

By contrast, George kept his stable at 133 West Fifty-fifth Street with six pairs of horses, eight carriages, and a saddle horse. The father, even with five children living at home, maintained a much humbler display than his eldest son. Jay's half-dozen horses shared the stable with only one other, a long-tailed gray thoroughbred belonging to Edwin, the second son. In these years, Edwin was at Columbia College, but he found time to become an active member of Squadron A, Troop A, of the Seventy-first Regiment, a captain in the unit, and the champion in wrestling on horseback, the sport of cavalrymen. Edwin's gray was fine and expensive but no more than that: George's display appeared a bit flamboyant for his years and obligations, although few people in New York were aware of it. The majority simply saw *Gould* display and did not differentiate.

Most of George's carriages and traps served to show off Edith Kingdon Gould. Each morning after an early breakfast, she strapped herself into her corsets, pinching in the famous hourglass figure that had brought her a princely fortune, donned her riding dress and furs, and called up one of the carriages. On West Fifty-fifth, coachman William Willis responded quickly. By 7:30, the carriage waited at the door of No. 1, and by 8:00, Edith had picked up her father-in-law at 579 and was heading for Central Park. There followed a half hour's brisk drive through the park, Jay chatting quietly with his daughter-in-law, trying in his own way to heal the wound that threatened to separate the family.

For Jay Gould had a dream, a dream of empire and a brilliant future for his family, and the translation of the dream into reality depended on maintaining the close-knit and affectionate quality of the family. Jay sensed that his wife's attitude was threatening everything, and in his own way, he set out to undo the damage.

Jay's dream was born out of his shrewd observation of the world about him. He had seen the fate of Daniel Drew, once most powerful of all the Wall Street princes. Indeed, he had led the hunt against Drew and had dealt defeat after defeat to the old man. Drew died a pauper. He had observed the wreck of Commodore Vanderbilt's empire, when, in 1879, William Henry Vanderbilt had sold off the margin of *control* of the New York Central and Lake Shore railroad systems. To be sure, William Henry Vanderbilt had been careful, and J. Pierpont Morgan had sold these securities through his father's banking firm in London, so it was assumed that Vanderbilt could control his railroad empire without actually owning most of it. But that was bankers' theory, and it was not shared by Jay Gould. He believed that the man who owned a property controlled it; otherwise there was nothing but trouble. He had certainly had enough experience in that!

Gould's theory called for common sharing of the fortune among the children, and he drew his will accordingly. He talked about the will and the empire, he instructed the older children in the ways of railroads, he gave them small sums of capital to use in practicing investment, and always he pounded home the theme of unity, unity, unity. A man who cared little for the trappings of power or even for power itself but who played the business game for the sake of the gamble, Jay Gould set about putting his affairs in order after George's marriage. His own grasp on life was precarious—even now he suffered from tuberculosis of both lungs, and he knew it. And he came more rapidly to terms with mortality as he observed Helen's waning health.

One day in 1887 at the dinner table in the Fifth Avenue mansion, Jay mentioned a railroad called the Cotton Belt. The correct name of this line was the St. Louis Southwestern Railroad, and in its day, this "trunk line," which reached from the Great Lakes to Tidewater, had looked good. But by 1887, the Cotton Belt had fallen on evil times, and Jay, who held a considerable amount of stock in it, told his children why he thought he ought to unload his holdings.

"I hope you don't do that, Father," Edwin said quietly. He was the quiet one, and it was unusual for him to make so bold an assertion about a business matter.

Jay looked at his second son sharply.

"Why not?"

"Because I own a piece of it and don't want to lose out," said Edwin.

Jay looked down the table again. He frowned, and then smiled.

"Well," he said, "If you are so interested in the Cotton Belt, why don't you come down to Broadway now and help me run it?"

So in 1887, Edwin left Columbia University and joined the Gould offices at the Western Union building to learn about railroads and business investment.

Two of the boys had now joined their father in the business world. It only remained to give the younger children ever-increasing doses of responsibility.

The passage of time was heightened even more in August when Edith gave birth to a son. (George was still so infatuated with his wife that he named the baby Kingdon, rather than George, Jr., or Jay, as one might have expected.) On that day, Jay marched up the steps of No. 1 and went inside to congratulate the young mother and to see his first grandson, while George went off to the office. George came home, stopped by the Windsor Hotel bar on his way home, "hoisted a few" with friends, then reported on the business day. That Jay was present on Fifth Avenue while

George went to work was extremely significant. The middle-aged businessman and grandfather was beginning to relinquish his hold on the empire, still keeping control, but leaving more and more detail to the boys.

Still, the father's education of all the children in family matters was essential, and Jay's move in this direction began in the summer of 1887. It was time again for another inspection of the southwestern railroads. The trip would be too gruelling for Helen, so she was left at home under the close supervision of Dr. Munn, George, and Edwin. Jay set out in the private car with Helen, 19, Howard, 17, Anna, 12, and Frank, 10. Also invited on the trip was Jay's niece Alice Northrop Snow—when there was room, Jay always liked to do something for his relatives. The Lyndhurst chef and second butler also went along. The trip was long, and every foot of it was chronicled by the New York newspapers.

For a man who cordially detested publicity, Jay Gould could never escape it except on the high seas, in the privacy of the mansion, at Lyndhurst, or in the wilds of the Catskills. This year, for the first time, Jay took his wife to Roxbury, the village of his birth. Spurred by a constant awareness of Helen's weakening condition, Jay now tried to atone for the years spent making money instead of spending it. There was a reunion with his cousin Maria Burhans, once Jay's intended bride, who had never married. One day Jay went fishing—an avocation he had not attempted for years. The air was relaxed and enjoyable, but a feeling of little time for such pleasant life underlay it all.

Home again on Fifth Avenue, Helen's pale listlessness increased, if anything, and Jay's efforts grew nearly frantic. He spent $100,000 redecorating the mansion just to please Helen. Dr. Munn suggested a sea voyage, a trip to the warmth of southern Europe, and the financier was only too pleased to drop all business and attend to his wife. But so suspect was Jay Gould in the business community that when his plans became known, nobody in Wall Street believed that he was going on a pleasure jaunt or that Helen's health occasioned the trip. Thus the newspapers had their usual field day of wild speculation. Said the *Times:* "There are people who insist that his announcement of a long absence from the land that owes him so much is a mere bluff intended in some mysterious way to affect the stock market."

Jay engaged passage on the Cunard steamer *Umbria* for himself, Helen, and the younger children. Captain McMickan had two cabins aboard the ship, and the senior Goulds took one of them. The rest of the family, relatives, governesses, and maids, occupied a suite of six rooms on the spar deck, abaft the saloon.

Early in the afternoon of October 30, 1887, Jay herded the family into three carriages at 579 and set out for the west side pier, where the *Umbria* was moored.

The reporters were there already when he arrived. Just before 2:00 p.m., the others boarded while Jay remained to talk to the press, an art he had at least partially learned.

Jay smiled.

"Are you certain you are going, Mr. Gould?"

"Well, I believe I am."

Another smile.

That was all. (The art was not totally mastered.)

Gould went on by to examine the quarters of his party, which included Helen's sister and brother, who had been brought along for Helen's pleasure.

"A more unassuming party than Mr. Gould's was not aboard the ship," reported the *Times* (October 30, 1887). "Mrs. Gould looked in splendid health, and, like her daughters, was dressed very plainly and in quiet, dark colors. The boys would have attracted no special attention anywhere, either from their dress, appearance, or manners. Like their father they are of very modest demeanor. Mr. Gould looked as he generally does, a trifle shabby as to clothes. It was noticed, however, that he smiled very frequently for him, as if going on shipboard he felt that he had thrown a load off his shoulders."

Russell Sage came down to see them off. The reporters noted that Sage was dressed in his usual "fifteen-dollar overcoat"—they never failed to call attention in one way or another to the penuriousness of Russell Sage or to the shabbiness of Jay Gould. The reporters observed them from a respectful distance as the two millionaires chatted. Then Captain Shackleford, the master of the yacht *Atalanta,* joined them. He, too, was crossing on the *Umbria* while his crew took the yacht over. He would then join them at Marseilles and make the yacht ready for the Gould party.

George and Edith then very noticeably joined Jay on deck to chat. (Helen had gone to the stateroom.) As the *Times* man somewhat unkindly noted: "Young Mrs. Gould looks much more matronly than she did as Edith Kingdon. She now probably weighs more than her husband."

Here was a hint of the impending tragedy of Edith Kingdon Gould's later life, for although the *Times* reporter was ungentlemanly, he was also accurate. Following the birth of little Kingdon, Edith corseted and struggled, laced and braced, dieted and took outings, and yet nothing could recall the hourglass figure she had had when George—who was still the mustachioed, slim dandy, and who weighed 145 pounds, just like Edith—had married her.

(One of the tragedies of a woman who tended to fat in the 1880s was the absolute interdiction against female exercise. Even walking was regarded as *de trop* in any dose larger than a stroll around the grounds of Lyndhurst. And then there were rich burgundies and champagne by the hamperful to be overcome at No. 1. The Gould household at 579 never saw such goings on, but George came of a different generation, and champagne to the young rich bloods of the nineteenth century was like beer to the workingman.)

The young Goulds left and Sidney Dillon appeared—he was one of Jay's trusted associates and employees who would help George and Edwin oversee the communications empire in the next few months. Finally, who should appear but J. Pierpont Morgan, nose aglow, for a brisk fifteen minutes of conversation with Jay Gould. He was followed by the three operating officers of the Manhattan Elevated System.

When the *Umbria's* warning whistle sounded, the visitors began to go ashore. Miss Helen, Jay's daughter, tearfully wrenched herself away from a group of school chums. The press began to close in on Jay again for some last words.

Jay stepped forward, smiling unflinchingly, and gave his hand to several reporters he recognized. Some later claimed they did not know whether to shake it or kiss it, but at the time they shook it.

"What will you do without me?" Jay asked.

The reporters laughed. It was a grand game, baiting him.

"We'll store up our energy while we wait for you," one wag said.

"Believe me, it's not necessary," laughed Jay Gould.

Then there were questions about health. Was he taking a physician? No, he was not, and he had no more need of one than the average reporter, he said. (Considering the whiskey quotient of the average reporter, the statement was probably true enough.)

The last warning sounded and the reporters debarked. Crowds lined the rails, and from the dock, the reporters could see the Goulds on the spar deck, watching as the ship pulled away.

Once gone, Jay was missed. Henry Clews, the editorial commentator and Emily Post of Wall Street, apparently regarded this particular sailing as potentially disastrous to the business world (as well it might be if the bulls were to raid every Gould stock in sight). So Clews warned the bears that Jay Gould would actually be absent only about seven days on each end of this trip, and that through the Atlantic cable he would be able to wreak vengeance on his enemies and protect his friends just as if he were in Wall Street all the time. *There* was an indication that if any man ever ruled that strange street it was Jay Gould.

If only he and Helen could regain their health. There should still be plenty of time.

14

Mrs. Gould Gives Up the Ghost

————✦————

*For the first time in his life, the middle-
aged millionaire gave himself over to enjoyment. He looked at the stock market
reports when he was abroad, but he firmly
declined to do more. He would not become involved in business. The trip was
helping his own health. He knew that.
But was it helping his loyal, long-suffering
wife?*

————✦————

FROM Liverpool the Goulds went to London where Jay shocked
the press by refusing to discuss business even in his usual monosyl-
labic manner. They spent a week in London, then headed south
for Marseilles where the *Atalanta* was waiting to begin their winter cruise. That year they saw Naples and Malta and Greek ports,
then back to Naples and Rome. They went to Alexandria and
travelled a little way up the Nile. They purchased bronzes and
collected artifacts, and the ladies bought silk for dresses and parasols to keep the tropical sun off their heads. In short, they joined
the score of other American millionaires in the 1880s who took the

celebrated tour of the Mediterranean to learn about the past and to collect some bric-a-brac for their mansions.

While Jay was gone, George learned the business quickly. The Kansas Pacific Railroad's bondholders grew impatient at nonpayment of interest on their holdings and raised a fuss. George tried to settle the matter with representatives of Mr. Villard, the principal agitator. During the conversations, George suggested that he might be willing to pay $30,000 to the attorneys for the bondholders—if they could settle the matter quickly. The chief attorney, one Mr. Fellows, chose to regard this as an attempt at bribery, and he broke off the negotiations. When Jay came home to this state of affairs, he announced to the press that the Kansas Pacific bondholders were trying to blackmail his son, and the fur began to fly.

So it was that Jay stepped off the boat into the customary turmoil, and he was content. But the winter's cruise, instead of improving Helen's health, seemed to have exhausted her. Her state of mind was improving, however, and on her return she became more reconciled to her daughter-in-law. Whatever Edith had been doing in the interim, it should be said, not one of those unsightly pounds had fallen away.

The Goulds had returned from abroad at the end of March. By midsummer, Dr. Munn clearly realized that he had two patients instead of one. Jay's tuberculosis was verging on a critical stage. His insomnia grew worse, and night after night in the spring and summer of that year, he paced up and down Fifth Avenue before 579, accompanied by two bodyguards, until he had exhausted himself and could sleep a little.

In August, Jay and the family went to Saratoga where he could take the waters and the baths. All but the two elder boys, who stayed on in the sticky heat of New York and attended to business, checked into the United States Hotel. The doctors tried a program of baths and exercise on Jay. Each morning he was awakened before sunrise to leap into a freezing bath. An attendant then towelled him briskly and rubbed him down to restore circulation, after which the ailing millionaire was sent out for a walk of at least two and preferably four miles. One day he walked five miles. Upon staggering home, he took breakfast at 8:00 a.m.

"I have an appetite now," he told the press in a burst of loquacity. "This air is working wonders for me. I feel more like myself than I have in a long, long time."

He did not look it.

The reporters came to the broad verandah of the United States Hotel and observed him as he sat in a high-backed rocking chair from morning until afternoon, reading and resting. His clothes hung on him as on a pole, and indeed, when he crossed his legs in his chair and his trousers came up, the reporters could see that his legs were stick-thin. "They seem barely more than pipestem thickness," one man wrote, "and there is a listlessness in the eye—that nobody knowing Jay Gould ever saw there before."

From breakfast until lunch, Gould sat, rocking and reading and sometimes dozing. At noon, he joined pale Helen and little Helen, Howard, Anna, and Frank in the big hotel dining room, but he seldom ate much. After lunch, he returned to the big chair; in midafternoon, a carriage took him over the roads outside Saratoga. At 8:00 p.m., he had supper with the family, then was whisked off to bed to rise again just before daybreak.

After three weeks of this, Jay felt well enough to undertake a change—although for the first time in years, while within arm's reach of a stock ticker on the American side of the Atlantic, he flatly refused to consider business problems. The press was mystified by Jay's attitude, alternately recalling his flat statement of a year earlier that he was out of the market and his record of depradations. They were more mystified when he headed for Kingston and the Catskills. He went to Arkville, located on the Ulster and Delaware railroad line, and from there drove to Furlough Lake, a wild spot eight miles deep into the woods abounding with trout. Dr. Munn went along, nodded briskly at reporters, and refused to be drawn into questions about Jay's physical condition. After a few days, Jay went to Roxbury. There, while he was attending services at the Methodist Church, visiting relatives, and loafing in the sun, the reason for Edith's continued avoirdupois was revealed. On September 1 the word came over Western Union:

Dear Father: Congratulations. It's a fine boy.

Mother and baby doing finely. GEORGE.

George's family piety made up for his bad grammar. This second son was christened Jay Gould II.

Edwin and Helen came up to Roxbury to join their father, then took him home, which at this time of year meant Lyndhurst, in the private railroad car. There Mrs. Gould was waiting, her health improved much less than her husband's.

It continued to deteriorate. Back in New York she suffered a stroke. A few weeks later, she suffered two more slight strokes within a matter of hours, and she was so nearly paralyzed that she could not receive any visitors. A specialist, Dr. Jared C. Baldwin, was called in. Each evening he visited, consoled the family, and offered them hope. But on the night of November 12 when he came to 579, Dr. Baldwin found Mrs. Gould's condition so serious —she had not been able to speak since November 6—that he remained at the house all night. At 4:00 on the morning of the 13th, he aroused the family. Helen's three sisters were called to the house. Helen Miller Gould lingered all day, then at 9:00 that night, she died, with Jay, the children, and her sisters at her bedside.

The funeral took place four days later at the mansion, fittingly enough, because in a special sense, 579 Fifth Avenue really "belonged" to Helen as much as Lyndhurst "belonged" to Jay. They had moved from house to house together without the slightest friction, but Helen Miller Gould was a New York City girl. Brought up in gentle Manhattan society, it was her private tragedy that her marriage removed her from much of the past, and made her prey, in the press, to comparisons with those *parvenus,* the Astors and the Vanderbilts.

The funeral was quiet, as Helen's life had been. The family came, including all her sisters and cousins. Jay's sisters were there, along with other relatives. Among the handful of friends invited were the Russell Sages; the Thomas Eckerts; Samuel Sloane, the merchant; Jesse Seligman, the banker; Cyrus Field, the investor; G. P. Morosini, Jay's confidant; and Sidney Dillon.

The two drawing rooms and the hall were arranged sparely for the funeral. The downstairs was hung in black with floral trimming but the whole effect was unostentatious. Two ministers read the services, the Reverend Dr. Paxton of the Episcopal Church and the Reverend Dr. Terry of the South Dutch Collegiate Reformed Church. After the short service, the casket was carried through the crowd on Fifth Avenue—that same crowd which seemed to assemble to observe and record the daily comings and goings of Fifth Avenue millionaires.

Jay Gould followed the casket, haggard and thinner than ever, escorting one of Helen's sisters. The procession entered the carriages that lined up at the curb and headed for Woodlawn Cemetery for this first burial of a member of America's most hated family.

15

Line of Succession

———◄••►———

The middle-aged millionaire's chest was wracked with coughing, night after night, and he knew that his end would come soon. How could he, in the few months he felt were left to him, arrange his affairs so that the great fortune would be safe?

———◄••►———

WHEN her mother died, Helen Gould was twenty years old, and she immediately took charge of the houses and the menage. Actually, she had taken charge in November after her mother's collapse, and even before that time, she had managed from backstage. At this time, Helen also took over the management of the family's good works—Jay passed over the mantle to her.

In past years Jay Gould had been about as generous as any millionaire of his times. He had given dinners for the poor of the city and money for various kinds of relief. But by 1890, he was becoming tired of the adverse publicity he received no matter what he did. For example, one day that summer, Jay gave two acres of land to the Protestant Episcopal and Presbyterian Churches of Irvington-on-Hudson, the village nearest Lyndhurst. The story behind the gift was this. The two churches were not far apart, and the land in question lay between them. For several years, each church had coveted the land and each had tried to buy it. The land owner had each time gone to the rival church, and the price had, concomitantly, escalated rapidly. Jay settled what was threatening to become a disgraceful dispute by buying up the land and splitting it between the two churches. He did so without a thought for publicity, without a press release or a murmur. He certainly did not expect an attack. Then, on July 8, 1890, the *Times* ran a little story about the gift. The headline read, typically, GOULD SOOTHES HIS CONSCIENCE.

Another attack came at a more unfortunate time. Jay and his daughter Helen had just given a reception, at her instigation, for the Presbyterian Board of Church Extension. Funds were raised for the work of the church, and in the course of the evening, Jay wrote out a check for $10,000 and slipped it into the hands of the chairman of the event. He wanted nothing said, but the next day the newspapers had the story, and as Richard O'Connor so aptly put it, it was "as though he had been caught robbing poor boxes." A particularly sanctimonious fool of a minister, the Reverend Charles H. Parkhurst called Gould's gift "an ostentatious display of wealth in the name of religion." Actually, Gould's gift was plain and simple; the fact was that Parkhurst's bleat was an ostentatious display of religion in the hope of publicity.

A day or so later, when the newspapers and publicity-hunting parsons had all finished their say, Jay sat in his parlor at 579 reading the usual account of his sins. His niece, Alice Northrop, described the scene:

> Uncle Jay was sitting in a deep chair near me. Suddenly he threw his paper to the floor, dropped his arms, and sank back wearily in the chair. I looked at him. His eyes were closed. He sat there for a long interval. He looked completely beaten. At

last he roused himself, and then, for a second time that morning
I was dumfounded.

"Alice," he said slowly, "I guess I'm through with giving."

"What," I gasped. "Why Uncle Jay, you can't really mean
that—not just because some newspapers are so unfair."

"Yes," he said, "I guess I do. It seems to cause nothing but
trouble, trouble. Everything I say is garbled. Everything I do is
purposely misconstrued. I don't especially care about myself, but
it all comes back so on my family."

Jay Gould was demonstrably tired. He was in the process of
reorganizing the Union Pacific railroad and putting his financial
house in order—trying to preserve the railroad empire and the
telegraph empire in order to leave them intact for his family.
Harried by the press, for the first time in his life he was becoming
sensitive about it.

The cynicism or outright disbelief of the press and the public
was clearly manifested in the view that editorial writers took of
the consolidation of the Union Pacific and the Kansas Pacific.
While Gould had been abroad, Oswald Garrison Villard had begun his efforts in behalf of the Kansas Pacific bondholders, using
material brought out by the Pacific Railroad Commission which
had recently completed its investigations of irregularities in the
management of the roads heading west. On his return, Jay Gould
had cut dividends in the Missouri Pacific and otherwise made a
stir. The *Times* and every other newspaper except the *Tribune*
took after him, referring to the Kansas Pacific deal as "larceny" and
indicating that Gould should stand trial. If he had a good defense,
said the *Times,* he had nothing to fear. "Why does he not meet
the charge squarely and face a trial?"

The point of the *Times* objection, the reason for the immense
national hatred of Jay Gould, was summed up in this editorial by
writers who had begun to echo a growing demand for a new view
of the "public interest" in America, a term that had not existed at
the start of Jay Gould's career:

. . . It is well known that Jay Gould has never made his
chief gains from the conservation of railroad property and the

legitimate profits of its management. His policy has been to wreck railroads and gobble up the remains; to buy stocks at low figures and sell them at high figures; to sacrifice stock to bonds when he has the latter in his possession, and all his movements and representations are naturally interpreted in the light of this policy.*

Gould's actions would always be so interpreted. The Gould methods, said the *Times,* had been successful for so long because of the ineffective state of law enforcement, the venality of lawmakers, and the flaccidity of public opinion. Yet after the election of Grover Cleveland to the presidency, public morality was changing rapidly and there was much talk, beyond that of newspapers, of resistance to big business, and "the vindication of justice and the protection of rights" which would protect the public from the excesses of capitalists like Jay Gould.

The people were growing tired of the Jay Goulds. And Jay Gould was growing tired of the harassment of the people.

Furthermore, he continued to be physically threatened by cranks such as Charles J. Dickson, who said he had come out of the wilds of Colorado to kill Gould in behalf of an organization known as Christ's Followers which had tried, judged, and condemned Gould in absentia. Such threats always grew in number following newspaper attacks.

So Jay Gould's hold on charitable feelings was weakened by the society around him. He had also been snubbed by the other society —Mrs. Astor's "400." Jay felt a growing obligation to his children's success in the world, however, and he made one attempt to join Society with a capital S. He was persuaded to give a grand reception at Christmas in 1891—the only such party the Goulds ever gave. Three thousand invitations were sent out for a huge reception at Lyndhurst to be held on December 26. Surprisingly enough, although Jay admitted to being the most hated man in America, most of the guests decided to come, including the Whitneys, the Carnegies, the Grants, the Rockefellers, the Pierpont Morgans, the Villards, and the Sloanes. The Astors and the Van-

* New York *Times,* March 28, 1888.

derbilts and their hangers-on stayed away, and the newspapers made much of this "failure" to achieve proper social success. But by any other standards, the party was successful.

It was all a matter of point of view and what the Goulds really wanted out of their relationships with the "400." They did not attend the same parties, largely because of the deep-seated enmity between Jay and William Henry Vanderbilt. No one in the Vanderbilt family had forgotten that Jay had taken the huge fortune that was Western Union away from William Henry.

But general interfamily relations were never really that bad, and the proof had come four years earlier, during the Christmas season of 1887, when Mrs. Frederick William Vanderbilt, wife of one of William Henry's sons, called on New York City's Grand Opera House to give her a box for the Actor's Fund benefit. Mrs. Vanderbilt certainly wished to attend one of *the* charity events of the season. A. M. Palmer, manager of the opera house, told Mrs. Vanderbilt that he was sorry, no more boxes were available. Every box in the house was sold and would be occupied—except one.

And whose box was the empty one?

Why, it was Jay Gould's box, said Mr. Palmer.

There was silence on the other end of the telephone.

Mr. Palmer offered to intercede, and he laid the request before Edwin Gould, the senior Gould in the city that season (Jay, Helen, and the younger children were in Europe and George was travelling in California at the moment). Edwin immediately sent Mrs. Vanderbilt a note inviting her to use the box. She did so, taking several young Vanderbilts with her. That very evening, a young man of the House of Vanderbilt appeared at the Madison Square Theater where Edwin was attending a play, and publicly presented him with a check for $100, a Vanderbilt donation to the Actor's Fund.*

It might be said, then, that if the Vanderbilts did not come to this Christmas party, it was largely in deference to the enmity between William Henry and Jay. The Goulds did not like the

* New York *World,* December 2, 1887.

snub, however, and they remembered it. Jay grew testy in this period and began to take exception to many snubs—from Society and from society—that had not previously disturbed him. The result was a withdrawal that colored the family attitude for the next three generations, a fear of newspapers, newspapermen, and even of plots and assassination. The Goulds became paranoid—to use a twentieth-century term—and all of their millions could not protect them from it.

So Helen Gould was consigned the responsibility for future good works. Helen was not pretty, but she had the gentle goodness of a nun. As a child she was plump, and the figure would never be like an hourglass. Her face was oval, and her nose seemed to be plopped onto the flat plane of her cheeks like a maraschino cherry on top of a cake. At a very early age, even at the Gardner School, she seized upon religion. As her cousin Alice Northrop Snow put it, "Helen's deep religious convictions were unfolding into active expression" even then. "She made me think of a lovely flower pushing out sweet-scented petals in the spring," said Alice.

Helen was active in the King's Daughters Tens, a religious service organization then popular. She worked for the New York orphans at the Home for the Friendless. She worked for the sick at Flower Hospital. Summers at Lyndhurst, she ran a Sunday School class at the Presbyterian Church and then went on to attend a Sunday School class run by a friend at the local Episcopal church. In New York, she attended St. Bartholomew's *and* the Dutch Reformed Church at Forty-eighth Street and Fifth Avenue.

The other children were going their separate ways. George Gould went on adding to his possessions. Jay had liked the 10-acre lake in the Catskills where he had fished in 1887 so much that he bought all the property around the lake and created a woodland paradise called Furlough Retreat. Two-hundred and fifty feet back from the lake, a disarmingly rough house was built of logs hewn on three sides, with the bark retained on the outside. The house was, of course, the most magnificent "log cabin" in North America, as befitted George, the son of America's leading Wall Street

figure. The house was 34-feet wide by 70-feet long, two stories
high, with a 10-foot verandah on three sides, a main hall 16-feet
wide and 32-feet long, and twenty-six rooms. The calculated
roughness of the exterior did not extend inside. The logs were
caulked, papered, furrowed, and celled over with strips of Norway
pine panelling. Floors were laid of finest quality Georgia pine. The
rooms were decorated in the Queen Anne style. On the front and
rear of the second floor hung 16-foot balconies. The main stairway
had a railing and balustrade cut from native trees and left with the
bark on for atmosphere, each baluster representing a different type
of tree growing within the perimeter of the summer estate. The
lake was stocked with trout and the grounds with two dozen deer
and elk.

George also moved from the house at 1 East Forty-seventh
Street to a far more sumptuous mansion on Fifth Avenue as befitted his new position of chief Gould manager. This great brown-
stone had fifty rooms, many more than the elder Gould's mansion,
but then George planned to have a large family in the Gould
tradition. He could easily afford it on his $500,000 a year salary
from his father.

The second son, Edwin, was married in the autumn of 1892 to
Sarah Canting Shrady, the daughter of an eminently respectable
physician of a conservative, upper-middle-class New York family.
The Shradys were not "Fifth Avenue," but they did live in a
comfortable New York townhouse on the East Side in what is
now midtown Manhattan but was then the near-suburban countryside only one step away from Millionaire's Row. Only the two
families attended the quiet wedding. The flowers, however, were a
Gould triumph. The bride and bridesmaids carried orchids from
the Gould greenhouses at Lyndhurst, and the Shrady parlor,
where the marriage was performed, was also decorated with
Gould flowers and rare plants. After the wedding, Edwin and
Sally went to the Caribbean and to Florida for a brief honeymoon,
then came back to New York to set up housekeeping at No. 1 East

Forty-seventh Street, which they took over from George and Edith.

Helen was more or less out of the marriage game by her own wish. Her idealization of a knight-in-shining-armor was matched by no one in the Gould circle—and no one known to be in the New York area. Howard, who was just 21, had gone downtown to join the family firm after studying under tutors, at the Browning School, and at Columbia University for a year. The young businessman and man-about-town still lived at home.

Anna, the next child, and Frank, the youngest, were still teen-age school children, not admitted to the family councils, and this gap in age soon became a matter of major importance in their futures and Jay's hopes for eternal family solidarity.

During the first months of 1892, Jay knew that he was mortally ill. He was scheduled to make a trip south to inspect the railroads and to journey through the Caribbean, but in late February, he took to his bed in the back bedroom of 579 Fifth Avenue where Helen had died.

The reporters were immediately at the door, but George came to the hall and assured them that it was nothing more than a "temporary indisposition." The same assurances were given representatives of Wall Street who showed up at the house at the close of the business day. Jay was up again from his "cold" in a few days, but after long and serious talks with Dr. Munn, the financier knew that only a matter of months remained to him—and how many months depended on his own conduct. The doctor argued again for a complete break with business and retirement to the life of an invalid. How much longer would he live, Jay asked the doctor. When that physician could make him no promises, he shrugged, smiled, and said he guessed he would go on and straighten things out for the family.

"I am not afraid to die," he told Alice one day. "I am not afraid to die. But the younger children . . . well . . . I don't like the thought of leaving them."

This worry for his children haunted Jay Gould's waking moments. He devised and redevised ways of assuring the continuity of the future, the promise that the children would all come into their shares of the fortune, and the establishment of a course of action that would make sure the fortune was worth coming into.

Jay Gould trusted his sons and their judgment. He trusted George most of all—George was oldest and should have the soundest head on his shoulders. George had done well, carrying out his father's orders. He had been a dutiful son, never going beyond those orders, never taking it upon himself to move on a questionable matter without advice. George seemed sound as a dollar. He was sturdy and athletic and a good family man himself. Jay trusted him implicitly.

During the Thanksgiving holidays of 1892, niece Alice noticed that a great change had come over her Uncle Jay. She had come to the mansion to visit for the holidays, and with the prescience sometimes given the outsider, she realized suddenly that he was about to die. The idea came to her one night when he came home from downtown, and sat down in his chair in the sitting room. The rest of the family was ranged about the big reading table in the center of the room, enjoying the light of the new reading lamp that had just been added to the furnishings.

"He sat down heavily, in a favorite armchair, and leaned his head against the back. His face was completely drained of color. I had never seen it so white."

Jay Gould once more passed off his illness as a cold, but it was not, and that night the household was disturbed by the coming of Dr. Munn and Miss Coots, a trained nurse. The patient was hemorrhaging from the lungs, and the doctor let the family know it was now only a matter of days or even hours.

Jay Gould struggled upward, renewing a little bit of the vitality that had made him the strongest, if most hated, man on Wall Street. He began issuing orders. The illness must be kept secret until the financial house was in complete order—he expected an immediate bear raid on the Gould holdings. Shaky or unnecessary holdings must be sold and converted to cash or government bonds during these last hours. The will of the great financier was done. Every day, George, Edwin, and Howard went to the office and did what was necessary to strengthen the western railroads and Western Union. All else was peripheral. They came back to 579 Fifth Avenue each night and reported, Dr. Munn fussing at their side, and from his deathbed with its huge black headboard, Jay Gould nodded and gave new instructions. Then, on the night of December 1, 1892, the hemorrhaging was worse than usual, and at 9:15 on the morning of December 2, Jay Gould died.

16

Jay Gould's Last Laugh

—————◆••••◆—————

The middle-aged millionaire was dead. Somehow it seemed that he had known his life was to be short, for he had tele-scoped all that others did in three score and ten into his fifty-six years, he had been virtually retired for a year or so, and all that concerned him in the last was the welfare of his family. What was there for them to share, what should be done with it, and who should do it?

—————◆••••◆—————

AT 9:20 on the morning of December 2, 1892, a sorrowful George Gould telephoned his offices in the Western Union building and announced that his father was dead. Two days earlier, he had informed the key executives of the Gould enterprises that Jay's condition was critical, and so they were not surprised, but the secret had been kept so well that the clerks, the errand boys, and the outside world of Wall Street suffered a thorough shock.

George's plans had been laid carefully. The three major Gould companies, the Missouri Pacific, the Western Union Telegraph

126

Company, and the Manhattan Railway Company, issued statements assuring the world that they were financially sound and their executives showed figures to prove it. Gould brokers bought Gould stocks heavily that day in behalf of the estate.

On Wall Street, the initial emotion was relief, "the sort of relief the Hebrew warriors felt when Goliath fell," said the newspapers. But after this brief hour of recriminations, worthier emotions began to emerge. Yet such was the hatred of Jay Gould by the press that even the facts of the financial world were twisted that day. At the end of the day's trading, Western Union was up 2 1/8, Manhattan Railway up 2 3/4, and Missouri Pacific up 1 1/2.

"No harder judgment was ever passed upon a departed millionaire," wrote Burton J. Hendrick in the *American Illustrated Magazine.*

"The advance of two or three points, upon the day when Gould's death was announced, in the quotations upon the securities of every one of the corporations with which his name was particularly identified shows that his death was regarded as the removal of a danger even from those corporations. . . ." the New York *Times* wrote on the day after his death.

The *World,* the *Herald,* and other media were equally uncomplimentary, none of them recognizing in their jubilation at the end of an old enemy that the tranquility in the marketplace could be attributed almost entirely to Jay Gould's arrangements before his death, and to plans carried out carefully by George, Edwin, and Howard in the hours afterwards.

The truth was not exposed to the public until three years later, and the facts came out only when David McClure, an independent lawyer, made an official report on the state of the Jay Gould fortune to the Surrogate of New York. The report revealed that in the last few weeks before he died, Jay Gould's every effort was turned to assuring the utmost strength of the fortune, and the least taxation, and that on the day of Jay's death, George behaved brilliantly and conservatively to save the values of properties that were really much shakier than anyone outside the companies believed them to be. George declared that the floating indebtedness of the Missouri Pacific and the St. Louis, Iron Mountain, and Southern could be paid off and that the companies would have sizeable cash surpluses even after so doing. But as McClure discovered, at that moment the indebtedness could not have been paid off without throwing these railroad companies either into reorganization or bankruptcy—and thus endangering the whole Gould estate.

So Jay Gould had the last laugh—his enemies were so busy congratulating each other on his death that they did not wreak the destruction they might have.

The funeral was held December 5 at the house, and several hundred of Gould's acquaintances, associates, employees, relatives, and friends came to pay their last respects. Railroad executives came from Denver, St. Louis, and Houston. The casket remained at the house that night, and next morning preparations were made to take it to the Gould mausoleum, an imposing structure modelled on a Greek temple which stood near those of Henry Clews, Austin Corbin, the Sloane brothers, and George H. Lorillard in Woodlawn Cemetery. Jay had caused this mausoleum to be built to a size large enough to accommodate the entire family. Its roof was 30 feet high and supported by granite columns standing on a broad base of three steps. The entrance was guarded by bronze doors with three heavy columns on either side. The tombs were in a vault beneath the surface, and the whole was very nearly secure from vandalism.

In 1892, tomb vandalism was very much on the minds of millionaires. Several years earlier the body of Alexander Turney Stewart, the wealthy merchant, had been stolen from his grave in New York and held for ransom, and the Goulds, having suffered so much from cranks already, were severely aware of the danger. So every necessary precaution was taken.

At about 9:30 on the morning of December 6, an undertaker's wagon drove up to the mansion on Fifth Avenue and picked up the flowers left over from the previous day's funeral, a broken column made of lilies and other flowers which had come from

George and Edith, a white pillow of roses from the grandchildren, and an orchid cross from Helen. The wagon drove out to Woodlawn where the undertakers deposited the flowers on the steps.

Just after 10 o'clock, a plain black undertaker's hearse and seven funeral carriages drove up before the mansion. A few minutes later, George's brougham, mounting coachman and footman, drove up behind.

George escorted the weeping Helen into the brougham. Edith Kingdon Gould, Edwin and Sally, Howard, Anna and Frank, Jay's half brother Abraham, several sisters, cousins, and other relatives all filed into the undertaker's carriages, and the undertaker, a Mr. Main, led the procession in a carriage all by himself, the hearse coming along behind, George behind that, and the mourner's carriages following.

They drove up Fifth Avenue, then cut over to Seventh, passing the Manhattan Railway Company repair shops, which were draped in black, then across Macomb's Dam Bridge to Jerome Avenue, and to the western entrance to the cemetery, where the vehicles stopped.

The casket was taken from the hearse and carried by hand to the door of the tomb where it was placed in an oaken box. Two half-tents, or marquees, had been set up in front of the tomb to protect the mourners from the vicious wind. Chancellor Henry MacCracken of New York University read the office of committal, and said a short prayer. Then the undertaker's assistants began *soldering the lid* on the coffin—a further protection deemed necessary against vandalism, and so long and grisly a process was it that even George lost his self-possession and began wiping his eyes with his handkerchief. The casket was deposited inside one of the twenty catacombs, the family marched out behind George, re-entered the carriages, and the ceremony was over.

But even in death, the newspapers could not or would not leave Gould's memory unsullied. The following day when the will was read and made public, the contents did not interest the newspapers so much as the fact that Jay Gould left no bequests to general charity. The implication was clear—more, it was stated—that Gould owed all to the American public and should have returned a large share of his fortune to the public. The charge was not quite fair to Jay Gould; while his charities had not been astounding, they had existed. In 1879 when Memphis was suffering from a yellow fever epidemic, he had given $5,000 to that town for nursing the sick and had authorized the town to draw on him for more. He had bought a parcel of land adjoining Mt. Vernon, George Washington's home, and presented it to the committee effecting the restoration. He had rebuilt the little church in his home town of Roxbury.

The presence of Chancellor Henry MacCracken of New York University at the burial ceremonies might have been a tipoff to an enterprising reporter, too, about another Gould charity. The chancellor was seeking funds from prominent New Yorkers to move New York University—at least partially—out of the ever-more-crowded Washington Square campus and up into the Bronx where land was cheap. A few weeks before Jay Gould's death, he and the chancellor had met, and Gould had authorized his attorneys to look into the best methods of making a large gift to the university. Gould's death did not disturb the plans—eventually the gift was made by Helen Gould in honor of her father.

Altogether, of course, these were not huge charities for a multi-millionaire, and Jay Gould would hardly go down in the pages of history as a grand philanthropist in the manner of John D. Rockefeller. But Jay's day of glory and the elder Rockefeller's were separated by more than a decade—a very important decade in deciding the public responsibility of great fortunes. While Jay Gould was not so generous with outsiders as he might have been, neither had he so black a character as history has depicted.

The disposition of the fortune had occupied much of Jay's thought in the past five years, and many of his waking moments in the last two weeks of his life. Two weeks before his death, on November 18, Jay Gould had handed his lawyer, Judge John F.

Dillon, a new codicil for the will. And right down to that last night he was thinking about the will. George, Edwin, Howard, and Helen were its executors, and later, if one of them died, Anna or Frank would take that one's place. George and Helen, further, were appointed guardians of Anna and Frank. No outsider was to be involved in family affairs.

Jay had been supporting his three living sisters for many years, and now he left each of them $25,000 and a $2,000-a-year income for life. His half brother Abraham, an agent for the Missouri Pacific Railroad in the west, received a like bequest.

As to the main body of the fortune, first came the special case of George, Jay's eldest son, who had been managing the father's affairs for the past five years. George received $5,000,000 outright, plus $500,000 for each of those years he had worked as manager of the Gould properties. He was to have a similar salary in the future. But deducted from this was to be the money Jay had put up for George's house at Sixty-seventh and Fifth Avenue along with other moneys advanced to George.

Because he was the old man's namesake, and for no other ascertainable reason, George's son Jay was singled out to receive $500,000 in his own right and the first son, Kingdon, passed by.

All these bequests, and debts within the family, came to $6,500,-000. Once these were subtracted, according to the McClure report, the estate was worth $73,224,547.08, this amount to be held in trust for the six children of Jay Gould. Each child was to have a one-sixth interest, except that it was not outright: that is, if Helen should die without children, then her one-sixth would be divided among the other five Gould children or their heirs, but the heirs of one line could never receive more than one-sixth, no matter how many of them there were. For example, if Helen died childless, Anna had one child, and Frank had six, Anna's one child would receive as much of Helen's share as Frank's six children combined.

There were two other important qualifications: that the children must be blood children, born in wedlock, and that George was to rule over the affairs of Anna and Frank (with Helen's help), and that his voice was to control in any case of disagreement about family matters.

As for the rest, Helen was given the house at 579 Fifth Avenue with all that it held, plus the use of Lyndhurst until Frank came of age. She had $6,000 a month from the estate to keep up both places.

The whole purpose of the will was to keep the family together. Seventy-five million dollars or so divided into six parts averaged out at about $12,000,000 per child and could be dissipated in two or three generations by nothing more than faulty birth control. But $75,000,000 kept intact was a sizeable sum that could sway kingdoms, and properly managed, it could increase more than the sum of the parts would indicate.

Of course, the fortune was really larger than these figures indicated—by far. For example, the *Atalanta* was valued at only $100,000 in the capitulation, but Jay had turned down an offer for $200,000 for her although he had scarcely used the yacht for three years. Furnishings and valuables at the mansion were listed at $146,000, although they were worth more, the antique furniture and art objects alone running up the value, and the contents at Lyndhurst were listed at only $117,000 though they were worth twice as much. The stocks and bonds included 101,000 shares of Missouri Pacific plus 14,000 bonds at $1,000 face value; 220,000 shares of Western Union stock, which meant control by a handsome margin; and 100,000 shares of Manhattan Railway Company stock, which also meant control. There were big chunks of Wabash Railroad stock, Texas and Pacific Railroad, Consolidated Coal Company of St. Louis, Wagner Palace Car Company, and perhaps $10,000,000 in bonds of the St. Louis, Iron Mountain, and Southern Railway Company. One could argue values far into the night, but a liberal estimate might have put the residuary estate at over $150,000,000. The $74,000,000 was certainly most conservative and calculated for tax purposes—the New York estate tax being roughly 1 per cent on an estate so large.

No one could say that Jay had not left his family well protected, financially, or that he had missed any considerations in his attempts to keep the family together. He had appointed a head for the family, George, and he had given his children very nearly equal shares in his estate. He had kept his houses, with the provision that Helen was to make a home for the younger ones, Howard, Anna, and Frank, until they married or went to live alone. And he had persuaded rather than ordered the older children to follow the course he dictated. George served him willingly. Helen gave up all thought of young men and marriage to carry out her father's wishes. Edwin was prepared to assist his brother in every way, and so was Howard.

Never had a family of substance been more close-knit than the Goulds. Never had such a family been surrounded by more provisions in the will of the father to assure the retention of the family ties.

Then how would they fare, the Goulds and their fortune?

17

"Miss Tyler Regrets . . . ."

---

*In the condition called metal fatigue, a
tool or a machine which has been working steadily and comfortably for years suddenly flies to pieces. Such things can also
happen with families.*

TROUBLE came from several directions almost immediately after Jay
Gould's body was interred in the catacombs of the Gould mausoleum in Woodlawn Cemetery, although there seemed to be no
visible reason for divisions to set in. Nevertheless, here is what
happened.

The change in physical affairs after the father's death probably
bothered George less than any other member of the family. That is
not to say that George was an indelicate or unloving son. It *is* to
say that the changes time wreaks in families began to set in by
1892. George was twenty-eight and married, with two children and
another on the way. He lived in a house of his own a mile up

Fifth Avenue from the old family home. He had his own friends, his own amusements. And although he was never welcome in the parlors of the Vanderbilts, he was living an intensely social life among thoroughly respectable people in New York. Furlough Lake in the Catskills had been the George Gould family's first summer house, and they had loved it. But with the increasing social responsibility that Edith Kingdon Gould felt upon her husband's emergence as head of the family, Furlough Lake seemed just too far away for entertaining. And George wanted a place from which he could commute to the office during summers. He might have to stay over in town during the week, but he could at least be out of doors on weekends.

The George Jay Goulds now discovered the pleasant community of Lakewood, New Jersey, where several millionaire families maintained homes. A Rockfeller summered there and built a house. And there were other pleasant people who liked the country life, doctors, lawyers, and inheritors of money. The community was very social and very horsey. It was not long before George was riding to hounds and had begun learning to play polo. Anyone who had ever seen Jay Gould striding purposefully down Wall Street in baggy pants would hardly believe that his son and heir would be found twisting his mustaches and "knocking them home" with other young bloods on the polo field. But times had changed. By the winter of 1894, George had decided to make Lakewood his home. In January, he gave a great ball at the Lakewood Hotel and brought a special train load of guests down from New York for the party. The whole public portion of the hotel was turned over to the Gould affair that night and the place was decorated in bunting and palms. A "Viennese Orchestra and Austrian Band" played behind screens. Champagne corks popped and the dance floor bustled until midnight when a late supper was served in the dining room. Never had Lakewood enjoyed a more successful affair.

As far as business was concerned, this first year or so after Jay Gould's death was spent simply in shoring up the investments.

George's concerns were to make sure the sharks of Wall Street did not learn how shaky Missouri Pacific had become and to retire some of the railroad's floating debt so that it could show profits and calm whatever fears might arise. Under the watchful eye of lawyer McClure, who represented the Surrogate's office, George concentrated his efforts on cleaning up the estate's loose ends.

Edwin simply helped him. Less flamboyant and much quieter, he was given to solitary canoe trips up and down the rivers of New York state. One time, Edwin even went canoeing alone down through New York Harbor, around Staten Island, past Navesink, to Sandy Hook, the end of the coastal waters, and then back again. He camped out and slept under his canoe at night. Given such evidence, one could scarcely say Edwin was without resources or interests, but he was a quiet one. His first child, Edwin Gould, Jr., was born in 1893, and Sally was happy keeping up the house at 1 East Forty-seventh Street, which Jay had willed them. Edwin went to the office in the Western Union building each day with more devotion than did George. He was seldom tardy and almost never absent—one could not say the same for his older brother. Edwin became the workhorse: watching the market, cleaning up details, he became the office man.

If George was the financial manager of the Gould family, Helen became the spiritual manager. Twenty-four years old when her father died, she quickly became plump and matronly. She did not want to live alone, so with George's help, she persuaded her cousin Alice Northrop to come and stay at 579 for a time. Alice was teaching school in Camden, New Jersey, and she thought she ought to go home. George was obdurate.

"Alice," he said, "you just can't go now . . . that's all."

When he wanted to exercise authority, George could be manly and persuasive. He told Cousin Alice that Helen needed her, which was true, and that Uncle Jay had suggested that she be brought to live at the house as a companion for Helen, which might not have been true. Alice hesitated, but before the will was read, she was persuaded to give up her career and come and help Helen raise the younger Goulds.

Of all the children, Helen was worst stricken by her father's death. She had been closest to him, sharing his love of flowers, assigning herself the role of substitute mother, and making Jay's interests and Jay's life her own. Hardly was he buried when she set about a life of good works. Her first task would be to rebuild the Roxbury Reformed Church in honor of her father. It was a charity close to his own heart, and he had done the initial planning, setting aside $100,000 for the project. Helen undertook its supervision, laying the cornerstone on September 2, 1893.

Helen's idea of an outing was to attend the Chicago World's Fair in that summer of 1893 and to spend gruelling hours trudging from one exhibit to another until she had seen everything. She went with Mrs. Russell Sage and Cousin Alice, returning with renewed vigor to Lyndhurst and the overseeing of the flowers and the management of the household.

About this time Helen also introduced Edwin into the ways of sweet charity during one of her brother's visits to the country home. In the acquisition of the estate lands, Jay Gould had purchased one substantial property with a big house that stood about halfway between Lyndhurst and the village of Elmsford. He had no use for the house, sturdy as it was, and it had stood vacant. Coming across it one day on a walk, Helen and Edwin had stopped and wandered through the empty rooms, and Edwin had thoughtfully turned his Prince-of-Wales profile to his sister.

"Sister," he said, "do you know what I was just thinking? I was thinking that . . . I could see children here. Poor children . . . with no one else in the world to look after them . . . or make them happy."

Helen's eyes brimmed with tears, so happy was she that her older brother was willing to join her in good works.

Helen's religiosity found kinship in Edwin's love for children, then, but that same quality in the oldest sister also brought about the first cracks in the family's solidity. Her houses at Lyndhurst and 579 Fifth Avenue were quickly filled with religious objects. On birthdays and other occasions, brothers and sisters were almost certain to receive a prayer book, a Bible, or some religious symbol from Sister Helen. Her very goodness forbade the use of liquor in the house and successfully quashed any gaiety. Consequently, while Howard, Anna, and Frank made their homes with Helen as their father had planned, Anna and Frank spent as much of their time as they could at George's house, where the atmosphere was lighter and more charitable toward the foibles of the young. Anna, in fact, grew quite sharply away from her sister.

Two girls could not have been more different: Helen was already matronly and settled in her life; Anna was frankly interested in young men, a fast social pace, and the delights of the world around her. Frank was a bit young for such tastes, but he shared Anna's general attitudes.

Howard fled Helen's virtuous household whenever he could manage to be away. In 1893, he joined the New York Yacht Club (there was no stigma on Jay Gould's sons like the one there had been on the father), and he kept a small sailing yacht. Sometimes he stayed at the club rather than at 579 Fifth Avenue. He managed to time his visits to Lyndhurst so that Helen was either absent or extremely busy.

In the winter of 1893, Howard spent much of his time going to the theater, and especially to Charles Frohman's Empire Theater. The twenty-three-year-old gay blade had been smitten by a beautiful young actress actually named Bessie Kirtland but who appeared in several of Mr. Frohman's productions that winter under the more euphonious stage name of Odette Tyler. Howard met Miss Tyler at a party early in the season. Miss Tyler was flattered, as any girl would be, by the young millionaire's attentions, and the acquaintance blossomed into romance. She appeared in *The Girl I Left Behind Me* and in *Gudgeons* that season, with, of course, Howard watching, enraptured, from his box at nearly every performance.

All winter long the theatrical community observed the budding romance. Toward the end of March, 1894, Miss Tyler accepted a $9,500 ruby ring from Howard, and let it be known that they were engaged to be married. At George Gould's house, there was much quaffing of champagne and celebrating. Edith Kingdon Gould kept up her acquaintances in the world of the theater, and she was happy enough to welcome another theatrical lady into the family.

Not so Helen. Helen was her mother's child. She alone among the Goulds had inherited the inhibitions of Murray Hill. Among them was a strong distaste for the theatrical community, although such poor opinions were no longer generally held. Helen did not like the notion of this marriage, and she said so.

Howard paid very little attention to his older sister. He spent more time at his club and less time at the house and went ahead with the wedding plans.

Apparently he did not fully appreciate his sister. Helen let it be known far and wide that she objected to his marriage to an actress, and when her objection became known, the press filled her in on the details of Miss Tyler's life. The actress was not Miss Tyler at all, or even Miss Kirtland. The lady was *divorced.*

A divorcee! They might as well have said Miss Tyler was a prostitute as far as Helen was concerned. She redoubled her outcries and called all the family to complain.

Miss Tyler was not pleased when she learned of Helen Gould's fuss. Odette Tyler was a vivacious and beautiful woman about whom there had been no previous scandal. When Helen hired a detective to look into the antecedents of Miss Tyler and her family in Virginia, the detective found that Miss Tyler had an excellent reputation, and that as far as her divorce was concerned, it had been granted on the grounds of desertion after her husband had abandoned her. No scandal could be found because there was none.

Having been subjected to such ignominy from her prospective sister-in-law, Odette Tyler called Howard Gould to account. Was it true, she asked, that his family was opposed to their marriage?

Not all of his family, Howard replied. Just some of his family.

Could this kind of harassment be expected in the future? asked Miss Tyler.

Howard certainly hoped not.

Miss Tyler observed and considered and decided she was not pleased with the prospects. She removed Howard's big ruby ring, returned it to him, and returned him to his sister.

"I would not consent to enter a family that harbors such unjust thoughts about me," said Miss Tyler.

Howard was so shocked that he could not even argue, and when he left his fiancée of a few minutes before he had nothing to consider but the unbelievability of womankind.

Miss Tyler might have reconsidered, but soon she began receiving letters and messages from what her friends called "the monstrosity managers" offering her huge sums to go on the stage and play the woman scorned, the woman jilted, or the woman who had thrown over the Gould millions. She could have had anything so long as *Gould* could be prominently displayed on the marquees. Miss Tyler was first surprised, then she wept. Finally, she broke down completely. Was it not enough that her happiness had been blighted by Helen Gould? Must she now accept the gibes of the world in her unhappiness?

Odette Tyler was scheduled to take *Gudgeons* on tour and to play the lead in the next season's production of *Shenandoah*. Suddenly all these prospects seemed abhorrent to her, and she told Charles Frohman she must take the rest of the season off. Frohman understood, and on April 14, Miss Tyler left New York for Sharon Springs, Virginia, to try to recover her aplomb and to forget that a family named Gould existed.

Moodily, Howard drew a little farther away from the other Goulds.

18

Anna Gets her Count

———◆•••►———

*The early signs of family dissension were
in evidence within a year after the death
of the patriarch. As always in these matters, the differences were occasioned by
disagreements in judgment, and the ability
of the younger generation to exercise good
judgment seemed to vary.*

———◆•••►———

GEORGE JAY GOULD, at the age of thirty, was a prodigiously busy
man—busy as a beaver—a comparison not too inept since he was
not only keeping the Gould financial house in order, he was also
building his own house.

Having purchased about 200 acres of land on the edge of the
lake at Lakewood, New Jersey, George employed Bruce Price, the
celebrated architect, with instructions to produce for him one of
the most notable country houses in America yet, at the same time,
a livable house. Price built a house directly in the pine forest on the
edge of the lake, an oblong structure with two long fronts and two
shorter ones. The kitchen buildings were built on one end of the

house attached to the dining room. A magnificent conservatory, with skylights and tile floor, occupied the other end of the family rooms. George wanted a country house but not a palace, and so he put strings on the architect to be sure he got no more than he wanted. From the entrance to the grounds, which were protected by an iron fence, the house was set on the left, overlooking the lake. On the right were the stables where George's polo ponies were to be housed. It was a day of bastardizing styles, and Price built the house of brick, terra cotta, stucco, and dark wood, giving it an English Georgian look—and then he put a French château roof on it. Inside, white and gold were the chief colors. The main entrance led off a porte-cochere, and this led into the great hall, done in white with crimson walls, with a magnificent curved marble staircase and a bronze and gold rail and balustrades. At the top of the wall was a frieze of the Canterbury pilgrims entering the town of Canterbury, the carpenter mounted on his ass and the others trailing along, all very jolly, as painted by Robert V. Sewall, a prominent muralist of the day. From the front, to the left of the stairway, was the billiard room, and to the right a handsome but very dark "library" where it would have been almost impossible to read without the most powerful of lamps—none of which was in evidence. The library's handsome burnt-wood walls were designed by J. W. Fosdick.

Across from the great hall stood the music room, sporting panel paintings of nudes in the Roman mode, and here a good deal of money had been spent, the artists alone having included Charles M. Shean, G. W. Maynard, Harper Pennington, and Irving R. Wiles. To the left of the music room was the dining room, which had its own frieze depicting the fruits of the seasons—each fruit painted in its own ripe colors, standing against the dead white of the dining room walls with its jade green tints for emphasis. (The green of the walls matched Edith's eyes.) The "morning room," where the sun shone only in the afternoon, was gilt with wall panels of white silk embroidery. Edith received here when guests and clergymen came to call.

The second floor was devoted to suites of rooms, bedrooms, sitting rooms, and bathrooms, with George's personal suite (including an upstairs study). Edith had her own rooms, and there were several suites for guests. The children, four of them in these early days, occupied a portion of the third floor with their nurses and governesses, and the servants occupied the rest of that floor.

The furnishings of the house were all that could be desired— the decorator was given a free hand. There were antique Italian walnut armchairs with spiral legs and stretchers, French Renaissance end tables, French marquetry tea tables, settees, and armchairs from the periods of Louis XIV and Louis XVI, beds of satinwood and ironwood, unglazed bisque vases, Chinese porcelains (mixed with American porcelains showing such scenes as Eliza Crossing the Ice) and this pièce de résistance: a pair of urns with *pâte sur pâte* decoration in the form of allegorical female figures of Cupids and stars in white relief on a blue background, with ornamentation on the neck, shoulders, handles, and foot in enameled colors and gilt in conventional *Egyptian* design. These were signed L. Solon.

There were Minton porcelain garnitures, Minton china oyster plates, Limoges china plates, Wedgwood fish plates, Wedgwood and Spode game plates, Staffordshire oyster plates, bouillon sets, soup sets, and all the equipment for serving any and every dish known to the George Gould chef. There were Persian rugs and Kazak rugs and Feraghans and Hamadans, Koulahs, Pekings, and French carpeting.

George was not then much of an art collector, so what was hung in the house went heavily to sporting prints and etchings, photographs of yachts, and a few oils, mostly of yachts and sea scenes.

The stable held no fewer than twenty-one vehicles, from a buckboard surrey to an opera bus, and included a tea cart, a Victoria, a road break, a buggy cart, a pony cart wagonette, a basket phaeton, and a breaking cart, along with several broughams of various kinds and makes. The stable was much more formidable,

really, than the house—its expense was quite out of keeping—
although the house itself was much simpler than the country
houses of such men as Cornelius Vanderbilt, who occupied the
magnificent Breakers at Newport, a huge place, its rooms three
and four times the size of those of Georgian Court, the name of
George's house. But the Vanderbilt stables were not nearly so
impressive. The Vanderbilt stables in Newport represented transportation; the Gould stables at Lakewood represented George's
greatest interests outside business: riding and polo.

George had one other major avocation, however, in keeping
with his role as a millionaire: yachting. The children had inherited
the *Atalanta,* and George was the one who used her. He also owned
a big schooner, the *Hildegarde,* which had once belonged to the
Prince of Wales. In the spring of 1894, George joined Howard, the
other older son interested in yachting, in the purchase of the 85-
foot racing sloop *Vigilant,* the successful America's Cup defender
in the races of the previous year against Lord Dunraven's *Valkyrie.* The American yacht had been built by the designer Herreshoff for a syndicate composed of Commodore E. D. Morgan of
the New York Yacht Club, C. Oliver Iselin, Adrian Iselin, Cornelius Vanderbilt, August Belmont, O. H. P. Belmont, Perry
Belmont, Charles R. Flint, and Dr. W. Barton Hopkins. James
Gordon Bennett had intended to buy the yacht from this syndicate
at $30,000, a bargain price considering the fact that she cost $67,000
at the Herreshoff yard, and her total bill ran above $125,000 before
the America's Cup season was over. But Bennett's offer was con-
tingent upon his being able to arrange a number of races in English waters during the summer of 1894. When he could not, he
backed away. George and Howard stepped in and purchased the
yacht for $25,000, apparently a bargain.

But what would they do with her?

They were both members of the New York Yacht Club, but
they had not been prominent in sailing yacht and racing circles.
George had sailed small boats since boyhood, as had Howard, but
their father's interest in boating had been confined to steam yachting, and they had not stepped out in this intensely competitive

field of ocean sailing before. For a time, George had raced the 46-foot sloop *Fanita* in local contests at the American and Eastern Yacht Clubs, but as his father grew to depend more on him in Wall Street, he had given up yacht racing.

The newspapers speculated that George and Howard might be buying the *Vigilant* to convert her to a cruiser, in which case she would not be so much of a bargain since her spars would have to be shortened and her cabin space rebuilt if she were to be safe and comfortable for offshore pleasure sailing.

No, George said, pleasantly but definitely, when questioned by the press. He and his brother were going to race *Vigilant*. Yes, he had the time now, or he would make it, and yes he and Howard were serious.

August Belmont pronounced the benediction of the New York Yacht Club:

"They have money and push," Belmont said of the Gould brothers, "and the reputation of the boat will not suffer any in their hands."

At this moment, George was still struggling to pull together the various parts of the estate, and until the taxes were settled and affairs put in order, he was more or less marking time as a businessman. Thus he *did* turn his eyes to the amusements of millionaires. And as for Edith, his wife, she had decided upon Jay's death that she was to become the *grande dame* of the Gould family, and she began to play the part. Edith had never pinched pennies. Now she secured from George a famous and many-stranded pearl necklace which was reported to have cost $500,000 at Tiffany's. She never travelled without a king's ransom of jewels on her person or in her bag. One day in the mountains, for example, Edith was driving between Furlough Lodge and Arkville when she suddenly missed her handbag. While the major domo of the lodge, Superintendent Keator, went back to look for the bag, Edith grew increasingly agitated. Small wonder—she had been carrying $81,000 worth of diamonds, just in case she wanted to dress up a little. The jewels were found, picked up by an honest farmer's wife.

The expansive feeling of power and wealth that sometimes

attacks the sons of the very rich had obviously begun to work on George. From all sides he was flattered as a brilliant businessman. Where such flattery would have meant nothing to Jay, who had been thoroughly experienced in the ups and downs of business, the constant stream of praise and obeisance of Wall Street persuaded the still-handsome George that he was something apart from ordinary men. His vast wealth and vast leisure to enjoy that wealth were also persuasive. Assisted by Edith, George set about to stage a series of entertainments for himself and those of his family who wished to come. Helen never budged from Fifth Avenue and her good works to attend George's parties, bemoaning all the while the fact that wines and even spirits were consumed at these affairs. Edwin was conspicuously absent, too, except when Sally, who was far more socially inclined, could track him down at one of his charities or at the office and force him to don his formal clothes.

Howard liked George's parties, however, and particularly the theatrical crowd that was to be found at Georgian Court on the weekends. The actresses were not all beautiful, but many were, not all intelligent, but some were, and the effect was generally stunning even if sometimes in the absolute sense of the word, as when one young showgirl from one of the current theater's more attractive chorus lines came to dinner on the arm of a prominent playwright.

Because all she had to offer any party was purely visible, the playwright had cautioned the young beauty to keep her head high and her mouth closed. The young lady promised, but as she entered the house, she gazed up in awe at the frieze in the great hall.

Edith, playing *la grande dame,* swept her arm up to the mural of the Canterbury pilgrims.

"How do you like the frieze?" she asked the young lady.

"Marvelous," replied the beauty. "Jesus going into Jerusalem on the donkey!"

Edith Kingdon Gould swept away, the playwright choked on his champagne, and the young lady moved serenely on to enjoy the rest of the evening's entertainment.

But while Edith's salons were not perhaps marked by the brilliant, literary talk of world-famous litterateurs, they were at least stimulating, particularly to Anna, George's youngest sister, who at nineteen was very much a young lady, very much interested in the wide world of society, and very much a "catch" for some lucky young man. Anna was not beautiful, being short and a little robust (as were all the Gould women), and her face was no match for that of Helen of Troy. But she was vivacious and pleasant, and her gaiety so thoroughly masked a will of iron that her young men were quite unconscious of this inheritance from Jay.

Earlier, in 1893, Anna had fallen in love with Frank Woodruff, a handsome young actor, but Helen complained so that Woodruff backed away just as Miss Tyler had backed away from Howard. Later that year, Anna had fallen in love with Oliver Harriman, a cousin of Edward Harriman, the Wall Street broker who was just becoming interested in railroads. Edward Harriman was a good friend of George's at this time, young Oliver was well-to-do and quite presentable, and as far as is known, all members of both families approved of the match. The couple became engaged—and Anna went off to Paris in the spring of 1894 to shop for her trousseau at Worth's and the other fashionable and expensive salons.

Anna liked *l'esprit parisien*. She stayed with Miss Fanny Reed, a lady who ran a salon catering to young American heiresses. Anna would be "finished" here and come home with *éclat* and *élan* enough quite to astound New York Society. To keep the young American misses happy, Miss Fanny Reed opened her house to the young nobility of Paris, and the less well-heeled young men came around in droves in this era of alliances between blue blood and yellow gold. At Miss Reed's, Anna was paid much attention by the Duc de Talleyrand-Périgord and by his young cousin, the Count Marie Ernest Paul Boniface de Castellane. The former was attracted to Anna, but the latter pursued her madly. She might be weighted down with debilities, she might have had warts and a clubfoot, any negative quality would have been immediately cancelled in the face of her twelve million dollars, give or take a few, and for that sum, Boni, as he was known, would easily sell his soul. Indeed, as it appears, he need not worry about selling it, it was sold for him by his bankers. Count Boni was twenty-eight years old and a poor relative of the Talleyrand-Périgord families. His own parents, unable to afford an apartment in one of the fashionable sections of the city, lived in a broken-down château outside Paris, and he eked out a miserable existence while he searched for a millionaire heiress who could relieve him of his need.

Boni settled on Anna as the best thing available on short notice, and the notice was short indeed—his creditors were closing in on him. He was notorious, he had had a score of mistresses, he gamed and fought and drank, and spent money like water. The only thing about the girl he saw at Miss Reed's that impressed him was her money. She had her father's deep-set eyes. *"Elle a les yeux d'un singe, un singe qu'on a pris en captivité,"* said Robert de Montesquiou in describing her. Boni was less charitable; he found her "shy, childish, a trifle malicious"—and he knew nothing about her. Boni's friend, the Marchioness of Anglesey, the former Mary Livingston King of the Livingstons, told him that he did not understand American women and ought to stay away from them, particularly Anna Gould, whom the Marchioness described as "essentially the child of her father," and "with a will of iron."

But Boni was in no position to cavil—he needed the money.

With all these noblemen about, kissing her hand and whispering sweet nothings, Anna's head was quite turned before long— away from Oliver Harriman. She broke off the engagement and remained in Paris on the excuse that George and Edith were coming over. Anna was still a minor, and under the terms of Jay's will, she could not marry and inherit unless George approved of her husband-to-be. George and Edith did come in the spring of 1894 with *Atalanta*. Anna dutifully joined them in yachting around England, then brought them to France. Whatever George thought of the dapper, almost effeminate Count, he kept it to himself, feeling either that a count in the family would be useful or that the fellow might make Anna happy and that was what counted. George met the Duc de Talleyrand-Périgord along with other French noblemen, but he paid most attention to the count, who was obviously the favorite.

Somewhat to the annoyance of Edwin and Howard, who were entrusted with the management of Gould affairs, Russell Sage, and, especially, the New York press, George went to the "other side" in the spring of 1894 with the announced intention of not coming home until autumn, and that is what he did.

Anna returned with her brother. Count Boni de Castellane was not far behind, his suit being looked upon by the elder Goulds with much favor. But, of course, the suit must finally be pursued in the United States, for it was of no use whatsoever for an American millionaire to make an alliance with noble European blood if all were done in Europe. So Boni, so poor yet so close to a fortune, borrowed enough money from his bankers to make the trip to America.

He arrived in New York in August without a sou. In the apartment of his friend, Raoul Duval, a well-to-do young Frenchman, he explained his prospects, whereupon he was granted another loan and was taken in as a nonpaying boarder.

Soon Boni was asked to visit the Goulds in the mansion on Sixty-seventh Street and Fifth Avenue. He sniffed in distaste at what he saw, the Moorish parlor, the opulent furnishings which were just too heavy and mismatched—mix-matched, one might say. He was asked to tea at 597 where he met Helen and Mrs. Sage. Helen took an instinctive dislike to Boni, thought him a fortune hunter, and did all she could to discourage the marriage. Her dear friend Mrs. Russell Sage quite agreed.

But Helen's currency was not particularly valid with the other Goulds—she had already meddled disastrously in family affairs and had virtually driven Howard away from home. And Boni was intelligent, so he took up the airs of "the virtuous curate," as he put it, and Helen began to believe that she had misread the poor young man after all.

Anna wished and waited. She liked the idea of marrying a

count, but she did not like the idea of leaving America. "I don't like foreigners and I won't live out of America," she said at one point. Such a statement struck panic into the breast of a man living on an overdrawn letter of credit. But Boni was made of steel, and he persisted; Anna's homeliness, her queer relatives, her strong character and wilfulness—nothing could turn him back from those twelve million dollars.

As for Anna, she still lived at 579 and was still more or less Helen's ward.

Boni thought he had confused Helen by his abrupt change of manner, and he was partly right. Helen asked the coachman, the footman, and the other servants to keep an eye on Anna, and she engaged one private detective to follow Boni and another to check up on him. Anna's discovery of her sister's concern infuriated her, and she behaved much more sweetly to this suitor about whom she had so many qualms.

To fan the fires in Anna's bosom, Boni decided to bestow some of his favors on other young American heiresses, although he could ill afford the respite from the main chase. He went to Newport for the season along with Raoul Duval, knowing that the Goulds did not go to Newport. The two Frenchman gave a dinner dance at the Café Renaissance which was declared by all to be the "most important of the season." In September, they returned to Duval's apartments near the Waldorf Astoria Hotel. Soon they were invited to Georgian Court, as Boni fully expected. After several days there, it was back to New York again. There were stays at other country houses, but the visits were most frequent and longest at Georgian Court, where the count went fox hunting with George and the Monmouth County pack.

Boni and Anna went to Lyndhurst, where Boni found life unutterably dull—there was nothing to do but go to church and walk in the conservatory, swim in the pool and play billiards. Helen regulated every activity precisely. He went back to New York in disgust. Time was running out—so was his patience.

At Christmas, Helen insisted that Anna and Boni come to

Lyndhurst again. They did, but the season at Lyndhurst was so overwhelmingly religious and so dull that Anna went to town, wired George, secured an invitation to Georgian Court, and they fled to New Jersey. Boni did not like George much—George represented the uncouth American businessman in Boni's eyes, and he thought Georgian Court a monstrosity. Boni did appreciate the gold plate off which they dined, but not the skins of bears and lions strewn around, particularly up and down the grand staircase. And the cement copies of granite funerary urns which lined the lawns of Georgian Court, along with the cement statuary in the gardens, repelled him.

Yet by this time the question was already framed in New York salons: when would Boni say the word that would give George and the other Goulds a title in the family to match the Levi Mortons and half a dozen other wealthy American families whose daughters had collected coronets? The coronet was already available. The Prince del Drago, a Corsican relative of the del Dragos of Spain, had brought over a coronet which he put on the market for $70,000, and George had picked it up in anticipation of the happy event.

The beginning of 1895 arrived and it was deemed that Boni had been courting Anna long enough to satisfy the proprieties. George organized a rail trip to Canada in his private car. George and Edith went, along with the count and Anna. Also present were Kittie Cameron, the vivacious daughter of Sir Roderick Cameron, then living in New York, and Richard Peters and Raoul Duval, Boni's friends. Somewhere between the Canadian Rockies and Montreal, Boni put the question, Anna answered, and the press was informed that the romance had culminated in an engagement to be married. Not one New York society editor experienced a tremor of surprise.

Boni was running out of his bankers' money, and it was fortuitous that the engagement had come when it did. The problem was to make sure that the marriage occurred before he was reduced to selling his extra pair of pants. In this contretemps,

George exhibited the deep understanding of a great financier: plans were made for the marriage to take place almost immediately, at the end of February—just as soon as the Count's parents could raise the money to buy passage over from France.

Immediately upon the return from Canada, Edith, acting as substitute mother, set about arranging the wedding, which was to be *the* social event of New York in the spring of 1895, and which would put the final seal on the Gould emergence into the "glittering society" of New York.

When the editors of the New York *World* learned of the plans, they made ready to enter into the spirit. ". . . A house which rivals the swellest establishments in town and a real live count ought to be a passport for them into the innermost of the inner circles, which privilege they so much crave," said the *World,* meaning apparently the Vanderbilt crowd. The brevity of this dispatch reveals the attitude of the New York press toward the gilded peacocks of Millionaires' Row—a combination of sneering and fawning, less admiring than jealous, like a palace *jongleur* who has been so long in the service of His Majesty that he has come to feel superior to the court and all its doings. Still, the newspapers knew what their readers wanted. Every shopgirl and every shoe salesman in New York panted over the doings of high society. It was the practice of thousands of poor young men and women to go strolling up Fifth Avenue on a Sunday afternoon, gazing toward the drawn drapes of the mansions on Millionaires' Row, and hoping the everlasting hope that somehow, in Horatio Alger fashion, the employer of the young man in question would see the youth's true merit, so he, too, might become a captain of business, and his lady, too, might drive out in a brougham in furs with coachman and footman up, in the fashion of Edith Gould or Alice Vanderbilt or Caroline Astor.

The Vanderbilts during that period might well say that the Goulds would never be taken into polite society, but in fact, by 1894, the Goulds had already been accepted nearly everywhere. Under the sponsorship of Mrs. Paran Stevens, they were accepted in even more places during this year, and they were invited to Mrs. Astor's ball—*the* accolade, as anyone in New York knew. The Vanderbilts might hold out for another generation or so, but the Goulds had come into Society, and if they chose to spend most of their time in summer places in New Jersey and up the Hudson River rather than at Newport, that choice was their own. The Goulds, including George, never felt terribly attracted to New York society and its amusements. They wished to belong, but they preferred polo and racquet games, canoeing and yachting to the coaching and party-going that were staple amusements among the Newport toffs. This wedding proved the essential modesty of the Goulds in matters of public display. When the William K. Vanderbilts married off Consuelo to the Duke of Marlborough a few months later, the pomp and ceremony at St. Thomas' Episcopal Church, before a huge crowd of guests from polite society, could not be rivalled. But the Goulds chose to make of Anna's wedding a family affair, as all Gould weddings before this, and it was to be held at George's town house at Sixty-seventh and Fifth Avenue.

The festivities of the bridal week began on February 23 when the Count and Anna gave a matinee party for a few friends at the Harlem Opera House where Mrs. Potter and Kyrle Bellew were appearing in *Charlotte Corday*. The Goulds occupied the two lower boxes at the right of the stage where they entertained the Prince and Princess Hartzfeldt, Mrs. Van Rensselaer Cruger, and the Prince Peppenheim and Count Hadik with their ladies. The word was out early, of course, due to the exertions of an active press agent for the theater, and the Harlem Opera House was jammed to the aisles for the matinee performance, to the surprise of the cast and the pleasure of the management.

That day, as Anna and the Count whispered to each other in the darkness of their box, Howard Gould sailed from Europe. Moody Howard had gone into business for himself the previous summer, putting up $100,000 and thus becoming a special partner in the firm of Julio Vale, a venture with breadth and aggressiveness enough to suggest Jay's shade. Howard had entered the import-export and ranching business in Colombia, and, really, more than that. The papers filed with the New York County Clerk showed the full extent of the undertaking:

> . . . for the development of a general merchandise, export and import business . . . . the establishment, maintenance, and development of a general commission and commercial exchange business in San José, Colombia and New York City, and elsewhere as may be agreed upon; the acquisition, maintenance, development, irrigation, and operation of cattle ranches, coffee plantations and farms for the purpose of grazing and general agriculture in the state of Colombia, Venezuela, and elsewhere, and the acquisition, maintenance, development, and operation of *railroads* [italics mine] and other means of transit and transportation in said states and elsewhere.

Howard had gone to Europe in the winter on business and to escape his family. The matter of Odette Tyler still hung heavy between them, and Howard had the feeling that he had not been given adequate support from George and Edwin against Helen. But Howard's attitude did not affect his affection for his little sister Anna, who was not involved in the dispute, and, having been the last to be informed of the coming wedding, he rushed home to be on hand.

Each day following the announcement of the wedding, the society editors vied for space to reveal the details. Anna's bridesmaids were to be her chum Kittie Cameron, her sister Helen, and Beatrice Richardson and Adelaide Montgomery, school chums from the Gardner School and her other school, Miss Greenough's Young Ladies' Seminary in Boston. Among the Count's ushers was Brockholst Cutting, which assured the success of the wedding as far as the *World* was concerned—"as far as can be recalled he has been an usher at all really notable matrimonial events for years." Cutting had been chief usher for the Marquis de Choiseul when he married Claire Coudert and chief usher for John Jacob Astor when he married Miss Willing. Cutting belonged to no fewer than thirteen clubs, and he was among the ten best dressed men in New York. Six feet tall, he wore long hair and a drooping mustache. He quite outdid the bridegroom, in fact, in manliness; Boni de Castellane was nearly as slender as a girl, and his pencil-thin mustache and peaches-and-cream complexion did not add up to what Americans considered a manly figure. The second usher was Raoul Duval, another handsome dandy who sported a short brown mustache and an accent the young ladies of New York termed "delicious." Howard would be the third usher, as soon as he arrived, and the Prince del Drago, of the coronet, would be the fourth.

On February 23, the newspapers reported with sympathy that the poor count had a cold. Nevertheless he was up early making new preparations and announcements. His best man, he said, would be the Count Henri de Castellane, his brother, blonde and mustachioed like himself. His mother and father, the Marquis and Marquise, were on their way to New York with Henri at the moment. The wedding date was set for March 4, and the Goulds sent out some two hundred announcements although not that many tickets to the wedding were included. The crowds were already gathering around George Gould's house every day—gaping, quiet crowds that did nothing but stand respectfully and wish away the hours, stirring when a member of the family came in or out. Anna went out that day and met her bridesmaids for lunch; then they all went downtown shopping. She was buying clothes at the fashionable Kraemer and Sterns, hats at Mme. Louise, and lingerie here and there. Her going-away gown was acquired that day, a gown, she told the lady reporters, of Scotch tweed.

On February 25, the de Castellanes arrived, and the elders went to stay at the Gould mansion while Henri joined his brother in the apartment near the Waldorf. The bridegroom-to-be spent the morning showing his brother New York. He was to meet Anna at 1:00 o'clock at Twenty-seventh Street and Fifth Avenue. He appeared on the corner at the appointed hour and waited, and waited, and waited. Anna and Beatrice Richardson finally arrived at 2:30. They had been out shopping, said Anna casually, and had not noticed the time. She pretended not to see the Count's obvious chagrin, and he swallowed it—there was no point in jeopardizing twelve million dollars just because he disliked being kept standing on street corners.

Then the busy time began. Edith Gould took the Marquise to the Bagby Musicale at the Waldorf, not a very happy occasion, as it turned out. The Gould party occupied a box, and so many were the comings and goings to meet the Marquise and so noisy was the conversation in the box that some of the ill-bred hoi polloi on the floor below began complaining and even *hissing*. The Marquise took umbrage, and the Gould party swept haughtily away from this congregation of the ill-bred. That night George and Edith, Boni and Anna, and the Marquis and Marquise all went to Hoyt's Theater (where George did not have a box). They sat in the last row of the orchestra on the left, and they enjoyed themselves, George, the Marquis, and Boni going off to the bar of the Fifth Avenue Hotel next door between acts and quaffing champagne. The ladies remained in their seats and gossiped. The newspapers gossiped, too, pretending to read the minds of the Goulds.

"What we insist upon is geneology. We want blood, the lady says," reported the New York *Recorder*. Edith's secretary dutifully cut out that remark, along with every other clipping about the wedding, and saved it in a scrapbook for posterity.

On February 26, although still nearly a week before the wedding, Boni gave a bachelor dinner at the Waldorf. Described as "simple but elegant" in the next day's editions of the New York *Herald,* the menu read:

Huîtres—Barsac, 1887
Tortue verte claire—Dagenet, 1880
Filet de sole, sauce crabes d'huître—champagne
Salade de concombres—more champagne
Coquille de riz-de-veau—still more champagne
Volaille et truffes
Carre d'agneau du printemps, Sauce Menthe

Pommes Palestine—still more champagne
Petits poulets, casserole, salade de laitue—
Château Pape Clément
Charlotte de pommes—champagne again
Fruits–fromage–dessert
Apollinaris—liqueurs

Twenty-one guests sat at one grand round table decorated with five stands of American Beauty roses. The party began at 8:00 that evening with a reception and apéritif in a room off the dining room. George's friend, A. Morris Bagby, acted as host and introduced everyone, since the Count, his brother, and even Raoul Duval did not know all the guests. According to custom, no members of the bride's family were present. But a good cross section of New York society *was* there. Belmont Tiffany was there, Perry Belmont was there, along with Brockholst Cutting and Creighton Webb. The dinner was relatively quiet, but by the time it was over, the young men were feeling the champagne. Creighton Webb went to the piano and began to play Lohengrin, and the Count threw roses around the room. More champagne. More music. More champagne. More roses.

While this bacchanal livened the dreary existences of the waiters of the Waldorf, back at Sixty-seventh and Fifth Avenue, the Marquis and Marquise unveiled for George, Edith, and Anna their wedding gift to the bride. It was to be a pearl necklace that had once belonged to Marie de Médicis and Henri IV and had come down into the de Castellane line for generations. That evening Edith gave a dinner for the Marquise, inviting only ladies, including Mrs. Paran Stevens, Mrs. Russell Sage, the bridesmaids, and the bride.

The newspapers reported everything, and in the interest of the Goulds and American society, they hired agents abroad to check out the de Castellanes. M. Lefebre, the agent of the *Herald* in Paris and editor of the *Dix-Neuvieme Siècle,* duly reported back that there was "nothing wrong with the de Castellanes," that Miss Gould had thrown over the Prince Bozan de Périgord for him, that Boni was not a gambler or a womanizer, that he was sometimes called "Powder Puff" by his friends because of his womanish appearance, but that he had also engaged several mere acquaintances in more-or-less bloody duels for so terming him.

The next day after Edith's dinner for the bride and bridesmaids, the decorators took over the front rooms of the mansion at Sixty-seventh and Fifth Avenue. First came the broad hall which opened on three connecting parlors on the south side of the avenue with a reception room on the left as one entered the building. The wainscoting of carved walnut in the big hall stood 10 feet high, with red damask wall covering running from there to the ceiling, which was laid out in mosaics. The hangings were of cardinal velvet, in silver and gold embroidery, and the floor was parqueted hardwood, strewn with thick oriental rugs. A glamorous settee with a figure of Mars defined on the back in embroidery adorned this hall. Two onyx pedestals supporting two big bronze Greek athletic statues guarded the entrance to the drawing room.

The reception room was done in gold and white, with panels of white moiré antique held by narrow gold beading. The chairs and divans in this room were of matching upholstery, made of silk stripe and vine-of-roses alternating with draperies and portières to match.

Into these rooms on February 27 came the florists and their assistants, building trellises and other attachments. Helen had insisted, and everyone else had been delighted, that this must be a floral wedding, and the flowers must come from Jay's greenhouses at Lyndhurst.

The wedding itself would be performed in an alcove in the Moorish drawing room where a small altar was erected. It looked small and drab indeed, undecorated, against the magnificent mother-of-pearl wainscoting of this dazzling room, its floor of alternative squares of parquetry of sandalwood and ebony, its mantelpiece of mother-of-pearl, and its fireplace flanked by glass cases crowded with figurines and high-priced souvenirs from

Egypt, Rome, Japan, China, and even far-off Hindoostan. The floor was spread with the skins of Bengal tigers, Assyrian goats, African leopards, and polar bears. To all this would be added trellises of orchids, carnations, lilies-of-the-valley, and other blossoms rare to New York in the icy days of winter.

The florists and their assistants worked away, and in the evenings, the families practiced for the wedding. Archbishop Corrigan of New York was to perform a Catholic service, out of deference to the religion of the groom and his family, but Anna would not take the Catholic vows.

Boni had suggested that she become a Catholic, and Anna had fixed him with an eye reminiscent of her father's in his most serious business dealings.

"I will never become a Catholic," she said, "because if I were to do so, I should not be able to divorce you, and if I were not happy, I would not remain your wife a moment longer than was necessary."

Boni had been upset, for the French thought of marriage as a lasting institution although they had sexual proclivities really polygymous in nature. Boni had been even more upset when he was forced to sign a marriage settlement leaving control of Anna's fortune in Anna's hands. How right the Marchioness had been. How little, Boni suddenly realized, did he understand about America and Americans. He had thought them soft and simple as well as tasteless—now he found himself being traded off like a horse for what he was worth, and not getting a penny's worth more than he was offering. He would be dependent on his wife's bounty, he who had lived for so long under the Napoleonic code where a wife's fortune became her husband's at the moment of their marriage. He was a count, and Anna was buying a count. He would be supported as a count ought to be supported just as long as Anna wanted a count, and not for one moment longer. The prospect was horrifying, and Boni had many sleepless nights over the sale. But his creditors were hounding. He forged ahead.

By March 1, all the unpleasantnesses of settlements and other difficulties had been ironed out, and Boni was as content as he ever would be in this unsettling marriage. That night the Goulds gave a dinner for twenty-five, including Archbishop Corrigan, the priest who would marry the young couple. A. Morris Bagby was there, along with I. Townsend Burden of *the* Burden family, and the various members of the wedding. The Count gave his ushers each a diamond pin bearing shield and crown, the de Castellane coat of arms, and the de Castellane motto, *Mai donours che donours.* Anna gave ruby and diamond monogram pins marked simply "C & C" to all the members of the wedding.

There was much talk of the gowns and hats of the members of the wedding as they moved from one function to another, and much Society talk, too. Boni would come to New York in a year or two and enter the Gould enterprises, it was said, and soon would be a railroad magnate in his own right. Boni read such news with puzzlement—did the newspapers really think that he, a de Castellane, would soil his fingers in trade? His family had not worked in two hundred years. Why should he start now?

"This will be a final wedge to bring the Goulds into New York Society," said the *World.* New York Society? The Goulds were already in as far as anyone could get, with the exception of the acceptance by the Vanderbilts. What they were doing now was entering International Society.

When Edith read these accounts, she accused the *World* of deliberately misinterpreting everything she said and baiting the Goulds. She refused to give out any more information to reporters. So Jay Gould's tradition asserted itself again, and the result was much as might have been expected—the more the Goulds objected to newspaper speculation and slighting remarks about their social station, the more speculation there would be and the sharper the remarks. Next day, the *World* carried the rumor that Boni was really just a "Canuck" on the "lam" from Winnipeg, with a fancy accent and no money. The *World* was right about the last point and did not know it, but as for the remainder, it was simply cut from whole cloth by an angry and frustrated reporter.

The reporters wanted to know *everything:* what Boni and Anna were getting for wedding presents; what the groom's parents thought about the marriage, about the Goulds, about America; who was coming to the wedding, who was not coming, and why; where the young couple was going to spend the honeymoon; how much Anna's trousseau cost, and what the bridesmaids were wearing underneath.

On the day before the wedding, someone prevailed upon Edith to relent and many of these details were released to the panting *World,* as well as the *Sun, Herald, Tribune, Times,* and every other paper in the city. The list of wedding presents was offered and it busied the reporters for an hour. Anna received pearls from half a dozen relatives, along with rubies and diamonds in rings and pins and chokers. She received a deluxe edition of Victor Hugo's works with raised gold-encrusted letters on the covers, and a hand-painted mother-of-pearl fan from one of her girl friends. George gave her the $70,000 coronet which she would ostensibly need for the things countesses need coronets for. It was a triple crown, the base made of solid gold, with a thin row of emeralds, pearls, diamonds, rubies, and Alexandrite from the Urals. The rest was platinum and silver. The newspapers promptly put the value of the coronet at $500,000, and there it stayed. Helen gave her a heart-shaped brooch which contained, among other stones, the famous Esterhazy diamond. No value was mentioned.

The bridegroom's family also gave Anna an old gold necklace that had been the property of Queen Margaret of Spain. The papers valued it at $100,000 (more like $10,000). The Marquis gave his future daughter-in-law a bronze copy of a Luigi marble statue the value of which was anyone's guess—to a modern world, it would be nil. Boni, hard-pressed emotionally as well as otherwise, gave Anna a girdle with a hanging ornament which had belonged to the Duchess Magdalen, the wife of Duke Wolfgang Wilhelm Schleissheim (1587–1628)—it was old, but its looks were disappointing, and a jeweler might find it difficult to value at all if he were not familiar with Duke Wolfgang. The Duke had

married into the Radziwill family which had married into the de
Castellane family, and the girdle was fraught with historical sig-
nificance and Old World values that an American would find
hard to understand. The ornament was six inches wide with
diamond—*shaped*—scrolls, each of which held the head of an animal. The only settings consisted of eyes made from chips of various precious stones.

The Marquise did better. She presented her future daughter-in-
law with five ropes of pearls dating back to 1763, and nobody gave
any valuations on them. Edith gave Anna a silver salver set with
diamonds and rubies and a full dinner set for a dozen to match.
Someone gave Anna a drinking cup of pure gold, and someone
else sent a tea service from Tiffany's of sterling silver lined with
gold. The sanctimonious Russell Sage gave a Bible. At least it
came in a silver box.

M. Patenotre, the French Ambassador to Washington, presented
an Egyptian hand mirror of rock crystal set in greenish gold,
studded with five scarabs, part of the loot of Napoleon. The Earl
of Gaithness gave a Greek loving cup girdled with gold dolphins,
chased in scallop shells and seaweed, inlaid with mello and copper,
with dolphin handles. The Prince Lowenstein gave a smelling
bottle of agate. George added a ten-strand necklace collar of eight
hundred pearls with seventy-two diamonds as an afterthought. But
of all the wedding presents, the grandest was the one Anna was to
give her husband—custody of herself and her $12,000,000.

In exchange, the de Castellanes gave her a name that was a
thousand years old.

On March 2, the gaping crowds outside the house at Sixty-
seventh and Fifth Avenue were larger than usual, and more enthusiastic as the wedding seemed to take shape. Mr. Cornell, the
florist in charge of decorating, hauled in one truckload of greenery
after another from Lyndhurst. Howard arrived from Europe.
Landaus, coupés, two-wheelers, and humble carriages came and
went from the house hour after hour as friends dropped in to pay
respects, leave presents, and go on along their ways. Photographers

jammed the park and the walk across the street to take pictures of the house, and the crowd was so dense that when the Marquis and the Marquise went out at 11:30 that morning, they had to fight their way through the crowd and into the Gould carriage.

About noon, the orchids arrived from Lyndhurst, a vanload of them, and the crowd oohed and aahed as they were carried inside. Most of the orchids were taken into the downstairs billiard room, which would be used as the dining room for the post-nuptial breakfast.

It was announced that day that Anna was giving ice cream and cake to the Home of the Friendless. That afternoon, 1,200 children at three different locations feasted and gave three cheers for Anna Gould.

On March 4, the Count arose early as usual, and by 9 o'clock he had gone over to Prince del Drago's to dress in formal day attire for the wedding ceremony. He and his ushers began arriving about 11:30 and milled about in the downstairs rooms, nervously waiting. Upstairs, all was atumble with the confusion of last minute packing and final preparations for the bride and her maids of honor. Their gowns were of pure white broadcloth, very simple, full skirts and blouses, but sable trimmed. The bridesmaids also wore big black picture hats of chiffon, very fetching, if a little unusual for a wedding. Anna wore a dress that looked simple, but cost a thousand dollars, and a $6000 lace veil. Upstairs at noon, they were fussing with the veil as the guests began to arrive.

It was truly an international wedding. The French, German, and Italian ambassadors, along with the Belgian minister, had all been asked. The Belgian minister was even a relative of the groom's family, Count Ruspoli, son-in-law of the Marquis de Talleyrand-Périgord, Boni's cousin. Bagbys and Burdens began to march in, along with Sages and van Rensselaers. Dr. Shrady, Edwin's father-in-law, was there, along with assorted Goulds and Kingdons and other relatives. Altogether there were to be one hundred and fifty guests, most of them close friends of one family or the other. The New York *Recorder* christened them "the Gould set" and prophesied that the Goulds would now forget about Mrs. Vanderbilt (Alice of the Breakers) and establish their own High Society, as Alice had done in defiance of Caroline Astor. The list represented eighty families, from the Goulds themselves to Pierre F. Collier, who was invited because he had taught George to ride to hounds and hunt.

Shortly after noon, Fathers Connally and Noonan arrived and announced that the Archbishop would be a little late. He was conducting the funeral of Judge Richard O. Gorman that day, and the mass was running overtime, so the wedding would not come off precisely at 12:20 as was planned. Boni brushed back his yellow hair, wriggled his shoulders a little nervously, and settled down to wait. Upstairs, the news was greeted with cries of joy, for the girls simply were not ready, and even ten minutes was a marvelous gift.

W. F. Perkins, the organist of St. Patrick's Cathedral who was to play the music, came in with his portfolio. Superintendent Byrnes and Captain Strauss of the East Sixty-seventh Street Precinct came in for a moment, then sent their men out to prevent intrusion and to handle the usual gang of pickpockets who could be expected to circulate through the crowd. The orchestra assembled in a gallery on the third floor above the hall and Moorish parlor. Victor Herbert directed.

From time to time, Edith flitted into sight, wearing a yellow gown, talking to her mother, who wore an antique brocade navy silk.

Outside the crowd, too, grew nervous. It was a wonderful day, quite unlike New York for March 4. The sun was shining brightly, and an optimist might even say it was warm.

Finally, nearer to 1:00 than 12:20, the Archbishop hurried in, doffed his cape, and made his way to the improvised altar in the nook of the Moorish room. The orchestra struck up Handel's *Largo,* the soloist of the day, Frau Rosa Sucher, began fingering her music nervously. Then the strings played, and she sang *Elsa's Dream* from Lohengrin.

That music was the cue for the wedding party to prepare to move into the improvised chapel. On the now-beflowered staircase stood Don del Drago, Raoul Duval, and Brockholst Cutting. Then came the bridesmaids, led by Helen Gould, and followed by Anna on George's arm. Anna was also followed by her 9-foot train borne by little Kingdon and young Jay Gould, eight and six years old respectively, dressed in white prince's costumes and white shoes with silver buckles.

Boni waited in the alcove with his brother, the best man.

The orchestra struck up the wedding march, the couple knelt on a cushion before the Archbishop, and the brief, truncated ceremony of marriage between Catholic and Protestant began. In a few minutes it was over, the ring was on Anna's finger, and she was a countess!

Then there *was* a celebration.

All went down to the billiard room now nearly afloat in flowers. The bridal party was seated at the head table, which was decorated with a vast centerpiece of electric lights and orchids in the shape of a fleur de lis. Smaller round tables had been brought in for the other guests, who sat eight to a table. Everyone received a gift: wedding cake in silver heart-shaped boxes sat beside each place, and each guest had a favor or a pin. It was announced that Anna had given 20,000 francs to the children of the Castellane village in France. Sherry's twenty men at the twenty tables began serving the luncheon and the champagne. First came *essence de Gibier,* the hors d'oeuvres, and canapés. For those who were breakfasting there were *les oeufs brouillés aux truffées,* and *éperlans à la valois.* For those who wanted more hearty fare there were *cotelets d'agneau du printemps à la Messena, poussins en cocotte à la Lyonnaise, asperges nouvelles à la vinaigrette, glace d'apricots en orchidées,* petits fours and bonbons.

In among the 30,000 feet of trailing vine and orchids, the waiters wended, carrying champagne for the guests, and the laughter was gay. As a surprise, Frank Gould gave his sister a chain with two hundred diamonds, and Howard gave her a cluster of diamonds. Outside, the watchers counted the hampers that held champagne as the minutes ticked away.

Eight.

Nine.

Ten.

"Hurray," they shouted as the waiters brought out the tenth hamper and threw it carelessly alongside the Sherry wagon in the service entrance.

The party continued. At about 2 o'clock, the bride and groom emerged and were whisked away.

Seventeen.

Eighteen.

Nineteen.

Went the champagne hampers.

The crowd cheered again.

Helen came out and went home, burdened by a faint look of displeasure. She was accompanied by the Russell Sages. Other guests began to leave, some of them definitely weaving as they marched across Fifth Avenue into their carriages there lined up for three blocks.

Twenty-six.

Twenty-seven.

Twenty-eight.

The crowd began to thin out. Then the ushers and the bridesmaids left the house, two by two, and headed somewhere with Howard and several of the other young guests.

Twenty-nine.

The last hamper came out.

Cheers.

Inside, Edith gave a sigh of relief. The servants began cleaning up the debris. George walked around the house hoping the Sherry men would soon be gone and he could have a little peace for the first time in two weeks. All the assorted Goulds remaining made ready to go to their homes.

Boni and Anna had fled to Georgian Court, where they would spend the first days of their honeymoon unobserved by any but George's servants. Then in a week, they would sail for France, where Anna would meet the other members of her new family, and Boni would begin paying off his bankers. How idyllic was life! Next day, March 5, Anna hauled Boni down to the Lakewood County Court and made him go through a civil ceremony. She was not taking any chances with those Roman rites that she did not understand.

19

The Mysterious Mrs. Cody

———◆●●◆———

The middle-aged millionaire had been in his grave for three years, the will had been probated and found sound, the fortune had been amalgamated and seemed to be holding together. How was the family faring?

———◆●●◆———

IN THE spring of 1895, Howard Gould was in a stew. The reason was still Odette Tyler. The beautiful young actress was playing in *Shenandoah* at the Academy of Music on Fourteenth Street, and Howard engaged a box there for the run of the show. Almost every night, almost every matinee afternoon, he went to the theater to gaze at his lady love and to yearn.

At first it got him no place. Miss Tyler's eyes roamed the audience as she played, but they remained ostentatiously removed from the top-tier proscenium box at stage right. She simply never looked there. One night she did look, Howard was there, and she smiled. That night, after the performance, Howard was at the

168

stage door waiting, flowers and candy in hand, asking to see Miss Tyler home.

So the romance began to bud again. Howard took Miss Tyler to dinner once, and then again, and soon he was a frequent caller at the house on West Thirty-sixth Street where she lived with her father, General Kirkland.

It was to be hoped that Helen would see the light. After all, General Kirkland was a thoroughly respectable man, he had served his country for many years, and as Howard knew well, his daughter Bessie—or Odette—was virtuous as well as beautiful. But what could be done with a sister who spent her days attending meetings of the Daughters of the American Revolution, the Daughters of Colonial Wars of the State of New York, the Dutch Settlers Society of Albany, the Daughters of Founders and Patriots of America, the Society of Magna Charta Dames, the Colonial Daughters of the Seventeenth Century, and the United Daughters of 1812, and went about distributing Bibles, prayer books, and religious songs and pamphlets in her spare time? Apparently nothing much. Helen continued unwavering in her opposition to the match.

And so nothing came of the renewed courtship although Howard stewed. While Howard would have thrown his sister to the lions as quickly as Odette Tyler could lift a finger, the young lady simply would not marry him if any member of his family objected.

Small wonder that Howard was unhappy. He continued to make his home at Lyndhurst, but he and Helen grew steadily away from one another. Whatever affection he had felt for her diminished as her activities in the religious and social fields increased at the expense of family understanding and sympathy.

Helen was turning into a busybody of the worst order. Over George's mild objections, she insisted that she knew as much about running the railroads as anyone and demanded the use of the private car *Atalanta* to make an "inspection tour" of the roads. So George signed the papers and gave the orders with a woeful shake of his head, and Helen, who really had nothing better to do with herself, set out with her entourage. She dragged along the eighteen-year-old Frank—he could not avoid it—and for company, she took Cousin Alice and her brother Cousin William. Cousin Alice and Cousin William enjoyed the trip as a country girl enjoys the Queen's reception, and for the same reasons: David, the chef, concocted the most marvelous meals en route, and Eugene, the butler, served them. If one is not used to being waited on, a month or so of such railroad travel, otherwise dull as a thimble, could still be highly enjoyable. But for Frank, who had seen all this before, it was a deadly bore and would have been unbearable had not he and Cousin William become friends. In the narrow confines of the car, there was no escaping Helen's Bible readings, no avoiding two or more church services every Sunday no matter where they might be, and no surcease from Helen's snivelly little Pekingese dog, Chinky, who marched around the car being fed candies and cakes all day long and who was exceedingly careless in his toilet habits.

Helen, in her element on this trip, played the grand lady surveying her realm. Wherever they stopped, railroad officials stood on the platform, leading porters in their black caps and starched white coats, carrying loads of flowers, fruit, and candy. The officials would stay aboard between divisions, going over reports with Helen, who absorbed every word of them, and making sure that Frank was also included in the conversation. Having six bosses where they had once had only one was difficult, and the divisional officials thanked their stars that, except for George and Howard, not many of the others chose to make frequent inspection tours.

Helen's party went west to Denver to check up on the Missouri Pacific, and then south, and then back east again and north—and Helen visited every station, round house, shop, terminal, and ticket office in her jurisdiction. She talked learnedly of ballast and ties and trestle repair, tensions and metal fatigue and freight-passenger ratios. She stopped the train frequently and talked to station agents, trackwalkers, and repairmen who were working on the roadbed. She *managed,* and there was absolutely no question about that, the trainmen could all agree, but eventually the tour of inspection ended, and the railroads got back to work while Helen concentrated on her charities, such as the million-dollar Gould Memorial Library which she gave New York University in her father's name. Helen also gave the University $200,000 toward a dormitory on the new Bronx campus. And she married off Alice to Professor Henry Snow, an engineering teacher at New York University. The last event was carried out quietly, for Helen hated notoriety of any variety.

After spending much of the summer on the road, Helen went to Atlantic City for "a change," then back to Lyndhurst for the remainder of the good weather. By the time she returned, Howard and Odette Tyler had parted forever, yielding to what seemed to be the inevitable, and a certain tranquility was restored to the household.

Howard sought solace in the true sport of millionaires (no matter what they say about horse racing) and was soon busily engaged in planning yacht races and racing. Having bought the *Vigilant* and having raced her in English waters during the summer of 1894, as George and Howard had done, the brothers felt it reasonable enough that they should be asked to join the syndicate that was preparing for the new defense of the America's Cup in 1895. The Earl of Dunraven had challenged for the cup in 1893 with a cutter named *Valkyrie II* when *Vigilant* had won. Lord Dunraven wanted to challenge again and did so, taking in with him Lord Lonsdale, Lord Wolverton, and Captain Harry LeB. McCalmont, the latter one of the finest of English yachtsmen.

To meet this challenge, August Belmont set about forming a syndicate once more. He approached George Gould, who said he would be glad to put up $50,000 or even as much as $100,000 if necessary to help hold the cup in the United States. Belmont checked around with builders and designers and soon had a figure for the building of a suitable yacht—at least $175,000.

Then Belmont began talking to other members of the New York Yacht Club. He talked to his relatives, Perry Belmont and

O. H. P. Belmont. He talked to the Iselins and former Commodore E. D. Morgan of the Club. He talked to Cornelius and
Frederick William Vanderbilt, and to Pierpont Morgan.

As he talked to the latter men, Belmont gathered that George
Gould's offer was not going to be met with relish by some of
them. They regarded George as a Johnny-come-lately in yachting,
even though he had played around with boats all his life. For one
thing, a man simply did not "take over" the America's Cup defense, particularly a tyro in international yacht racing. These were
testy and not particularly pleasant words, but there was reason for
them, particularly in the case of J. Pierpont Morgan. Morgan was
just a year younger than Jay Gould had been, and he was quite old
enough to be George Gould's father. Morgan was just coming into
his prime as a reorganizer of railroads, and this year he was re-
vamping the financial structure of the Erie to rescue it from the
huge liabilities placed on the railroad by Jay Gould in earlier years.
The memory of Jay haunted Morgan these days, but that did not
cause his coolness. He had asked George to come to his office
several times, and George had displayed a lack of tact and a lack
of respect for Morgan's wishes in railroad affairs which annoyed
the banker more than a little. Morgan was not, in 1895, a good
man to annoy—he did not differentiate between levels of vexation
and resentment, and he made no attempt to keep his business and
personal lives separate. George had acted like an insolent young
pup: therefore George should be taken down.

The problem with George's proposal, from other points of
view, was that if he became the senior member of the syndicate by
putting up the most money, he would also have the most weighty
arguments in the counsels of the syndicate members, and several of
these gentlemen did not believe he had enough experience yet,
even though *Vigilant* had run up a respectable record in yacht
races at Cowes and other English ports the previous summer.
Some members of the club wanted to modify the plan: they
wanted the syndicate to be a club proposition wherein everyone
participating would have an equal voice.

George had considerable ground for resentment at the way he

was being treated. After he bought the *Vigilant* and took her to England, he might have expected that as a purchaser and as a member in good standing of the New York Yacht Club he would receive the full support of the club in his delicate negotiations with the English yachtsmen. But he had been supported only half-heartedly. Yachtsmen are sensitive to any slight, no matter how unintentional, and George felt that he had truly been badly served by his associates. The proof of it came when he had been eager to challenge in England for the Royal Victoria Gold Cup. When he could not produce enthusiastic support from home, however, the challenge was accepted so halfheartedly that George withdrew.

It was expected, then, that George would flare up as had General Paine and others in years past and cut loose from other challengers to build his own boat. But George was too sensible to become involved in such an affair. The Club formed the syndicate, thus giving each participant an equal vote, C. Oliver Iselin was appointed manager, and he went to Herreshoff again for a design and construction. George accepted the decision with good grace and agreed to pay for the fitting out of *Vigilant* to serve as a "trial horse" against the new yacht.

These difficulties resolved, George sailed in May on the steamship *New York* for Southampton. From there, he and Edith and the children went directly to Paris to stay with Anna and Boni, now ensconced in a mansion on the Avenue Bosquet. George's plan was to spend several spring weeks in Paris, then to join the *Atalanta* at Le Havre and cruise for a time. The Kiel Canal was opening that year, and he wanted to go there for the ceremonies, which would be attended by the Kaiser and other sea-going nobility. He would go on to Norway to steam up and down the fjords, then to St. Petersburg. He promised to be back in time for the racing season, and he was. In a gesture of considerable generosity, he commissioned his yachting skipper, Captain Charles Barr, to race *Vigilant* against the syndicate entry. The new boat would undoubtedly win, for Herreshoff was learning each year, like any great designer, how to make a boat a little slicker and faster.

George was back, too, on August 24, well in time for the

America's Cup races, which would not begin for another two weeks. He came home lithe and tanned. Edith and the children went to the house on Sixty-seventh Street and Fifth Avenue, and the five servants they had taken with them supervised the unloading and delivery of the one hundred pieces of luggage which held the Gould belongings. The Goulds had enjoyed a long and restful vacation, they had dined with the Lord Mayor of London, visited the American warships at Kiel for the ceremonies, and had steamed off Scotland and Ireland.

The minute George landed, the reporters got after him about the Manhattan Elevated System. New Yorkers were growing annoyed with the Gould management, and the reason was understandable enough. New York's elevated railroads were still running on steam, while those of other cities were running by electricity, which was faster and cleaner, and even Chicago was electrifying its system.

"What about electricity for New York?" the reporters asked.

"I must ask Colonel Hain about that," George said. (Colonel Hain was chief operating officer of the Manhattan Elevated. Hain had inspected the Chicago system and could be expected to know more about it.) But George displayed that day his basic distrust of electricity as a motive power for transportation—a distrust extending back to the days of his father.

In 1885, Jay had allowed a young fellow named Frank Sprague to experiment with electric motive power on a short branch of the Manhattan Elevated. After several months, Sprague announced that electric power was perfected for running the cars, and he had asked Jay and the traction officials to come to the spur line for a test.

Jay had stuffed on his stovepipe hat and shambled uptown to the test site. He had climbed into the lead car of the short train that was rigged up for electricity, the other officials making way for him and trailing along respectfully behind him. Young Sprague had moved to the controls.

The scene was remarkable. The handsome young Sprague, a

graduate of the Naval Academy, a brilliant inventor, had begun his work with electricity at the Brooklyn Navy Yard, had studied in London, had worked for Thomas Alva Edison, and had been experimenting with electric traction for five years. He now faced Jay Gould, maker and breaker of men and companies, ruler of thousands of miles of railroad and hundreds of miles of New York City traction line. This was the opportunity for the Horatio Alger story of 1885, young Sprague would manfully seize the controls, turn the energizer in its sprocket, and the cars would shoot ahead smoothly and painlessly, quietly, smokelessly. Jay Gould would be so impressed that he would sign immediately for the new service.

Alas! Frank Sprague stepped forward and turned his energizer, the train carrying Jay Gould began to surge forward, a fuse blew with a blinding flash of blue light—and Jay tried to jump out of the car, certain that he was about to be incinerated. The capitalist was held back by his subordinates and calmed in a few moments, but when the car was brought to a safe landing place, he walked stiffly down the steps, shaking his head, and went back to 195 Broadway, never again to set foot in an electric car or to listen to the crazy men who talked electricity.

Consequently, ten years later, George labored in the shadow of the blue flash. He did not believe in electricity, even though Richmond and Brookline, Mass., had electrical systems that paid good dividends, not to mention the one under way in Chicago.

On this day, however, the reporters continued to cluster around George. He was very patient with them, although he kept looking at his watch and protesting that he must go to the office—he had been away just one hundred and fifteen days.

"What about subways?" asked the reporters.

"I will do anything to accomplish what the public wants, if the people and the officials are with me. I do not believe, however, that the underground idea is at all feasible in this city."

So much for foresight. The reporters filed away and let George go to the office in the Western Union building. There he did devote his whole attention to business for a few days before the last trials of *Vigilant* and *Defender,* the syndicate's Cup boat.

As it turned out, the America's Cup races of 1895 became a matter of much controversy. Lord Dunraven's *Valkyrie* unintentionally fouled *Defender.* The committee ruled for *Defender.* Dunraven said it was *Defender's* fault. Oliver Iselin offered to resail the race, but Dunraven retired in a huff and would not accept the offer. In the second race, the excursion fleet interfered with both boats, and Dunraven became angrier. Finally, he quit cold and would not sail the third race, which meant the series was over and the Americans had won, but it was not the kind of victory that anyone liked to brag about. Many charges and counter-charges were filed, and an investigation of the races was undertaken. Nothing new resulted from the investigation, except that tempers flared, and British and American yachtsmen bristled at one another across the Atlantic so fiercely that it was three years before another challenge was made. In all this controversy, one man stood out as a sportsman: George Gould. George's enemies admitted that he had comported himself with the utmost dignity in this racing season. Even his old enemies on the New York *Times* praised him:

"It is not necessary," said the *Times* on October 1, "to tell anyone who has watched the progress of yachting in the course of the season just ended that in spite of the remarkable work of the *Defender* and her owners, the most conspicuous single figure in American sea sport has been Mr. George J. Gould. The thoroughly sportsmanlike nature of his employment of the *Vigilant* as a trial horse for the *Defender* aroused general admiration, and when Mr. Gould returned in time to sail in his own sloop in some of the trial races, he was received with public enthusiasm. He does not court publicity but his potentiality as a factor in next year's yachting has aroused much expectancy."

Howard, too, came in for praise as a yachtsman. He had gone to Europe in the late summer to forget Odette Tyler once and for all, and had occupied himself with sailing the 20-meter yacht *Niagara* that had been built for him a few months before.

Howard had done very well indeed. He had sailed *Niagara* in fifty races in England that season and had won thirty first prizes, eight seconds, and one third. Of the prizes, twelve were silver cups, most of which he brought home. The rest were flags and purses, and whenever there was a purse, he divided it among his crew, which in the fashion of the time consisted of paid sailors. He had good reason to be proud of himself and his yacht: among his most important races were those off the coast of Scotland, where he met Lord Lonsdale in *Eucharis,* a 20-meter boat that had been built specifically to race against Howard's *Niagara.* They raced fourteen times that season, and Howard won thirteen of the contests.

Of all the American yachtsmen of the year 1895, the Gould brothers had come away with most honors, and they knew it. Next year, in spite of the stickiness that generally disturbed relations between American and British yachtsmen, Howard took *Niagara* back to England for racing. But this year, the British Yacht Racing Association paid a visit to Howard's yacht one afternoon when he was not aboard (a distinct breach of courtesy) and checked his water tanks, port and starboard. They asked that the tube connecting them be disconnected in racing—the implication being that somehow Howard was shifting his ballast during the races (this was a charge made by Dunraven against *Defender* in the America's Cup controversy). The only way Howard could thus shift ballast would be to make water run uphill from the lower, or leeward, side to the higher, or windward, side, or to illegally pump it up. He did not appreciate the implied accusation and addressed a protest to the association. A stiff letter came in reply. He decided then that as long as the association continued with those members and officials he would not race again in English waters, but as the aggrieved party, he conducted himself with such dignity that he won reluctant admiration again from the British, and to show it, that year he and George were both elected to membership in the Royal Cork Yacht Club, the oldest in England. The club's active membership was limited to the Prince of Wales, the Duke of Edinburgh, the Lord Lieutenant of Ireland, the admiral, flag captain, and staff officers of the Queenstown naval station, the general commanding the Cork District, and the commodore and vice commodore of the Royal Yacht Squadron. George and Howard, as Americans, were simply honorary members, but the honor was great indeed, and shared by only a handful of Americans in history. This was one arena in which the Gould boys won success not through their fortune, although it took money to race yachts, not through contacts or family power, but through their own efforts and gentlemanly behavior.

With all this activity, Howard had managed to forget Odette Tyler, and in 1896, he began to devote himself more seriously to business. The yachting season over, he put his boats away and accompanied George on a long, thorough examination of the family's railroad holdings in the West.

Howard and George then became the "partners" who, for the most part, managed the Gould railroad interests. Busy with her good works, Helen let the men run the business except to demand periodically that she be given obeisance as one of the executors. Edwin was deeply involved in his own business enterprises—and very successfully, too. Among other investments, he put a considerable amount of money into a new match company called Continental, which began showing profits almost immediately and within a year or so was expanding into new plants. The company started at Passaic, New Jersey. Soon a new plant was built in Ogdensburg, New York, and then one in Chicago.

George and Howard both followed a policy of work hard, play hard. As the younger bachelor member of the team, Howard might be forgiven for indulging in more high jinks than his brother. Back in New York, Howard also met a new actress, Kathrine Clemmons, who was not impressed by Helen's outcries. Far more sophisticated than Odette Tyler, far more a woman of the world, Kathrine lived alone in an apartment at New York's fashionable Holland House and was quite capable, without assistance, of planning a dinner of terrapin and asparagus with four fine wines—and she did so just before Christmas.

As to high jinks, one night, Howard went out sailing on George's yacht *Hildegarde* and, after a brief cruise, had anchored off Larchmont. Someone had suggested a party, and a group, largely of young women, came aboard to help celebrate. The champagne glasses were raised high. The laughter grew louder as the evening went on, and finally Howard was struck by a brilliant idea: why not have fireworks—he had a supply aboard.

"Mowbray!" he called.

Frank Mowbray, the steward on the yacht, disengaged himself from the champagne bottle he was passing around, and came to see what his master wanted.

"Set off some fireworks," Howard said. "We must have a ton of them in the hold."

"But, sir," said Mowbray, "they have been down there for five or six years and I don't think . . . ."

"I said set off some fireworks, Mowbray, if you want to continue working here," said Howard.

Mowbray bowed briefly and went below to secure the fireworks. He came back up on deck with an armload. He lighted a rocket that would not explode. Then he picked up another skyrocket which also sputtered and died. Picking up a roman candle, a very large one of the size used aboard ships to send distress signals, he lit the fuse, and like the two skyrockets, it sputtered out. Mowbray looked down at it and prepared to throw the candle away. Just then, it exploded. One of the balls struck him directly in the left eye and a second burned a hole in his chest before he fell to the decks while the remainder of the fireballs spurted over the side.

The women screamed, and the men rushed to pick up the stricken unconscious steward. Howard, suddenly sobered, called the captain of the yacht, and in a few minutes the ship was under way, headed for Manhattan and the West Twenty-sixth Street pier. When the ship arrived in the very early hours of the morning, Mowbray was transferred to Bellevue Hospital. After his recovery he remained in Gould's service for some time, with the promise that he would have a position for life. Then he was fired. The fly in his ointment, apparently, had been Kathrine Clemmons. She and Mowbray had quarreled in London about a fish bill. She said she had given him the money to pay. He denied it. Also, when Mowbray shampooed her hair aboard the yacht the yellow color came out and she blamed him for "putting something in the water."

Mowbray brought suit for $50,000.

At about the same time, two events of major importance occurred in the lives of the Goulds. Howard's engagement to Kathrine Clemmons broke down the family solidarity. And another suit against the family threatened to destroy the family fortune.

Howard had been running around with Kathrine since shortly after he was finally jilted by the proper Miss Tyler. But where Odette Tyler was a lady who happened to be in the theater, perhaps not quite the same could be said of Miss Clemmons. On stage, she showed a figure that would put even the young Edith Kingdon's hourglass form to shame, her features were regular, and her hair long and curling. In 1896, she had her first starring role, long after she first appeared on the New York stage in a bit in *The Lady of Venice* (February 12, 1894). The critics unanimously cheered her undeniable attributes—but histrionic skill, unfortunately, was not one of them.

"A fine figure of a woman," said Jo Gargery, the wit of many tales of Manhattan.

"She has an interesting face," said the *Times* reviewer, "a large quantity of pale hair, a large mouth, which is generally wide open, and a full set of very handsome teeth."

How in the world did Kathrine, with so little talent, get on the stage? The story started with "Buffalo Bill" Cody, Kathrine's "backer" and "protector" at the beginning of her career. Buffalo Bill thought very highly of Viola Kathrine Clemmons in those early days, and after their friendship cooled somewhat, he made it possible for her to leave his Wild West show and make her way in New York.

Howard continued to pursue Miss Clemmons for months, although the chase was never difficult. They went off on other yachting expeditions *à deux,* and they went to Europe together, although Miss Clemmons made her reservations on the *St. Paul* under an assumed name.

On January 14, 1897, Miss Clemmons' mother in California announced, proudly, that her daughter had hooked her millionaire, although she did not put it just that way, and back in New York, Howard confirmed the engagement. Helen exploded. She threatened to invoke Jay's will to disinherit Howard, but when the lawyers got into the matter, they discovered that Jay's will, giving power to the older children over the activities of the younger, affected the personal lives and decisions only of those children who had been minors at Jay's death. Howard had been over twenty-one in 1892.

Then another difficulty arose. Edith Kingdon was a *lady* of the stage, like Odette Tyler, and while Edith Kingdon had not objected to Miss Tyler, she did object to Miss Clemmons.

As an actress, Miss Clemmons had turned out to be a press agent's charade. She could not act. And yet to Edith Kingdon, this was not the decisive matter. What turned Edith against Miss Clemmons was Kathrine's previous association with Buffalo Bill and her general deportment. Miss Clemmons was indeed one of those free spirits among actresses who gave the group their bad name.

So Edith opposed the marriage, and that meant George must oppose it, too.

What a contretemps! George and Howard had fared well together in business as senior and junior partner. They had fared equally well as gentlemen yachtsmen. They had been friends as well as brothers. But when George tried to interfere in Howard's romantic life, the once-burned Howard bridled, and the family unity was shattered forever. To avoid an open breach, George persuaded Howard to promise to "think about" the romance for a while. Then George took the family off to Europe in the spring of 1897. Howard thought about the romance, with Miss Clemmons' assistance, and he decided to persist. The family fought a delaying action and managed to stall until October of 1898. Then Miss

Clemmons put on the pressure, and Howard married her on October 12.

Not one member of the Gould family attended the wedding. No bridesmaids, no ushers, no flowers from Lyndhurst.

The couple was married in Miss Clemmons' apartment at the Holland House by the Reverend Doctor Wilton Smith, pastor of the Central Presbyterian Church. A handful of people unknown to most but Miss Clemmons stood by. The bridal party went out for a brief wedding supper. Then Howard and Kathrine fled on Howard's new steam yacht, the *Niagara,* for a honeymoon trip—which may have been a little anticlimactic.

They returned to build a castle at Sands Point, Long Island, an exact replica of Kilkenny Castle in the old country—after all, Kathrine wanted a castle. At this Howard's separation from the rest of his family was complete.

Under the terms of Jay's will, the money was all in trust, and that saved Howard's share of the fortune. In these early years, the Goulds lived off the income from the estate, and as long as George could manage to keep together the stocks and bonds that represented Missouri Pacific control, Manhattan Elevated, and Western Union, the income was sufficient.

Howard's defection was not nearly so immediately threatening to the fortunes of the estate as the second difficulty that arose in these last years of the Mauve Decade. It began in 1895, or, at least, it then came to the attention of the Goulds.

In that year, a woman named Mrs. Margaret Cody decided to cash in on the Gould millions. For a number of years, Mrs. Cody had earned a precarious living by blackmailing certain millionaires. Her business was to rummage through the forgotten closets of history finding family skeletons. Where she could find one, she clothed it fully and presented it to the family. Usually the family paid. In the case of the Goulds, Mrs. Cody went farther than usual. Unable to find a scandal in Jay Gould's pristine personal life, yet refusing to give up on her planned assault on one of the greatest fortunes in America, Mrs. Cody decided to fabricate a scandal—and anyone with a grain of imagination must honor this dark lady's creativity.

First, Mrs. Cody began a public-relations campaign, sending small reports of New York happenings to far-flung newspapers, in Nebraska, Wyoming, Montana, and the Dakotas—places far from the big cities, places where it would be expected that the doings of millionaires in the East would cause jaws to drop and eyebrows to raise. In these dispatches, Mrs. Cody included "news" of the Lost Dauphin variety, indicating that every day or so an heir turned up out in the hinterlands who could lay claim to vast chunks of some great New York fortune. Then Mrs. Cody became more specific. She had discovered, she said, that deep in the past of Jay Gould lay a secret: Jay had been married before he was rich, and he had a child before he came to New York and made his fortune. That child had disappeared.

If the child had not disappeared, he or she would have claim to a large portion of the great Gould fortune. Mrs. Cody indicated, in her helpful little hints, that a marriage had been performed in some upstate New York county in the 1850s, and that a child had resulted soon after.

The opening was extremely inviting, and before very long, Mrs. Cody had just what she wanted. A Mrs. J. F. Pierce of Rock Springs, Wyoming, was in touch with her, indicating tentatively that she might well be the long-lost daughter of Jay Gould. Mrs. Pierce said that she was born in 1854 in New York state and that her mother had married a man that she thought must be Jay Gould.

Her mother's name had been Sarah Brown, and she had been born in Cooperstown, New York, she thought, or somewhere around there. But as a girl, Mrs. Pierce had been bound out as an indentured servant, and she had drifted with her "family" west to the Missouri country and finally had married and gone to live in Wyoming. Could Mrs. Cody help her prove that she was the lost daughter of Jay Gould?

Mrs. Cody was enraptured. If she now could convince various

people that Jay *had* married early, she might then set her trap. Mrs. Cody went upstate to Clinton County and began to get the lay of the land. At Rouse's Point, she found a Catholic priest, Father Charbonneau, who spoke very little English (since this was French-speaking territory). Taking the good father on a carriage ride to Cooperstown, she explained that she was searching for records of a marriage of Jay Gould either at Cooperstown or somewhere around there. She carefully did not ask Father Charbonneau to examine any records—all she was doing at this point was establishing, by her manner of speaking, the fact that Jay Gould *had* been married before he met Helen Miller in New York City. Mrs. Cody made much of looking through the records of the 1850s at St. Joseph's Catholic Church in Cooperstown, but she was also careful not to let Father Charbonneau see what she was doing.

Later, Mrs. Cody wrote Father Charbonneau and asked him to look for a baptismal record of a child born to a Sarah Brown and Jay Gould. The good father went to the church, and lo and behold, there in the records of 1854 he found just what Mrs. Cody had predicted, the record of birth of a daughter to this couple.

How pleased Mrs. Cody was!

Mrs. Cody wrote the father again asking this time for a certified copy of the baptismal certificate. Father Charbonneau wrote Father Constantine at the Cooperstown Church, and secured the copy (no questions asked between one priest and another) and sent it dutifully along to Mrs. Cody. He was a little puzzled, but, after all, a very amiable man.

Mrs. Cody then set out to track down Sarah Brown, the mother of the child who had gone off to Wyoming. It took her a long time, nearly three years. Meanwhile she had other closets to examine, and other millionaires to consider during this period, and so could devote only part of her time to helping the Goulds recover their lost relative.

Finally, Mrs. Cody discovered a former Miss Brown who had married a man named John Angell and was still living in upstate New York. Mrs. Angell was not very bright, and it was not hard to convince her she had once been married to a man named Jay and that she had a child. Mrs. Cody persuaded Mrs. Angell to sign a paper declaring that Mrs. Cody was her lawyer and that they would make an even split of the proceeds.

Mrs. Cody then wrote Mrs. Pierce and informed her she had found her mother. Mr. and Mrs. Pierce roundly congratulated her, overjoyed as they were to learn that Mrs. Pierce was the lost princess. The Pierces were determined to secure every penny coming to them from the Goulds, and they employed Denver lawyers of their own to help pursue this fortune. In due course, Mrs. Cody contacted these lawyers and made her own arrangements with them.

Mrs. Cody spent some five weeks at Rouse's Point in the summer of 1895, and other papers came to light. She found an ancient, tottering clergyman, the Reverend M. Leighton, who conveniently remembered marrying Jay Gould and Sarah Brown. The Reverend Leighton knew, he said, because Miss Brown was a servant in his house at the time—which was 1853.

By 1896, Mrs. Cody had her skeleton sufficiently prepared to exhibit it to the Goulds. She wrote to Helen Gould and asked for an interview. She was refused. She wrote George, and he also refused.

By this time, for reasons that had nothing to do with Mrs. Cody, the Goulds were thoroughly sick of the public and the public demands made on their fortune. One day, Helen made a list of the mail that came across her desk in *one week*:

1	wishes to form colony in Cuba	$1,000,000
231	requests for money, (149 not naming sum)	187,880
91	requests for loans, (16 not naming sum)	156,203
91	requests to raise mortgages, (4 not naming sum)	77,575
43	requests to aid churches, (27 not naming sum)	56,981
27	requests to aid educational institutions, (22 not naming sum)	35,400
26	donations to libraries, (24 not naming sum)	10,000

5 requests to buy places	5,200
1 anti-saloon league of Idaho	5,000
34 requests to aid religious and charitable institutions, (30 not naming sum)	3,000
1 wishes to sell farm	2,600
4 wish help toward trousseau, (3 not naming sum)	2,000
11 requests for pianos, (3 not naming sum)	1,400
12 requests to buy inventions, (10 not naming sum)	1,200
1 wishes to sell ring	1,200
1 wishes to sell brooch	525
1 wishes donations to patriotic league	500
1 wishes to sell Sèvres vase	500
1 wishes monument to parent	500
1 wishes help to redeem jewels	280
1 church organ	175
13 treatment (cancer, morphine, Keeley, etc.,) (12 not naming sum)	150
1 wishes passage to England	75
1 wishes to sell quilt	50
1 wishes expenses defrayed to secure prisoner's release	30
1 wishes to get goods from storage	30
1 wishes help to publish music	25
1 wishes to buy set of teeth	15
1 wishes help to get watch from pawn	8
10 requests to aid church fairs	
107 requests for aid, presumably money	
34 requests for old clothes	
3 requests for watches	
14 requests for scholarships	
17 requests for advice	
15 requests for tickets or passes	
1 request to buy railroad stock	
18 requests to have embroidery or lace work sold	
18 cranks	
8 requests for autograph	

17 German letters
 6 French letters
 4 Russian or Swedish letters
 5 wishing to sell manuscript
 3 silk for quilt
 7 naming child after Miss Gould
 5 want sewing machines
 2 help to publish book
 3 want Bibles
 2 want bicycles
19 advertisements, circulars, etc.
53 requests for positions
32 requests for interviews
 5 wish to sell books
 5 wish to use Miss Gould's name
10 donations toward church organs
 1 wishes help to become medical missionary
 1 wishes help to bring out opera
 1 wishes help to bring out oratorio
 1 wishes electro plates
 1 wishes 550 "America" cards
 1 wishes farm and three cows
 1 wishes to sell hay claim and cows
 1 wishes help to open photographic gallery
 1 wishes peddling horse and cart
 1 wishes money to print 2000 hymnals
 1 minister wishes horse and buggy
 1 wishes house so that girl can marry at once
 1 wishes money to enter old folks' home
 1 wishes invalid's chair
 1 wishes position to get up time table schedule
 1 wishes to sell photographs of Miss Gould for
   his own profit
 1 wishes air pillows furnished to regiment of
   soldiers
 1 wishes team of horses
 1 wants to go on shares on Alfalfa in California
126 personal letters

25 newspapers, marked copies
2 almanacs
6 books
31 catalogues, pamphlets, etc.
8 magazines

<u>1303</u>

Total amount demanded $1,548,502

It would surprise no one who knew the Goulds that Helen and George consulted and decided to take a strong stand in the Cody case. When the Angell-Brown claim failed to move the Goulds, Mrs. Cody suggested that she had means of forcing the Angells and Pierces to drop their claim. George and Helen Gould became angry. This was blackmail.

Poor Mrs. Cody. She did not know that she had stepped into a hornet's nest. She presented her letter and wrote another. George Gould took the letters and presented them in turn to his lawyers, De Lancy Nicoll, John D. Lindsay, and D. D. Duncan. The lawyers consulted, and as a result, the matter was turned over to the New York District Attorney.

There were delays and difficulties, but finally a case was brought against Mrs. Cody for blackmail in Albany County Court before District Judge Clifford D. Gregory—Albany because it was nearest the area where the alleged crimes had been committed.

The case was tried a second time after the first ended in a hung jury. In the second trial, the lawyers brought out the following evidence:

When Mrs. Cody had taken Father Charbonneau to Cooperstown and rummaged through St. Joseph's Church's records, she had seen what she wanted, the baptismal book for the years 1853–57. Later, without the good father, she had returned to the church and, rummaging more, discovered the register of an illegitimate child born to one Sarah Brown. Mrs. Cody had carefully eradicated the letters *I-l* from the beginning of the descriptive adjective, and had inserted Jay Gould's name in the registry so the *legitimate* child was purported to have been born to Jay Gould and Sarah Brown.

Then Mrs. Cody had encountered a problem. Sarah Brown had disappeared. No matter how she searched, she could not find Sarah or any trace of her. Suddenly, Mrs. Cody encountered Mrs. Angell, who had been *Mary* Brown, and it was not too hard to convince Mrs. Angell that she had changed her name from Sarah to Mary to please one of her husbands. But when the case came to court, Mrs. Angell suddenly could not remember ever having been married to anyone named Jay Gould. Her first husband, she said, was a French Canadian named Vidas—and he beat her. (She would certainly remember him!) Nor was her name Sarah. It was Mary.

Most of this was new evidence. For months, the Gould attorneys and private detectives had been taking a hand in the case because George was willing to spend a small fortune to put an end to victimization of his family once and for all. The Rensselaer County District Attorney's office could not be expected to scour northern New York for witnesses, but after George's men did it for them, a huge array of prosecution witnesses was brought in for the second trial.

Handwriting experts testified that the records of St. Joseph's parish had been tampered with by someone, and that the forgeries were not even very good ones. When the defense produced a marriage certificate between Jay Gould and Sarah Brown, the experts pronounced that a forgery too, written with ink that had not even been manufactured in 1853. The Reverend Mr. Leighton tottered up to give his testimony about the marriage, and the prosecution brought on a younger woman, a Mrs. Millie Hoyle, who had been a servant in his house at that time. Sarah Brown had been small boned and very dark of complexion, she said, and this Mary Brown, or Sarah Brown, or whoever she was, was big boned and light of skin!

Finally, on March 9, 1899, Mrs. Cody was convicted of at-

tempted blackmail. Helen was delighted. The public insisted that
Mrs. Cody receive a light sentence because she was no longer
young. George Gould did not want blood but simply to be left
alone. There was no objection. The next day, Mrs. Cody's sentence
was suspended and she was allowed to go free. But when Helen
was credited for her mercy, she said she wanted no such credit and
denied that she had anything to do with the matter. Helen was an
eye-for-an-eye Christian, unlike George.

Anyhow, it was over.

George and his attorneys and Helen and her household went
back to the New York City area, hoping at last for respite from the
various invasions of their privacy.

20

George Gives a Party

———◄••►———

*The Goulds wanted simply to be left alone
to enjoy their fortunes, but it was not
America's way to allow millionaires to escape so easily. The price of fortune was to
become a public figure. The Goulds continued to live in a goldfish bowl, or a
series of goldfish bowls. Yet, in truth, the
capitalists brought their publicity troubles
on themselves.*

———◄••►———

THE year 1898 started out for the Goulds—as for all America—
with a bang when the pocket battleship *Maine* exploded in
Havana harbor in February. Then there was a series of other
explosions. Helen Gould did the spectacular: she gave $100,000 to
the United States government to spend in any way the government
wanted, just as a token of her wish to contribute to the war effort.
This done, she set out to win the war almost singlehandedly. She
organized the Irvington Auxiliary of the Women's National War
Relief Association, dragooning sixty of her friends and relatives as
the initial cadre. They took over the library at Lyndhurst and

turned it into a sewing room, creating what Cousin Alice called "badly needed articles of clothing" for the poor soldiers in Cuba and the Philippines. Since the government had been unprepared for the emergency, Helen had to step in. The ladies made chicken broth, fruit, jellies, and wool mufflers for the soldiers abroad. Helen went to New York, opened an office in the Windsor Hotel, and began telephoning generals, admirals, senators, and governors to speed things up. When the wounded and sick began to come home from foreign climes, Helen gave the government the use of Woody Crest, the big house at Roxbury. She went to Montauk on Long Island to help out at the government hospital. She built a camp there with her own money because she was disgusted with government red tape and said she could do it quicker and better than Washington. (And she did.) She forced New York officials of the Missouri Pacific so heavily into the war effort that they scarcely had time to run their trains. She rented a house on Sixteenth Street and used it as a convalescent home. And when the war was over, "the government," or at least Congress, responded by voting a special gold medal to be signed and struck by the mint "in recognition of the patriotic devotion and bounteous benevolence of Miss Helen Miller Gould to the soldiers of the army of the United States during the war with Spain."

Helen's good works continued. She joined the New York Historical Society and the Daughters of Holland Dames, the Colonial Dames of America, and the Allied Patriotic Societies, the American Bible Society, and the American Christian Literature Society for Moslems. She became a vice president of the Women's Board of Foreign Missions and a member of the Kashmir-Ludhiana Fellowship, and a grand donor to the causes of the YMCA and YWCA. During her thirties, the tempo of her good works increased. Having married off Cousin Alice, Helen took on a pair of social and business secretaries who lived in the house as companions and went everywhere with her. She was a single woman, but she had no time to be lonely, even though that year her last ward, Frank, reached his majority, which meant free use of the accumulated interest on his fortune even though the principal remained in trust.

When he was ready for the world, Frank was about 5 feet 9 inches tall, one of the largest of the Goulds, but slender, with the facial features of his father. He had been tutored in his early years, then sent to the Berkeley School. He had finally gone to New York University, from which he was graduated, studying in the engineering department under Cousin Alice's husband. He had enjoyed himself at NYU and showed it, giving the engineering department some $4,000 worth of equipment, even before he reached his majority. He was prepared to continue in the railroad business so he had studied engineering. His thought was that some member of the family ought to be familiar with the technical problems of railroading if George were to follow Jay's design and create the new transcontinental railroad system that Jay had always believed ought to be built further south than the Union Pacific, to drain the rich lands of Kansas and the heavy-lode mining country of Colorado and Utah.

As for the rest of the family, Edwin was hard at work with his useful but dull charities and his dull but immensely profitable businesses and investments. Howard was buying a 77- x 130-foot vacant lot at Seventy-third Street and Fifth Avenue and planning to build a house on it. He paid $450,000 for the property, then the most desirable single piece of residential property left in Manhattan. George had given the *Atalanta* to the government during the Spanish-American War, and Captain Shackford had joined Howard's employ as master of the fore-and-aft rigged steam and sail yacht *Niagara,* a big yacht fitted out every bit as luxuriously as *Atalanta* but far more modern. The Howard Goulds were going abroad this spring of 1899 on an extended cruise to the Azores, British waters, and most particularly the fjords of Norway which George had spoken of so highly after he returned a few years earlier from a similar cruise in *Atalanta.* Howard made several gestures to the public: he gave $5,000 to endow a bed at the Woman's Hospital and a check to the City Mission to send city

children upstate for summer camp. Then they were off, Howard
and Kathrine, on a summer excursion that promised to be most
exciting, given Kathrine's love of men and parties, and Howard's
proclivity for "a good time."

The truly notable activity among the Goulds in that summer of
1899 was to be seen in George's activities, which were puzzling in
the extreme. For three years after the death of his father, George
had marked time while he pulled the communications empire together. No one had criticized the young businessman for such cau-
tion. Rather, he had been lionized in Wall Street as a prudent manager of his father's investments, and since his personality was so
much less abrasive than Jay's, he had brought the Goulds to a
position where they were no longer the most hated family. George,
indeed, was fairly well liked.

George had made that serious mistake, however, of quarreling
with J. Pierpont Morgan over a business matter, and the resulting
ill-feeling deprived George of the support of the man who was
becoming the strongest banker in New York, and the banker who
had most interest in George's specialty of railroads and wires.
Morgan was an arbitrary man: quarrel with him once and he left
you strictly alone ever after. He would never "go after" anyone:
life on Wall Street was too hectic for vendettas. But never again
would he help a man with whom he had broken. So George could
mark the Morgan bank off his list of potential business allies.

Although Helen and Mrs. Russell Sage continued to be the best
of friends, Sage grew a little irritated with George, too, for a
reason that he had expressed a year or so earlier: George's propensity for long vacations and his disinclination to hard work.
And in the summer of 1899, it did seem that George was spreading
himself a little.

A New York art dealer named H. M. Earle contacted an old
Negro junk dealer in New Orleans who had in his possession
nineteen paintings which the old man claimed he had purchased
from former plantation owners down on their luck after the Civil
War. They were reputed to be early Italian and Dutch works,

Correggios and Rubens, Raphaels and Turners. The elderly black, Marcel, had been hanging on to the paintings for years, certain that he had a fortune on hand. Earle looked them over, got in touch with George Gould, and made an agreement with Marcel. He would pay $5,000 for the nineteen paintings as they stood, on behalf of George Gould. If the paintings were declared by New York experts to be what they were claimed, George would pay $600,000 for them.

George Gould immediately became the subject of talk in the art world. What were these paintings? Were they real? In London on Bond Street, the Duveens said they might well be real. They had been offered these paintings years before, but under conditions which made them believe the works might have been stolen—so they had no more than looked at photographs and then broken off negotiations. If the paintings were real masters—nineteen of them —the price, said the Duveens, was a bargain. Nonsense, said other dealers. The highest price paid for a mass of old masters had gone at the Lord Dudley sale of 1892, when ninety-one pictures sold for $500,000.

For a few days, the art world was agog. In London, Christie, Manson and Company waited to hear the verdict of the American experts. The Duveens watched and waited, and so did a dozen other art houses.

In New Orleans, art expert Armand Hawkins pooh-poohed the whole story. "I have known those pictures for the last forty years," he said. "If the New York experts pronounce them to be old masters, I will be the most astonished man in Louisiana."

And then one old resident of New Orleans told all:

"I think I have heard of these pictures before," he said. "Some forty years ago an Italian artist, Torriani, made quite a comfortable income by copying pictures by the old masters and selling them to wealthy families. Almost all of the old houses in New Orleans contain some of these Torriani canvases. I imagine Torriani had something to do with these 'old masters' of Marcel."

And that is how it ended. At $5,000, nineteen good copies of old masters was not such a bad bargain for George, although they meant nothing at all to the art world. But it had been an opportunity for George suddenly to become a dominant figure in the world of collectors—and he sorely regretted missing it.

George did want to make his mark on the world. He did not want to go down in history simply as the conservator of his father's estate. His polo playing (at which he was very good), his riding to the hounds, his yacht racing, all indicated this frustration, and his casting about for ways to express himself.

In 1899, George was known as "the patron of Lakewood polo." He bought the old Lakewood Golf Club grounds when the club moved and organized the Lakewood Polo Club. He bought and equipped some forty polo ponies and built three polo fields. Soon he had the most complete polo outfit of any man in America and was planning to challenge the Meadowbrook Polo Club of William C. Whitney.

That December, George gave a grand house party at Georgian Court to celebrate another acquisition, a $250,000 building which he called the Casino. One day a year or so earlier, George was giving a lawn party at Georgian Court when it began to rain. George and his guests went inside, but the party was ruined, and George vowed that this should not happen again. Thus, the Casino. The building was built of brick, stucco, and iron, and given the alternate name Bachelor's Hall, although neither name did it justice. A huge amphitheater, it contained living quarters for guests as well. Where Georgian Court contained some thirty rooms, the Casino had twenty sleeping rooms for guests, with bathrooms, hallways, and lounges, ice rooms and a pantry. Besides living rooms, the Casino had a tanbark ring inside—as large as that of Madison Square Garden. Above the ring were archways and balconies from which spectators could watch the polo games. Polo.

The ring was, after all, built for polo (although on one occasion George brought a whole circus into the ring for the entertainment of his guests). But Bachelor's Hall also contained a 110,000-

gallon indoor swimming pool, three bowling alleys, a gymnasium, a Turkish bath, a billiard room, a squash racquets court, a squash tennis court, and a Court Tennis court—one of half a dozen in the country.

To celebrate the completion of this facility that would have sufficed for a small university's athletic program, George gave a huge Christmas party on December 21, 1899. The guests began arriving by train at 3:30 in the afternoon from New York and Philadelphia. They were met by carriages from the estate and driven either to the Laurel-in-the-Pines, the local resort hotel that George had taken over for the occasion, or to Georgian Court. A handful would stay in the big house, and more would stay in Bachelor's Court. Among those who would stay with the Goulds was Mrs. Stuyvesant Fish, one of the grand ladies of New York society. Also representing society were the Sydney Smiths, the Hermann Oelrichs, Lispenard Stewart, the Charles Snowdens, assorted Burdens, Pomeroys, Depews, and Clews; the Marquis de Talleyrand, Posts, Hewitts, Webbs, Cuttings, and dozens of others, including Whelans, Colliers, and Drexels of Philadelphia.

The party began in the afternoon with cocktails and informal gatherings in the lounges at Laurel-in-the-Pines. Dinner was served at the hotel for everyone, the Goulds, their house guests, and the guests at Bachelor's Court coming the few hundred yards by carriage.

The guests were seated at two tables of twelve and twenty tables of four. A Hungarian orchestra assembled inside the dining hall to play, and this group struck up Rossini's Overture to the Barber of Seville, then went on to Liszt's Hungarian Rhapsodie No. 2, and other selections.

George presided over the dinner: Edith felt poorly and would save her strength for the later events. Dinner finally ended at about 8:30, the last dollop of champagne was poured out, and coffee was served. After liqueurs, the guests were treated to a three-pronged theatrical performance. Edith, coming out of retirement, was to play a leading role in this amateur production.

For the evening, Edith (as producer, too) had converted the carriage house into a theater, and here the audience saw three plays, *A Pair of Lunatics,* featuring Captain Fielding, one of society's brightest stars; *The Marble Arch,* featuring Miss Emily Key Hoffman; and then *The Twilight of the God,* with Mrs. Gould.

George served as an usher. He put on a bright scarlet satin-faced coat like the ones he supplied for all the ushers and led guests through a long covered archway lit by electric bulbs and decorated on all sides by yacht flags and burgees, conspicuous among which were his own private flags. These were hung against a background of holly, mistletoe, and palms, interspersed with bows of red ribbon. It was, after all, the Christmas season.

The play had been selected carefully to show off Mrs. Gould's hourglass figure and to provide her with marvelous and ringing lines. Her part, that of Isabel Warland, was almost the whole play. Well, it was her playhouse, and her money.

Edith's performance was judged by all to be magnificent. Her costume was magnificent, too, made especially for the occasion of the most costly materials. (Edith had the habit of spending: one time when doing a charity performance in Lakewood, she had had made a gown of purple velvet, trimmed with semiprecious stones, and a 10-foot brocade train lined with *real* ermine, all for a single benefit performance. It is said that when George got the bill for the costume, even he complained.)

The guests all agreed that their hostess, so long absent from the theater, did wonderfully well; her diction was clear, her voice rang out loud, her gestures were well timed, and she *was* the Isabel Warland who persuaded an old lover to grant her husband a political office, even in the twilight of this "God."

The last clap of applause had been heard and the last curtain calls taken at 10:30, and the guests then walked to the house. Mrs. Gould, ahead of them, had changed her costume. She now wore a low-cut ball gown of lace-trimmed white satin that revealed new aspects of sizeable breasts and her wasp-waist. Around her neck was the $500,000 string of pearls, and on her head, a diamond diadem that must have set George back $100,000. Elisha Dyer, Jr., led the cotillion with Mrs. Fish, who was as close to being a guest of honor as the party boasted, and the dancing began. Santa Claus, in regular costume, showed up after a time with his pack full of trinkets and handed out gold golf sticks, horseshoes, and pins for the men, and gold and silver bonbon boxes for the ladies—it was, after all, the Christmas season.

There was a Waldteufel waltz and a Sousa two-step, a *lancier* from Herbert's *The Fortune Teller,* and one piece and another until about 1:00 when the party broke for a dainty late supper.

> *Canapés d'anchois*
> *Tortue verte passée en tasses*
> *Consommé printanier*
> *Radis, céleri, pinjolas*
> *Grenouilles aux crabes d'huîtres Newburg*
> *Ailes de volaille sauce Périgord*
> *Fonds d'artichauts florentine*
> *Bécasses, et canards canvas back*
> *Tomates farcies au céleri mayonnaise*
> *Petits aspics de foie gras*
> *Asperges nouvelles vinaigrette*
> *Glaces de fantaisies*
> *Bonbons devises, fraises, petits fours*
> *Café*

All during the meal, the waiters poured champagne. After dinner, the bar opened, and the crowd went back to dancing until 5:00 in the morning when the host and hostess said their good-nights and the orchestra packed up its instruments. The partygoers were then decanted by carriage either to their rooms in the Bachelor's Hall or the hotel uptown, or were helped up the long circular staircase beneath the smiling frieze of the jolly Canterbury pilgrims. The party had been a grand success.

21

How Anna Went into Debt

So the second-generation members of this famous business family relaxed, mixing with the high society that the middle-aged millionaire had always eschewed. But almost immediately, there were indications that this attention to gaiety was going much further and much faster than anyone would have expected.

HOWARD GOULD'S wife Kathrine was a bad buy. She dyed her blonde hair but only when the roots showed abominably, quarreled with her servants, lorded it over those she thought her inferiors, lapped at the feet of those she thought superior, and rubbed herself against all available men like a cat coming in for a saucer of cream. Kathrine could not wait to go abroad that summer of 1899, and when they did go, she played the *grande dame* with her guests in the great yacht lounge with its player pipe organ, long settees, and rich velvet furnishings. The *Niagara* ran into a storm at 36° 31'N 41° 30'W, and Kathrine was confined to her cabin for several days, much to the delight of Captain Shackford, who found Howard a genial and friendly young man, but who had not nearly so many pleasant things to say about his employer's consort.

The Gould party went to the Azores, to Bangor, to the Royal Ulster Yacht Club, to Kingston, to the Isle of Man. There they went climbing from the Head Hotel up the bluff, on which stood a sign advertising Ivy soap. When they reached the top, they picnicked there with an entourage of a dozen people, including the butler who had the hampers of champagne and cold cuts.

They visited the ruined Dunallie Castle at Oban, Scotland, and they went to Norway to Vartdale Fjord, to Tromso, then to Alexandrosk in Russia, visiting more glaciers and fjords, and then coming to Molde where they anchored next to the German Kaiser's yacht *Hohenzollern*. Kathrine Gould's trip was quite made on the day that the Kaiser chose to visit the Goulds as a gesture of friendship toward Americans. Along with the Prince Albert of Schleswig-Holstein and sixteen German noblemen, the Emperor came aboard, piped over the side with all the pomp that Captain Shackford could muster from a civilian crew. The Emperor held Kathrine's hand for just a moment longer than he might have—she impressed even kings that way—and then his majesty presented her with a large autographed picture of himself, worth its weight in gold pieces to her for the new Fifth Avenue house. When a few hours later the *Hohenzollern* pulled out, she hoisted the Stars and Stripes at her foremast, and her royal master waved his cap at the Goulds as he sailed away.

What a triumph! Mrs. Vanderbilt (the former Grace Wilson) maintained that she, Grace, was "something like the Princess of Wales" when abroad, and that she and the Kaiser were on a first-name basis. But no other American millionaires made such lavish claims, and Kathrine Gould really had something with which to lord it over the neighbors when she got home.

When they did get home, Kathrine could not wait to move to the new house, a building on Fifth Avenue, from the old one on Fifty-seventh Street, so she rented a place, the house of Mrs. Catharine L. Kernochan at 824 Fifth Avenue, and there she installed her old drab furnishings and her new picture of the Kaiser, and began inviting people in to regale them with her adventures.

So went the winter for the Goulds. It seemed, too, that every branch of the family spread itself a little bit during these days, possibly excepting Edwin. But the champion spenders were the Count and Countess de Castellane. Actually, it would be more nearly correct to say that Boni was the world's champion spender, while Anna learned the role of gracious chatelaine.

Shortly after the wedding, Boni had taken Anna to Rochecotte on the Loire to visit the rundown château the de Castellane family kept there. The villagers put on a fête for Anna, and she dutifully sat on the bandstand and gave out the prizes for the various contests. But she hated it—she still did not like foreigners. She did not like the plumbing at Rochecotte, she could not bear the concept of *vie de famille,* in which she was expected to share the drafty old ruin with her mother-in-law and assorted other de Castellanes. She considered the local costume frumpy. She had no interest in the wine tasting. The hunt bored her, she found the occupants of the neighboring châteaux dull and provincial, and, in seven words, she insisted on going back to Paris.

Boni argued.

When he argued, Anna simply clamped her Jay Gould lips together, fixed her husband with a cold stare, and began packing. By the time Boni realized that she had made up her mind and was leaving, he was far behind and had to hurry to catch up.

So they went to Paris, the words of Boni's old friend, the Marchioness of Anglesey, ringing in his ears:

"Her soft exterior hides a will of iron. She is essentially the child of her father."

Boni shuddered.

If this was going to be the course of their marriage, then he would go his own way, he said to himself. One of his first excursions along that way was to the Faubourg St. Honoré and the antique shop of M. Guiraud. Not long before, Guiraud had bought some very valuable Gobelin tapestries of blue and pink at the sale of one of the Gunsburg mansions. These two tapestries, called the Bouchers, bore the royal arms of France along with pastoral scenes. To Boni, the connoisseur, they seemed "to breathe the sensuous charm and artificial grace inseparable from the period to which they belonged." Boni had to have them and he hurried his coachman along. The slim young aristocrat, dreamer of the days of Louis the Sun King, lover of beauty and Frenchman of Frenchmen, pictured himself very well in his book *How I Discovered America:*

> M. Guiraud welcomed me in the nature of treasure trove, as the sensation of my marriage with millions had preceded me to Paris, and everyone was curious to know how I should spend them. Nobody, needless to say, credited me with a desire to become a patron of arts!
>
> I suppose I must have secretly amused the famous dealer, I was so terribly in earnest, so anxious to buy, so young, and, to him, so inexperienced. I had already changed my letter of credit, and my pockets literally bulged with bank-notes. I pulled them out by handfuls.
>
> "Why, M. le Comte, you have become a Croesus!" exclaimed M. Guiraud.
>
> "What do you want for the tapestries?" I demanded.
>
> "Two hundred and fifty thousand francs," replied the dealer.
>
> "Here is the money," I said, and I began to count out my packets of notes; indeed, so greatly did I hurry that the floor was strewn with them. Guiraud could find no words!
>
> The tapestries were folded and transferred to my carriage. I wanted to feel that they were mine *that very instant,* and I hurried away with my spoils.

Boni showed the tapestries to Anna, who was only mildly impressed. Her interest went more to those other artists, Paquin and Worth, whose creations had at least the value of being wearable.

At the moment the de Castellanes had no place to put Boni's

tapestries. They had rented the furnished house of the Marquise d'Hervey de St. Denis in the Avenue Bosquet while Anna saved up enough money to build a house of her own.

And save she did. Although Anna was reputed to be one of the richest women in the world, and was indeed very rich in terms of capital, her fortune was in trust, and she could withdraw nothing but the interest or earnings of her share—one-sixth of the Jay Gould holdings, or, as it was now, the whole fortune as managed by brother George. The management was adequate, that much is certain, because Anna's income from her one-sixth portion was nearly three quarters of a million dollars a year, which indicated that the earnings on the fortune were running somewhere between 7 and 9 per cent.

But they went into rented quarters. Boni was very much displeased with the Marquise's mansion. He disliked the staircase and the high windows, but it would take Anna some time to save enough money to build the house he wanted, which was no less than a palace. He vowed patience, and put away his tapestries.

It soon became apparent that it would take Anna a very long time indeed to save the money for their house if Boni's spending were not curtailed. Boni bought a very expensive dinner service of green Sèvres at Stettiners. He bought rare furniture, tables inset with Sèvres plaques, Chinese vases, silver soup plates from the famous Russian Demidoff collection. He even competed against that collector of collectors, Pierpont Morgan, for the exquisite Crasse Fragonard panels. (Anna was lucky, and Boni did not get them.)

In his defense, however, it must be granted that never did mortal man spend money with better grace. On the birth of his first son, Marie Louis Jean Jay Georges Paul Ernest Boniface de Castellane, for example, Boni felt impelled to stage a truly grand celebration that would impress all Paris, and, hopefully, that cold-eyed wife of his (her twenty-first birthday came shortly after). The kind of fête he had in mind was too much for one poor man to handle, so he took his uncle, the Prince de Sagan, into his confidence and secured his influential uncle's assistance in breaking through the red tape of Paris officialdom to secure his end, which was no less than the use of the Tir aux Pigeons on the lake in the Bois de Boulogne on the edge of Paris. Since the Bois belonged to the French people, officialdom must be consulted, tiresome as that was.

Boni and the Prince appeared at the offices of the President of the Municipal Council and unfolded their project. They would rent the Tir, they would build a stage on the banks of the lake, and they would display there an "illuminated" ballet for the amusement of their guests.

So impressed was the Council President with the magnificence of the proposal that he promised an added attraction, an escort of mounted police in the Bois on the night of the fête. The President gave the necessary permission for the use of the woods with a flourish and promised even to appear himself, a prospect that the Prince deigned only to acknowledge by an extraordinary squint through his monocle.

Boni and the Prince rented the Tir aux Pigeons for several days before the night in question to make preparations. They then set workmen to transforming the area, meanwhile sending out 3,000 invitations to the fête and 250 invitations to "intimate friends" for an earlier dinner party.

Boni ordered 80,000 Venetian lamps made for him at Murano, and when they arrived, several dozen electricians were put to work attaching them to the trees to outline the walks and avenues leading to the Tir aux Pigeons. Scarlet livery was ordered for sixty footmen who would attend to the liquid refreshment of the partygoers. A total of *nine miles* of carpet was purchased from Belloir, upholsterer to the wealthy, and he promised to have it ready.

On that day Belloir called the Count. It was raining. What were they to do?

The moon would shine for him, said the count placidly. It was early afternoon. An hour later, it was still raining. At 5 o'clock, it was still raining.

"Put down the carpet," the count ordered. "I'll take the risk," he said.

And then, of course, as the carpet was being laid, the heavens cleared and the sun came out for an hour, just enough to dry the trees and make it perfect for the party. It was the luck of the Castellanes.

Boni's party was a grand success. The bluest blood in France arrived. At dinner, served under a large marquee decorated with red roses, Anna chatted busily with the Duc de Dodeauville and Baron Alphonse de Rothchild, while the Count turned his attention to the lovely Countess de Greffuhle. Everyone pronounced the fête the finest of the season—everyone except one.

Anna was really not at all impressed. She was far more interested in what Boni had been doing after dinner with the Countess de Greffuhle, especially when the 80,000 lights came on, the ballet was presented, and Boni and the Countess disappeared into the woods.

The Count did his very best, within the limitations of his ardently romantic nature, to captivate his bride because he truly desired that precious possession, her fortune, and wished one day to secure control of it for himself. Boni never did understand that Jay Gould had drawn his will specifically with people like the Count in mind and that there was no conceivable way, barring a legal overthrow of the will, that the fortune could be removed from trust. So he continued the chase.

Boni had always wanted a yacht. The *Walhalla,* a three-masted auxiliary-powered ship of 1,600 tons, was on the market. She was so large and so built (with that full ship rigging) that she was often mistaken for a warship, and she was so expensive, taking a crew of a hundred men, that she cost $150,000 a year to operate. So Boni bought her for 2,500,000 francs ($500,000) and became the undisputed king of the world's yachtsmen.

Boni took Anna yachting. They went to Norway with the Count and Countess Jacques de Pourtalès, the Marquis and Marquise de Chaponnay, and the Prince and Princess de Poix.

They encountered Kaiser Wilhelm cruising around Norway on the *Hohenzollern,* but far from being crazy to meet him as Kathrine had been, de Castellane ignored this son of the nation that had stolen the French national fortune in 1870. They went to Russia, they cruised the Baltic, and they were happy enough the first summer. But by the end of the second summer, Anna was sick of yachting, and she spent most of her time criticizing the morals of her noble guests, shooting sidelong glances at Boni.

In St. Petersburg, they dined with the French ambassador and then invited the Grand Dukes for an evening of fun and frolic aboard the *Walhalla.* The merriment was sustained into the wee hours, and in doing a jig on deck, Prince Orloff fell down and broke his leg, an accident deemed unfortunate at the moment but of no lasting concern. The festivities continued, day after day. The de Castellane party travelled by special train to visit Moscow. They came back and visited the Hermitage. The Grand Duke Alexis gave a supper for them, and they dined at the palace of Tsarskoe Selo with the Grand Duke Vladimir and his duchess.

Anna was bored by it all.

They returned from cruising and rented a villa at Deauville where Boni went out in his carriage every day, postilions up in their powdered wigs, to Madame Doucet's antique shop where he met various pretty young *baigneuses.* Anna, all-knowing although she stayed at home, saw to the education of little Marie Louis Jean Jay Georges Paul Ernest Boniface and ran her household.

Although the crowd at Deauville was exclusive and rich, Boni's pretensions impressed them, and soon they were calling him the Grand Duke of Gerolstein, a distinct slap at his theatricality. And Anna especially disliked being called the Grand Duchess of Gerolstein.

There were many things about their marriage that Anna did not like. She did not like *Frenchmen*—in her heart she really felt that all of them (all she knew, anyhow) were *bad*. She did not like the tales recounted to her by other ladies of Boni's previous affairs. It seemed that Boni had slept with every woman in Paris before he married her. She did not like Boni's disappearances with other ladies into the woods, or along the beach, or into odd rooms —and these disappearances were very, very frequent. The one thing Anna never complained about was the way Boni spent her money. Money meant nothing to her.

But that spending soon became a problem to all the Goulds.

Before their marriage, in order to be sure that Anna brought him a proper dowry, Boni emphasized to Anna again and again the rules of French society: she would never be accepted in the Faubourg St. Germain (the equivalent of the Fifth Avenue crowd in New York) simply because her husband was a member of that rich society by right of birth. Anna must dazzle all Paris with her riches, and then she would be accepted by the Rothschilds and Sagans, the Gunsburgs and the others. This argument succeeded enough to bring Boni a dowry of $2,000,000 along with Anna's acquiescence in his lavish use of her annual income from the trust. (The dowry represented accrued earnings of the trust between Jay's death and Anna's marriage.)

But with all this, with an income estimated to be about $600,-000–$700,000 a year, depending on the rise and fall of the dividends and interest paid by the Gould securities, by the spring of 1899 the de Castellanes were in serious financial trouble. They had bought the yacht for half a million dollars, and they spent $150,000 a year maintaining her. They had bought a piece of land at the corner of the Avenue du Bois de Boulogne and Avenue Malakoff for $950,000 and were building a pink palace modeled on Le Petit Trianon of Versailles, Marie Antoinette's playground. The building and the furnishing cost another $2,000,000. Boni gave another party for 3,000 guests to witness a mock wedding of Maria Thérèse of Austria and Louis XIV. He hired 1,000 people to work at the affair, either as servants or as actors, and the bill came to $300,000. Anna, in a gesture reminiscent of sister Helen, bought a piece of land for $200,000 and started work to build a permanent Bazar de Charité which would be dedicated to the memory of her mother. Meanwhile, the de Castellanes spent $300,000 a year to maintain the house on the Avenue Bosquet. And Boni was an inveterate optimist, always willing to back his beliefs and even his guesses with hard cash. So he lost huge sums at the Paris Bourse on faulty guesses, he lost at the gaming tables, he lost at the track. Every time he lost, he either gave a party or gave some fabulously expensive gift to a friend, usually female.

The road had not been entirely free of obstacles during these years. Several times, work on the palace had to be suspended while Boni and Anna waited for a quarterly payment from New York. The *Walhalla* was laid up more often than it was sailing—and twice it was attached for debt and docked.

Each time Anna bailed the yacht out along with the other debts.

By summer Boni was in trouble. A fervent Royalist, he held a position as a Deputy in the House, a position he used to try to wreck the Republican government of France and bring back the monarchy. Boni had been involved in 1898 in a sticky plot to overthrow the Republicans by force. Although the plot had been uncovered in time to prevent any violence, Boni had escaped jail largely because of the power of his wife's money. This summer of 1899, Boni argued at the Automobile Club with Henri Turbot, a dedicated Republican and editor of *La Petite République,* and when the argument was finished, Boni laughed in that narrow-faced, well-bred way of his and told Turbot he did not know what he was talking about, being an idiot of a Republican.

Turbot, who took his Republicanism very seriously, whitened. *"Dégénéré!"* He spat the insult between clenched teeth.

Then Boni whitened. Picking up his suede gloves, he slapped Turbot across the cheek, bowed, and turned away.

They met in the Bois with rapiers, and after a spirited encounter, Boni, who was an excellent swordsman, ran his opponent through the arm and honor was satisfied.

Still, that encounter became a part of Boni's trouble. Turbot was very popular in the Bourse and along the avenues, and some of Boni's creditors began to show their distaste for the aristocratic habits of the de Castellanes, and Boni's politics, by calling their notes. Boni could not pay. Harried and attached, he was threatened with bankruptcy.

In January, 1900, affairs had come to such a pass that Boni and Anna sat down for a long money talk, distasteful as it was to the latter. Anna heard Boni out, looked at him coldly, and said she would see what she could do to save the situation. She wrote to George in New York, asking his advice.

George refused to prescribe for their ills at long distance, and suggested that they make a trip to America to talk over the problem. Boni rather unhappily agreed. In New York, George looked over the de Castellane affairs, whistling in wonderment. Edith was known as a big spender in the United States and so was he, but he had never seen anything quite like this before. The thing to do, of course, was to consolidate these debts, secure a loan of some kind to take the pressure off, and then begin paying them. But what debts!

Boni and Anna owed 3,702,000 francs in connection with the building of the mansion on Avenue Malakoff and the charity bazaar. They owed 6,585,260 francs in mortgages, some of them past due. They owed 4,293,155 francs on bills to suppliers and notes payable to banks. Boni owed 9,100,000 francs to curio dealers.

Altogether the debts came to 23,000,000 francs, or $4,485,000.

George then called a meeting of the executors—Helen, Edwin, and Howard—and Helen pursed her lips. (She had never liked that Frenchman.) Edwin whistled, too, when he saw the figures, and even Howard, by far the most easy-going in matters of money, was visibly impressed.

The only way the situation could be salvaged was to make Anna a loan—the trust was inviolate. The loan would have to come from the others of the family, too.

So it was done, the pressure was eased for a time, and the de Castellanes went back to Paris. When the creditors continued to be restless, George took one more step: he had himself appointed trustee for the Countess by the Civil Tribunal of Paris, which meant that all debts concerning Anna would be referred to him for payment.

George cut Anna down to an income of $20,000 a month, with the rest of the earnings of her share of the estate to be paid into a fund from which the debts would be retired. With approximately half a million dollars a year for the purpose, it was estimated, then, that it would take ten years to pay off the debts Boni had run up in four years.

22

George, the Big Wheel

———◆◆◆———

*By 1900, the estate left by the middle-
aged millionaire had withstood many as-
saults of different kinds: blackmail, vanity, waste, and religiosity. Yet the burden
was growing noticeably heavier as the
years went by, particularly on the oldest
son, for with him rested the major share
of responsibility for the wellbeing of the
whole family and the health of the trust
funds that kept them well.*

———◆◆◆———

ANNA, as might be expected, was not particularly pleased when, in
the autumn of 1900, George told her that her allowance was going
to be cut. She sometimes spent $20,000 a month on dresses—if Boni
had done anything for Anna, he had given her a sense of high
fashion, and brought to her, by the power of his name, the highest-
fashion couturiers in Paris. They came to Anna, not she to them.

But Anna's case was not unique within the family. Howard
had overspent: he had built Castle Gould at Sands Point and used
up most of the accumulation of his interest and dividends, and

then the house he built for Kathrine on Fifth Avenue had gouged another hole.

With the fifty-room house on Sixty-seventh and Fifth Avenue, Georgian Court, his yacht, the summer shooting lodge in the Catskills, Edith's taste in clothes and jewelry, and five children, George had financial problems, too. Edith had some very definite ideas about raising the children. They were taught by tutors, of course, and they were all learning five languages: English, French, German, Spanish, and Italian. George had some special ideas, too. He believed in the out-of-doors, and the children were thus taught to excel in sports. This meant swimming teachers, tennis teachers, squash teachers, riding instructors, and boxing masters. Kingdon was thirteen, Jay, eleven, Marjorie, nine, Vivien, seven, and Georgie, five. There would be two more children, Edith and Gloria, and they would have the same careful education under the same kind of guidance. George and Edith were good parents, even if the children were growing up taught largely by strangers, in the manner of the very rich.

When it came right down to it, the large family created a whole new set of financial problems for George. When he died, how much would he be able to leave these children? Figured conservatively, his share of the general estate was worth about $15,000,000, although since he was in charge, he also was able to take expenses out of income each year for his services as financial manager of the fortune. But that was income and little of it could be saved, given the family spending pattern. True, George had inherited another $5,000,000, but altogether that put his share of the fortune at $20,-000,000, and when he died, this would go to his children in trust in equal amounts—that much was clearly stipulated in Jay's will. With five children already and his eye still gleaming it was apparent that none of them would be very wealthy unless George did something drastic to improve the fortune. So in 1900, George Gould set out to increase the Gould fortune on behalf of his children and the children of his brothers and sisters.

There were two conceivable ways to build up this fortune. One was to travel with the drift of the times, to build up the existing rail lines and make more profits from them. The impressive railroad empire Jay had amassed amounted to a line extending from Detroit in the East to Pueblo in the West. It touched Chicago, Omaha, Kansas City, New Orleans, and El Paso. It touched every important place on the Mississippi from Keokuk to New Orleans. The Wabash, for example, extended across northern Ohio, Indiana, and Illinois to Omaha and Kansas City, then down into the Iowa corn belt. The Missouri Pacific crossed the Missouri and spread out through Kansas into Nebraska, while the main line provided an artery into the heart of Colorado, ending at the steel town of Pueblo. From Kansas City south, the Iron Mountain, the Texas and Pacific, and the Southwestern drained the cotton fields of Arkansas, Texas, and Mississippi.

It was, in short, 15,000 miles of track, the largest empire controlled by *any one group in the United States.*

The other way was to expand the empire still further.

Which way would George choose to go?

Late in the 1890s, George began working on the dream of Jay Gould: the transcontinental railroad.

No transcontinental railroad existed then in the United States nor is there one now. It was, and is, possible for a man to travel from San Francisco to New York by train, but not without stopovers, interminable delays, and usually changes of cars. Railroads grew up in the United States, financed by limited private capital and limited dreams, so that they connected one big town or city with the next and sometimes went no further. To connect New York City and Albany, for example, Commodore Vanderbilt had to buy up three railroads, the Harlem, which controlled the entrance to New York City, the Hudson River, which ran from the outskirts of New York to Greenbush on the Hudson, and the New York Central, which ran from Greenbush to Albany, and then east.

George proposed to put the Missouri Pacific and Wabash systems together, run the Wabash to Pittsburgh, and connect it there with a new line which would go over the Allegheny Mountains and connect to the Western Maryland, with a terminus at Baltimore. On the west, George would build from Denver to San Francisco.

From San Francisco, then, one took a ferry to Oakland and boarded a Western Pacific railroad train, which carried him as far as Ogden, Utah. At Ogden, there was a direct connection with the Union Pacific, which carried as far as Omaha, and there an agreement between the Union Pacific and other lines allowed a Union Pacific to travel east as far as Chicago. That was the end of the line and the passenger changed trains, and often stations, taking the Lake Shore or the New York Central or another line east. This clumsy system had always annoyed Jay Gould who would have changed it in his day had he lived long enough. Completed, the line would be amalgamated and turned into America's first truly transcontinental railroad, where a man could get on at the western end and ride all the way to the east coast without changing trains or stations, or laying over.

George began, in 1899, to make plans for the system. It would be expensive. Jay would have gone about this program by looking over all the railroads and buying up competing lines and fragmentary lines, but this was not George's way. Jay had started in Wall Street at the bottom, and he knew every trick that his competitor railroaders were capable of, having used most of the tricks himself. But George had started at the top, and with the huge fortune to manipulate, it was quite inconceivable to him that he should be beaten in any endeavor by lesser men.

Suddenly, in 1899, George found himself presented with a natural ally. The heavens seemed to have sent him a gift. That ally was Andrew Carnegie, owner of the nation's largest steel company, and one that was basically self-contained. Carnegie owned or controlled its own iron ore, coke mills, railroads, and steamship lines. But the company did not control the Pennsylvania Railroad, the link with New York and the central east coast. The Pennsylvania was independent and extremely powerful, and its shrewd managers, over the years, had staved off a half-dozen attempts to infringe on their territory.

In 1899, the directors of the Pennsylvania sought to force Carnegie to share some of his enormous wealth. They doubled their freight rates from Pittsburgh to the eastern seaboard. The only other conceivable route was by way of the Baltimore and Ohio, and that line, acting in concert with the Pennsylvania, also doubled its rates.

Carnegie professed to be infuriated, and perhaps he was—one could never tell with this shrewd old Scotsman who was capable, like Jay Gould, of pursuing several apparently contradictory schemes at once. George did not consider this aspect of the Carnegie character. He did not see how anything Carnegie could do might affect him, except to help him if Carnegie promised to ship annually what was then about 10,000,000 tons of steel across the new line to the east. Such a commitment would immediately make worthwhile any expenditure at all in railroad building. So with Carnegie backing, George went ahead to build the Wabash east.

In the meantime, however, another development in American business was taking shape which did not augur so well for George in the long run. His father's one-time banker and George's enemy, J. Pierpont Morgan, turned his attention from railroads to the steel industry. As the railroads had ruined themselves by overcompetition, so the steel companies were killing each other by price cutting and equally hazardous competitive methods. Morgan wanted to create a great steel cartel, centrally managed with all assets in one grand company, with the various manufacturers confining themselves to their own territory and to fabrication of what they were best suited to make.

So while George was busy putting the wheels in motion to build the new rail lines east, Morgan was planning the super-steel company.

At the end of 1900, the new tracks were moving east. Then on

December 12, Pierpont Morgan attended a dinner given in honor of Charles Schwab, Carnegie's principal operating officer. Morgan got Schwab aside and began talking about buying Carnegie out.

Morgan was energetic and determined, and it was not many months before Carnegie was persuaded to sell his steel company for half a billion dollars in bonds of the new super-company. The announcement rocked Gould, but he was still well financed. He had allied himself with James Hazen Hyde, Louis Fitzgerald, and other men who held huge interests in the Equitable Life Assurance Society. This syndicate had raised $20,000,000 for the purpose of "rescuing" Pittsburgh from the clutches of the Pennsylvania Railroad. Gould then bought the Wheeling and Lake Erie Railroad, which extended from Toledo to the little town of Jewett, Ohio, sixty miles west of Pittsburgh.

He was coming close.

As George expanded east, he also moved in the west. A small railroad named the Denver and Rio Grande ran south from Denver to Pueblo, tapping the coal and mineral resources of the Colorado Rockies. This little road followed the Arkansas River west from Pueblo. One line ran north to Leadville and south to Trinidad and Durango, with Creede in the center. The Denver and Rio Grande controlled all the important gateways toward the Pacific out of Denver. Much of the stock of this line was held in England, and in 1900 and 1901 when George went to England, he took time enough from his vacationing to visit the city and pick up 30 per cent of the common and preferred stock of the Denver and Rio Grande without making any great fuss about it.

The road had been reorganized out of bankruptcy in 1886 by an Englishman named George Coppell who died in 1901, the year that George Gould first bought a third of the stock and then, coming home, equally quietly acquired a controlling interest for about $10,000,000. At the same time, George bought into another little road, the Rio Grande Western, which ran into Salt Lake City and Ogden, Utah, where it met the Central Pacific Railroad that had been built to connect with the Union Pacific—or to put it another way, to connect East and West, because the proprietors of the Central Pacific did not care who carried the goods and passengers once they went off that line.

At this point, George truly seemed to be following in his father's footsteps. These western purchases were made quietly and inexpensively, and once accomplished, George held a foothold on a route through Loveland Pass in the Rockies, which his father had favored, and had opened the way west.

For some time, George had been very friendly with Wall Streeter Edward H. Harriman. Anna had once very nearly married into the Harriman family. In 1897, Harriman had decided to try to take over the Union Pacific Railroad, in which George had some interest but not much concern, and the banking firm of Kuhn, Loeb and Co., and the Rockefellers had backed Harriman in this attempt. By 1900, Harriman had firm control of the Union Pacific. But the Union Pacific ended at Ogden and from Ogden west, the traffic was controlled by a monopoly. The road had been built as the Central Pacific by Leland Stanford, Collis P. Huntington, Mark Hopkins, and Charles Crocker back in the days of Jay Gould. In more recent years, these gentlemen had bought up nineteen separate railroads ranging from the 1,250 miles of the Central Pacific to the 4 miles of the Berkeley Branch Railroad and incorporated them under the name of the Southern Pacific.

This road had been milked by its builders, as had all the other railroads, and on February 1, 1899, the officers of the Southern Pacific had been hard-pressed to meet federal government loans of $58,000,000, but they had done it. Monopoly had its advantages.

At the start of the Harriman expansion of 1897, George Gould and Harriman had been very close. George sat on the board of the Union Pacific. Harriman was made a member of the board of Western Union, the Denver and Rio Grande, and the Missouri Pacific. Common interest was possible because the two systems drained different regions and were not necessarily competitive.

That was true, however, only under the conditions that existed in 1897 and the three or four years following. George and the other

Goulds, perhaps unconsciously, were doing what old Jay would have called "skinning the roads." The Missouri Pacific system paid a 5 per cent dividend each year. Meanwhile, Harriman, backed by Kuhn, Loeb, and the Rockefellers, was undertaking a $250,000,-000 expansion program of the Union Pacific, which meant double tracking, new heavy rails, straightening curves, flattening the roadbed for more speed, purchasing new equipment, and building new stations to handle more business. George did not know it, but a difference in the quality of railroad operations was growing between the more northern Union Pacific system and the more southern Missouri Pacific. Some shippers in between were thus persuaded to use the former road.

George felt that his associations with Harriman adequately protected him against any surprise moves. And was he not, quietly, moving both west and east to the Pacific and the Atlantic?

In 1900, however, when Collis P. Huntington was very old, the various estates and trusts of the other members of the Big Four of California (as the owners of the Southern Pacific were called) wanted to pull out of the risky railroad business.

George was still not concerned.

"Look here," his friends warned. "You must not trust Harriman. He isn't working for the Missouri Pacific. He's only interested in his own roads. He'll wipe you off the map the first chance he gets."

George only smiled.

"I'm in there on the Union Pacific board," he would reply, clapping the other on the back, "and nothing can happen that I don't know about."

His friends told him that Harriman was making Huntington's life miserable with requests to buy the Southern Pacific. Huntington refused. Harriman then asked for a perpetual agreement that the Union Pacific could always have access to the Southern Pacific. Huntington refused that too. Then Harriman began to sweat. He looked at the railroad map, and saw that George and he were really competitors for the goods of the far west. Devil take the drainage basins of Missouri Pacific and Union Pacific. What was important was to carry *all* those goods from California and Oregon and Washington.

Harriman also worried that George Gould might get hold of the Southern Pacific and shut *him* out. George was very amiable, but who knew what he was planning? George may have been planning to force Harriman to the wall, but he was not frightened enough to see that he must move quickly, while Harriman, further frightened by his bankers, saw all the dangers and was willing to take the risks in the manner of the old Jay Gould. The silver spoon in George's mouth made him immune to the taste of fear that bedevilled a man like Harriman.

At the time that the Southern Pacific affair was coming to a head, George was bemused by other considerations, it is true. He considered Harriman a friend, and he was inclined to leave that friendship alone as protection enough for his rear. George's problem, *prima facie,* was on the other end of his projected transcontinental system where he was *building* new lines of the Wabash.

Then suddenly, Huntington died. Within two months, the majority interest in Southern Pacific stock was brought up by Kuhn, Loeb, and Harriman, much of it from Huntington's widow.

When George Gould woke up, he went over to Harriman's office for a chat.

"I think you ought to let me have half of that Southern Pacific stock," he said. "Or, if you don't want it, I should be willing to take the whole thing off your hands."

Harriman smiled.

George went away, surprised that his friend should treat him so, but not entirely defenseless. He had now acquired the *control* of the Rio Grande Western, which took him into Ogden.

Not long afterward, Harriman dropped into George's office.

"You bought the Rio Grande Western for both of us?"

"Not at all," said George innocently.

"Well," said Harriman, "I should like to have a half interest in it."

George smiled.

Harriman went away, and George went back to considering his problems on the eastern end of the transcontinental system he proposed to complete. He also went to Europe. After all, a man needed a little relaxation after so hard a winter as George had gone through.

23

Playboy Howard

———◆•◆•◆———

The dream of empire that the middle-aged man had held for so many years seemed to be coming near to fruition. How long would it take the eldest son to build the transcontinental railroad? And would it not help if the others of the family would come in to assist him in these endeavors?

———◆•◆•◆———

WHO WAS there to help George build the railroad across the country?

Edwin was busy with his own investments and doing very nicely at them. Still the quiet one, Edwin lived a rather mysterious life in New York and up the Hudson in a big, unpretentious house. In 1900 and 1901, he was building a "cottage" at the exclusive Jekyl Island Club off Georgia. A handful of millionaires who liked privacy and nature had bought Jekyl Island (Pierpont Morgan was among them), and they hoped to keep it a quiet, luxurious retreat. Sally Gould went to New Orleans to shop for furnishings. In one Royal Street antique shop, she spent $4,000 in a few minutes one day, buying furniture and bric-a-brac. She bought a 100-year-old mahogany sideboard, a grandfather clock of the Revolutionary period, side chairs that predated Andrew Jackson and the War of 1812, a solid silver piece that once belonged to the unfortunate Joseph Bonaparte, a mahogany davenport, and a cordial set from one of the pre-war Louisiana plantation mansions.

Helen was also busy. She established the New York University Hall of Fame at about this time, much to the disgust of the New York *Times,* which found it a mawkish enterprise. Helen also took a new trip across the country in the *Atalanta* surrounded by adoring railroad officials, visiting shops, establishing a YMCA here and there as she did in Little Rock, and poking into things in her usual busybody way—but *this* could scarcely be called help, unless she had come back to report that the Missouri Pacific was becoming a bit dowdy—and she did not. Howard might have helped, had he not been so busy with domestic affairs that he could scarcely think about railroads. Kathrine Gould was leading Howard a merry chase, keeping his name in the papers in the most awkward fashion, and making him one of the most talked-about playboys of the western world.

In the summer of 1900, Howard had taken Kathrine yachting as was her custom. They left New York on May 8 on the *Niagara* with Dr. and Mrs. Clement Cleveland aboard as their guests. They steamed to Queensland, then to the Isle of Guernsey, then to Dartmouth, to Cowes for the races of the Royal Yacht squadron, then Southampton, Le Havre, and up the Seine as far as Rouen. They went to Ostend, to the Orkney Islands, to Iceland, where a quartermaster of the yacht was scalded in a geyser, and where the governor of the island came aboard at Reykjavik for a visit.

Then the yacht went to Norway, and Howard was back in the news again, for they went aground, most embarrassingly, while moving ahead at full steam about 80 miles from Bergen. Mr. Caws, the master on this trip, had been a little off in his navigation, and there they were, high and dry, atop the rocks off Halsin Fjord. At first, the yachtsmen shook with consternation, for it appeared that the ship might slip off the rocks and go down to the bottom. But the fear was soon quelled when Mr. Caws discovered that she was high aground.

Luckily, she did not leak, and they had time to radio to Bergen for tugs. As the three tugs started out, the steam yacht *Varuna* hove in sight. She belonged to Eugene Higgins, an acquaintance of Howard's, and Higgins suggested that he might be able to pull the *Niagara* off. Howard was willing to try, even though there was a certain amount of danger in case a seam had come loose in the keel, and she might leak badly enough to sink.

Still it was worth the attempt, and the *Varuna* ran a line which was taken aboard the *Niagara,* while the *Varuna* headed out to sea, straining with all her might. There was a crunch, a long, sliding sound like fingernails on a blackboard, and the *Niagara* was afloat. The captain and passengers were jubilant. The radio was set to work to send the tugs back to Bergen and to be paid the price of a day's work for their trouble, and drinks were brought out to celebrate.

The Gould party was not out of it yet, however. *Varuna* had to tow *Niagara* to Bergen to go into dry dock. There she sat for two weeks, getting a new keel laid on by 80 men, while Kathrine fumed that her summer was being ruined by that idiot, the master. Howard listened calmly, without any intention of taking action. By this time he was used to Kathrine's constant fulminations.

Kathrine was only partially mollified when King Oscar of Norway came into port and invited the Gould party to visit him aboard his yacht. She did, however, acquire another souvenir, an autographed picture of the King to add to her growing collection in the house on Fifth Avenue.

Finally, they got under way again. Then the imbecile master managed to lose the propeller while passing through the Kaiser Wilhelm Canal at Copenhagen. No royalty showed up to entertain Kathrine who left for London, leaving Howard aboard. Howard ought to have accompanied his wife. Loose in London, she went on a shopping spree, buying innumerable capes, cloaks, and dresses, a terrier puppy and three pugs, one of which, the Princess Zora, cost $1,250 and was said to be the second best pug in the world. It was a good thing for Howard's pocketbook that the best pug was not momentarily available. Kathrine rejoined the ship at Copenhagen, and shortly thereafter, the cruise came to an end. They steamed home to Sands Point to debark in a small boat and go back to Castle Gould while the yacht lay offshore awaiting orders. One thing must be said for Howard: he was no part-time sportsman. When he went yachting, it was all the way. The *Niagara* steamed across the Atlantic, and there was none of this "meet me in Marseilles" to the captain. Where the yacht went, Howard went.

Back home, the Goulds were in trouble again. James Mowbray, the valet who had lost his eye in the fireworks prank a few years earlier and was subsequently promised a lifetime job by an anguished Howard, was fired for drunkenness. He sued Howard. In the suit, the real reason for Mowbray's discharge came out: Kathrine's and Mowbray's quarrel over his shampooing of her hair. Eventually, Howard won the case. A jury had awarded the verdict to the ex-valet, but an appeals court overturned the verdict. Mowbray, they held, had relinquished his right to sue for damages to his eye at the time he accepted the "lifetime" job with Howard. When he was fired for misconduct, Mowbray had erroneously claimed the old damages. The defense counsel complained to the newspapers about the case, calling it a miscarriage of justice, but men of property everywhere cheered. As a letter writer signing himself "FORUM" said in the New York *Times* ". . . Too many actions are brought where the defendant's liability is, in the main, predicated upon his wealth or standing, rather than upon the merits of the plaintiff's own case." This was 1901, and then it was possible for the case to end a complete victory for the millionaire against the one-eyed valet. Hurray for the rights of property!

Kathrine Gould, who had been responsible for Mowbray's firing, continued to cut a wide swathe. She hired a butler named Eric Hamilton because of his fine figure and appearance. One night she

gave him ten dollars and sent him to the drugstore for some medicine for a sick maid. Butler Hamilton went out of the house and did
not show up again that night. Next day when he returned, Kathrine was livid—this was the second time in a week that Hamilton
had broken a house rule, 10:00 curfew for the servants. She fired
him on the spot, but he insolently refused to go until he had seen
Howard.

So Kathrine called the Port Washington police who came and
took poor Hamilton away. In court, he was arraigned for trespass,
disorderly conduct, larceny (the ten dollars), and might have
been charged with murder had Kathrine willed it. He was jailed
until his trial a few days later. His sentence required him to pay
$400 and to keep the peace for six months or to serve six months
in jail. (This was Port Washington, home of the millionaires, and
the Justice of the Peace Allen knew how to deal with unruly
servants.)

Being a drinking man, Hamilton did not have $400, so into the
town dungeon he went.

Two weeks later, Mrs. Gould received an abject letter from him
saying he had been wrong, and that he was in terrible straits being
caged up with these horse thieves, burglars, highway robbers, and
drunkards in the common jail cells.

Kathrine read the poor creature's scribbling and took mercy in
hand. She had her new butler telephone the Judge and ask for
mercy for the poor devil. In a trice, Hamilton was out of jail, and
on his way God knew where.

Such *noblesse oblige*.

It was not more than three or four months later that Kathrine
was in court herself, again bedevilled by the common herd that
would never let her alone, never give her a few moments of tranquility.

Mary Smith and Margaret Dillon, the dressmakers to Mrs.
Howard Gould, kept their establishment on West Forty-fifth
Street just off Fifth Avenue, and there Mrs. Gould went week
after week, whenever she felt that she needed a little frock or

peignoir to spruce up her wardrobe. Kathrine kept a running account with the ladies, perhaps $2,000 to $3,000 owing at any given time. The rich were never hurried about paying such accounts, and such permissiveness was understandable. Miss Smith and Miss Dillon, like all purveyors to society, knew that one of the responsibilities of those who serve the wealthy was to act as their informal bankers, without interest.

All went well until Kathrine began putting on a little weight from too many champagne parties, and suddenly she found that she could squeeze into nothing she had bought in the fall.

It must be those vile dressmakers, out to take advantage of her. Kathrine went storming down Forty-fifth Street, confronted the seamstresses, and said she would not pay.

They took her to court, asking payment of $1,775 and naming Howard as defendant.

Howard did not choose to defend, and the case was settled out of court, just in time for Howard to worry about a $1,000 suit brought by the Brewster Carriage Works against Kathrine, who had ordered a new landau that, on delivery, she did not like.

Was it any wonder that Howard had no time to help George manage the railroads?

24

The Goulds in Trouble

The elder son's activities in railroads awed the general public if not his immediate competitors. He was basking in the high sun of his public glory.

IN the summer of 1900, an election year, George's Republican constituents in Lakewood tried to persuade him to run for Congress. He listened to them, smiled beneath his curling mustaches, then frowned.

"Under no circumstances," he said. "I was not cut out for a politician, and besides, I have other business to attend to."

So saying, George Gould clapped his derby on his head and walked up the gangplank of the steamer, bound as usual in the summertime for Europe, where he would remain until fall.

On the continent all summer, George went yachting. He sent his children to Scotland, sometimes, and sometimes to Paris. He

went bicycling through the fields of France. He went art collecting
in the galleries. He went sailing and shooting and fishing. He did
precisely what he wanted to do, all the while remaining a thought-
ful and beloved father of the children, who received a personal
letter, a postcard, or a gift from him every few days. Every summer, George and Edith visited the Count and Countess de Castellane, either in the palace on the edge of the Bois de Boulogne or at
the château of Marais, in Touraine, which Boni had acquired with
Anna's money in 1897—in spite of the creditors. Boni and Anna
had three children now. The eight names of the firstborn had been
shortened to Boni. Then came Georges Gustave Marie Antoine
Boniface, and then little Jason Honoré Louis Sever. They were,
respectively, Boni, George, and Jay, but around the house they
were called Pittypat, Tippytoe, and Tittymouse—at least while
they were small.

Anna was still suffering over Boni's infidelities with some
compassion—she knew, but she preferred not to think of them. Sex
to her was strictly a requirement of marriage, and if Boni kept his
mistresses out of sight and did not upset her or the children with
his peccadilloes, Anna could put up with him for the decent place
in French society he had brought her. After seven years of marriage, Anna was settling down to enjoy society.

Anna did, in fact, become what even her foppish and super-
stylish husband termed "superelegant." The couturiers who made
her gowns were forbidden to copy them for anyone at any price.
She suffered Boni's hunting friends, a peculiarly hard-drinking
crowd, and his dressing up of the servants in eighteenth-century
costume with powdered wigs. Anna was not the only one who
complained about these arrogations. On one occasion, a particularly amusing guest stuck a pin into the white-silk leg of a footman
just to see if his calf was padded. (It was not.)

In 1902, after several years of George's trusteeship, and with
most of the debts retired (the result of good years for the
Goulds), Anna went to her lawyers and secured a court reversal
of the trusteeship decision. George was not particularly pleased

with this action—he did not trust Boni very far even now—but he was his usual amiable self and did not let Anna's hotheadedness about money disturb their relationship. Anna was very happy with the change, for in those years of trusteeship, no matter how much George earned for the family, Anna was held down to $200,000 a year—and Boni could go through that in a month. So the de Castellanes returned to their former style of entertainment. They sometimes invited 2,000 guests to their soirees, and on those days, the carriages were backed up from the Avenue du Bois de Boulogne to the Arc de Triomphe, and the five hundred footmen laid on for the occasion jostled one another in their hurry to serve the guests as they entered.

Boni went back to his big spending. He began running into Pierpont Morgan in the galleries and looking over the same priceless works of art—but Morgan had the money to buy them and Boni had nothing that did not depend upon his wife's pleasure. He contented himself by secretly hating Morgan and comparing him unfavorably to other American collector-millionaires, such as Daniel Guggenheim and Otto Kahn. He was also contemptuous in the extreme about George, Edwin, Howard, and Frank in matters of art. As he put it:

> One day I showed George Gould a set of four arm-chairs and a settee upholstered in yellow tapestry treated with decorative parrots and garlands of flowers. This wonderful set was one of Berain's finest examples, and I gladly purchased it for 60,000 francs. But this American merely glanced at these lovely products of a decorative age, and remarked, with a smile of peculiar contempt: "Why, the whole caboodle isn't worth twopence."
>
> To-day Seligmann (The Dealer) is asking 1,500,000 francs . . . for these same pieces. They may therefore be said to have increased in value, and as facts are stubborn things, it is incontestable that an investment which in 1898 stood at 60,000 francs must have justified itself by representing what it stands at, twenty-six years later.

"Why ever do you buy these old things?" continued my brother-in-law. But by this time I was almost speechless with rage, and when at last I found strength to speak, I voiced the historic remark of the Prince de Sagan. "For my own pleasure," I said. George Gould gazed at me in positive horror . . . .

Boni was mistaken in saying George had execrable taste. Or, at least in the matter of art, George followed the advice of someone who did have excellent taste—perhaps the Duveens. He was one of their valued customers.

Four years earlier, George had allowed some of the works of art from his Fifth Avenue mansion to be exhibited at the Union League Club. There was Van Dyke's portrait of the Count D'Alligre, then regarded by the art critic of the New York *Times* as "the finest example of the great Dutch master that has ever been brought to America." A second painting of George's was Rousseau's *Le Soir,* one of the "hundred masterpieces" exhibited in Paris a few years before. Others included Corot's *L'Arbre Brise* and *Ville d'Avray,* a Fromentin, a Fortuny, and a Gérome. All were pronounced superb by the critics.

This summer of 1902, as George visited his foreign relatives, his railroad builders were hard at work and the new lines of the Wabash Railroad extended from Toledo to Montpelier, Ohio, and from New Haven to Butler, Indiana, thus completing the Chicago-Toledo-Detroit triangle that proved so valuable and that made the Wabash anathema to half a dozen rail lines.

It was said in railroad circles these days that George was suddenly perking up and behaving like his father. But it was also said that no one who spent as much time abroad as George could conceivably run a railroad empire. The Puritan tradition in America dictated that to be successful, a man had to keep his nose to the grindstone twelve months of the year, begrudging himself even the slightest vacation. This was the American way. The fact that Europeanized Americans, such as the six Guggenheim brothers and the Goulds, did not do so caused hard-working Wall Streeters to predict bad ends for the lot. Secretly, of course, these slaves to office routine yearned to know how the Goulds and Guggenheims managed to increase their fortunes while seeming scarcely to work at all.

In 1901, George was still hoping that he could work out an arrangement with Edward Harriman and Kuhn, Loeb to split up the valuable western trade at the Ogden gateway. George had two reasons for wanting to come to terms with the Harriman interests on Southern Pacific traffic: first, the direct western trade that could go either by Union Pacific or Missouri Pacific system from Ogden; second, the valuable traffic that could be picked up by the Missouri Pacific system at El Paso, where the end of the line met the Southern Pacific's south spur. So George treated Harriman genially, inviting him onto the board of directors of the Denver and Rio Grande Western, and playing the game as though Harriman had not attempted to "put one over on him." And there are some indications that the advantage seeking was not Harriman's desire so much as that of Kuhn, Loeb.

George realized that his confidence had been abused in the Huntington purchase, and he took note. Yet he was anything but defenseless, for from the Utah gateway, he could build a route of his own west. It would be expensive, but all railroad building was expensive—the Central Pacific had been expensive. And if anyone in the United States had the money with which to build such a line it was a Gould. So George took Harriman into the Denver and Rio Grande and waited.

Now came three years of watching and careful maneuvering on both sides. George hinted that he might build west from Salt Lake City, and each time he seemed prepared to act, he found the Southern Pacific officials more interested in shipping across the Missouri Pacific. So the contest seesawed. George was grateful for the respite because he was fighting a stiffer battle in the east.

The sellout of Andrew Carnegie in the organization of United States Steel was an unpleasant blow to George Gould because the sale deprived him of a powerful ally in his fight to build to Pittsburgh and the sea, and also because he could expect no favors from U. S. Steel with Pierpont Morgan in charge. In addition, George had learned something from Kuhn, Loeb and Harriman: never to trust another man in business. So one day at a dinner party, A. J. Cassatt of the Pennsylvania asked George point-blank if he was the person who was stirring up a sale of the little Western Maryland line that extended from Baltimore to Cumberland, a spot 120 miles east of Pittsburgh. George looked Cassatt in the eye and said he had not the slightest interest in buying the Western Maryland. Six months later, George had a controlling interest in the line.

Cassatt fumed and fulminated and planned vengeance on George Gould as Commodore Vanderbilt had planned revenge on George's father. In Wall Street, there were mumbles of approval and disapproval as the little men gathered on the sidelines to cheer the giants in their battles and to gossip endlessly about these giants, then to rush to the exchanges to hedge their bets.

Cassatt's vengeance was a while in coming, but it came surely. For years the Western Union Telegraph Company had served the Pennsylvania Railroad and had built its poles along the Pennsylvania right-of-way, poles which also led to the various towns in the area and gave service to the general public. When the contract between the Pennsylvania and Western Union was about to expire in 1902, Cassatt warned Gould that under no conditions would the Pennsylvania renew the agreement. The Pennsylvania would give the business to the lesser Postal Telegraph Company instead.

Gould went to court to protect Western Union's property right in its telegraph poles and miles of wire. In the manner of the old robber barons, Cassatt did not wait for the courts, but sent an army of men all along the Pennsylvania lines. In less than two days, they hacked down the Western Union telegraph poles and sent them crashing, with lines attached, to the ground. Even Pierpont Morgan could not stomach such crudity. The Pennsylvania had wrecked 60,000 poles carrying 1,500 miles of line.

"I don't like George Gould," said Morgan, "but I do not like a man who destroys $5,000,000 worth of vested property."

Thus Cassatt had only a pyrrhic victory, and both he and the Pennsylvania suffered for it by incurring Morgan's enmity.

George Gould went ahead with his plans. He began building into Pittsburgh.

25

Frank Defies the Family

———•••——

And what of the youngest child, the boy who was only fifteen when his father died, who had gone to live with his elder sister who was truly of a different generation?

———•••——

FRANK GOULD was the most handsome, the most debonair, and the most disaffected of all the Gould children. He came by his looks from his mother. He came by his éclat from the training he received in Browning and other schools, New York University, and in Helen's house. How many other young men in the United States toward the end of the nineteenth century were making tours of a 15,000-mile railroad empire with the knowledge that it would one day belong to them? Not one. He came by his disaffection through quarrels with his elder sister and George over many, many things.

In December, 1901, when Frank was twenty-four years old, he

decided to get married. He had fallen in love with a young lady of seventeen, a Miss Helen Kelly. Her grandfather, an old Wall Streeter, had known Jay Gould back in the days when both were young and not very wealthy men. Her grandfather had prospered, not as much as Jay Gould, but he had left a comfortable fortune of $1,500,000, and when Helen was to be married, she had an income of her own of $50,000 a year, which meant she could be as independent as she wished.

After a promising beginning, Frank had deserted the family railroad enterprises and become a New York clubman with his headquarters at the Union League Club. He kept a kennel and showed dogs. He had ordered a $150,000 yacht from the Charles Seabury yard in Morris Heights, New Jersey, and he was planning to get married and take his bride on a honeymoon cruise to the Mediterranean.

But in November, 1901, Mrs. Kelly was suddenly ordered by her doctors to go to the south of Europe for her health, and Frank and Helen decided they would be married before her mother left for Europe. A hurry-up call went out for the various relatives to attend the ceremony.

Frank called for his cousin William Northrop to be his best man. Northrup had accompanied Frank on one of those very early tours of the Missouri Pacific system in the car *Atalanta,* and the boys had become good friends. Bill Northrop, one might say, was closer to Frank than any member of his own family with the possible exception of Helen, and Helen's attitudes toward life created a number of special problems for a young clubman in 1900. Bill Northrop rushed down to New York, sure proof of *his* family loyalty—he had been in no less exciting a place when the call came than the Klondike.

It was a very simple wedding, held at the Murray Hill house of the bride's mother at 17 East Thirty-second Street. Helen Miller Gould would have been pleased; the bride was the daughter of a former commodore of the New York Yacht Club, and her society credentials were impeccable.

Helen Gould attended, as did Edwin and his wife. George and Edith did not, and Howard was buzzing off somewhere else too. The happy couple was married by Dr. Edward H. Greer of St Bartholomew's Episcopal Church in the living room of the house which had been decorated by Helen's orchids from the greenhouses at Lyndhurst.

When it was over, the small wedding party went down to Jack's Restaurant on Forty-fourth Street, a favorite hangout of Frank's, and there the bridegroom conferred with Jack himself.

They sat down at a table in the back but not in a private room, and the waiters began bringing the nuptial feast. First came blue point oysters and Johannisberger Riesling. Then they had stewed terrapin, and burgundy. They ate artichokes Hollandaise and woodcock and drank champagne. They had celery salad and Camembert and drank more champagne. The bill came to $29.80 for the whole party, and Frank gave George the waiter an immense $5 tip to celebrate the occasion before the bridal pair headed for the Essex Hotel on East Fifty-sixth Street and Madison Avenue where they stayed until evening when they took a train to Jersey City.

Edwin gave them the use of his yacht *Nada* for a wedding trip, and they went to Bermuda. Back a few days later, they went on one of those tours of the railroad, as far as Salt Lake City, to look over the new Denver and Rio Grande. Frank might not be exactly happy with George and his management of the railroads, but he was interested enough to go out and see for himself what George was taking on.

26

The Count Is Out

A decade after the death of the progenitor of the fortune, how far apart had grown the children! The eldest son was engaged in a titanic struggle. The second son eschewed the railroad business and sought his fortune far afield. The third son was a playboy with a shrewish wife. The fourth son, hardly out of college, was also a playboy with no interest at all in the history of the fortune or the preservation of an ideal. Of the two daughters, one was proceeding on her road to heaven; the second, having married a foreign noble, revelled in the wicked city of Paris and grew to like it more each year.

ALWAYS the good father, George Gould encouraged his boys to excel in sports. As a result, fifteen-year-old Jay was forever coming home from the polo field banged up, and after being hit with a polo ball in the spring of 1903, he walked around with a splintered tibia for nine months before he could be persuaded to have it looked at and operated on. Young Jay was sent to bed for two weeks and was resting in his room at Georgian Court on the night of January 2, 1904, when Nurse Margaret Burrows suddenly stepped too close to an alcohol lamp, and caught her hair and dress afire. His leg in a plaster cast, young Jay burst out of bed as the nurse cast her head into the sheets to stamp out the flame. Jay hobbled to the door to summon help.

The newspapers acclaimed young Jay for his heroism—he and George's other children were favorites with the press because they were growing up to be strong, handsome people of the kind that newspapers adore, and their father's generosities with them—not to say extravagances—made good copy. For example, at this same Christmas season, little George, six years old, received a train—as did thousands of young Americans around the land. There was a difference, however: Georgie's train ran by alcohol, its cars were 3 feet long, and the engine was big enough for him to ride in and operate as engineer in the cab. Good training, one might say, for a boy who was destined one day to be an heir to the greatest railroad empire in the land. Georgie's train was erected on the grounds at Georgian Court, and soon he was running it around with great spirit. Spirit was indeed one of the major attributes of the boys that Christmas.

Kingdon, in 1904, was just seventeen, a slender youth who very much resembled his father in his late teens. He was good natured, courageous, and intelligent, and he was enrolled as a student at the School of Mines at Columbia University

At Columbia in 1904, it was the practice of the sophomore class to "haze" various freshmen, particularly those who somehow called attention to themselves as class leaders, especially good athletes, or even as scholars. Kingdon had refused to wear his freshman "beanie."

The sophomores planned a banquet just before Christmas, and their entertainment committee also planned that Kingdon Gould should provide the principal entertainment by being captured, spanked with hard wooden paddles, and then put on the stage to sing and dance. The program, thought the sophomores, would provide much amusement for the class, and would bring young Gould down to the level of the other Columbia students. Kingdon, however, learned of this attempt to haze him and decided to foil the sophomores.

The sophomore dinner was planned for the evening of Wednesday, December 21, just before the beginning of Christmas vacation. That day, Kingdon went to classes as usual, then to Library Hall, which he left at 12:30. As he and a friend came out of the hall, they noticed half a dozen sophomores following them, and they quickened their pace, heading toward Broadway.

The sophomores followed, gaining on them.

The two freshmen reached the subway station at One-hundred sixteenth Street, where one sophomore darted up and asked Kingdon to stop because the sophomores wanted to talk to him.

"No," said Kingdon, and started off again quickly.

He began to run and the sophomores ran after him. Heading down Broadway, he reached One-hundred fourteenth Street.

The sophomores gained again.

Out of his waistband, Kingdon drew a revolver. He pointed it at the sophomores and told them to stop or he would shoot.

The sophs laughed and kept coming.

Kingdon ran on.

When he saw that they would soon be upon him, he stopped short and pulled out his revolver.

The sophomores came on, grinning.

Bam!

The shot went over the heads of the pursuers, but Kingdon was making ready to fire another.

Over their heads or at one of their heads, the sophomores wondered.

They stopped, turned, and began walking swiftly in the other direction.

Kingdon and his friend kept moving down Broadway until

they could duck into the Delta Kappa Epsilon house at One-hundred thirteenth Street and disappear.

In a few minutes, the word was all over campus that Kingdon Gould had taken a pot shot at the sophomores who were trying to haze him. In an hour, the street around the Deke house was filled with students.

Meanwhile, the sophomores held a rump council further up the campus and decided that they must capture Gould, even at the risk of life and limb, or their authority to continue hazing would be undermined.

The sophomores began to assemble in the street outside the Deke house. Several dozen stationed themselves at One-hundred thirteenth and Broadway, and another crowd moved to Amsterdam Avenue to cut off Gould's retreat from the rear. Still others moved into the exit to the fraternity house, and another detachment went to the front, standing just outside the door.

Kingdon remained inside the Deke house all afternoon, and the sophomores remained outside.

Finally at five minutes to six, a carriage drove into Broadway and then down to the front of the Deke house. It was the Gould carriage. Inside was George with three Pinkerton agency detectives. Two of the Pinkertons went up to the fraternity house and escorted Kingdon down to the carriage, while the other Pinkerton stood at the door of the carriage and warned the crowding students away.

"We don't want to tackle them," cried the sophomores.

The driver whipped up the horses, and the Goulds drove away for Christmas vacation.

While Kingdon was commiserating with young Jay over his broken leg, sympathizing with the burned nurse, and taking rides on brother Georgie's model train that vacation, four of the sophomores were soaking in hot water. President Nicholas Murray Butler of Columbia learned of the incident, as did everyone else in New York, and he investigated, discovered the names of the perpetrators of the hazing idea, and ordered Algeltinger, Cauchois, Doty, and Finch suspended from the University for violation of the rules.

The punishment seemed harsh to Kingdon, particularly since the sophomores had not mistreated him but only tried to, and on his return to the University after Christmas, he interceded with Dean Hutton, the disciplinarian, and secured their reinstatement.

When Kingdon came back on January 10, he was surrounded by a bevy of his own classmates shaking his hand and congratulating him for helping end a most unpleasant practice. The sophomores left him alone, too—for a little while.

Then, one day in March, Kingdon was walking from the campus to the Deke house when an acquaintance came up and began discussing some campus problem with him. Kingdon did not pay any attention to the fact that the other was a sophomore, and he did not notice when two more sophomores came up—until they declared that he was "pinched."

Kingdon did not have his gun with him that day, and so he submitted.

The sophomores gave Kingdon an option: he could come with them then or he could agree to meet them that evening in the park without saying a word. He agreed to meet them later and the upperclassmen took his word. He did meet them, and he was hazed by this special group called the Black Avengers—self-appointed guardians from the sophomore class out to make sure that no freshman got away with destroying the time-honored practice of hazing.

Kingdon was lectured on the proper conduct for freshmen. He was forced to relate the geneology of the Goulds. He was forced to read the police regulations about the carrying of firearms. He was blindfolded, set astride a barrel with a broom, and told to give a polo exhibition. Then the barrel was kicked out from under him. He was given two toothpicks, placed on a shingle, and told to "row." He was paddled and mistreated for two solid hours, then released on the promise that he would not reveal the identity of his captors. And he never did, although the administration asked him to do so.

Kingdon's days at Columbia were strange ones in a way, as must always be the lot of rich young men. Who else among the freshman class could afford to present the class crew with a new $600 shell? Who else went to watch the races at the boathouse given to the university by his own uncle? Kingdon did well enough to lead any normal kind of life at all.

More and more, the six children of George and Edith came into the news. The two older girls, Marjorie and Vivien, were fifteen and eleven this year, and it was reported when they rode for the first time with the county hunt. The George Gould children were growing up, and being introduced to the world.

Growing up—that much could not be said for Kathrine Gould —who was still quarreling with servants, dressmakers, and even the architect Abner Haydel who built Castle Gould to her specifications and after going through Ireland's Kilkenny Castle with her. The castle cost a million dollars in the building, and the architect had sued for his fees because Kathrine claimed, *ex post facto,* that he had done it all wrong and that she would not pay. Architect Haydel secured $25,000, which represented 2½ per cent of the construction cost. He won partly on the basis that Kathrine had sworn at him and had him thrown out of her suite at the Waldorf the last time he called. And then there was a new suit by new dressmakers for another total of $3,700 for more gowns that did not fit. . . .

Kathrine was a problem to all who knew her.

There were other problems, other difficult characters in the family as well. By 1905, the storm brewing in the household of the de Castellanes was ready to break. Two years earlier it had been apparent to any who knew the couple that their days together were numbered. They quarreled constantly, and on one occasion Anna bit Boni on the hand. In 1902, Anna came home to America for a visit, bringing Pittypat and Tippytoe with her, while Boni stayed in Paris to stir up as much trouble as possible for the Republicans in

Parliament. Early in 1903, Boni came over on a French ship from Cherbourg after announcing his arrival date and time—no one met him at the pier. He called a cab that day and drove to the hotel where the family had rooms to find Anna and the children in the dining room with the nurse.

"Oh, how I regret not being able to live in my own country now that I have married a foreigner," she greeted him—or so *he* said.

The de Castellanes lunched at Delmonico's, and Boni objected to the ladies who stared at them from behind their picture hats. After they had consulted with George, who was warm to his sister and cold to her husband, the de Castellanes went back to France, and Boni that summer took Anna on a yacht cruise to the Middle East. She was not impressed. They went to Constantinople at which she sniffed. They sailed to Piraeus by way of the straits of Euripus, and went aground on a sand bank between the Isle of Negropont and the mainland. With the insouciance of the rich who are not really yachtsmen, they abandoned *Walhalla* to her professional crew and went on to Athens by train.

By the end of 1905, Boni knew that the days when he would be husband to one of America's richest women were drawing to a close. Anna was thoroughly disgusted by his parading of his many affairs, and when Boni took up with a certain lady and it became common gossip, she put private detectives on his trail and got ready to end the marriage.

On Twelfth Night, in January, 1906, Boni and Anna dined with the Comtesse Robert Fitzjames in her flat in the Rue Constantin. During the dinner, someone at the table asked Boni what he was doing these days.

"Oh, I've been to the *chambre*," said Boni, referring to the Chamber of Deputies.

Then, to Boni's horror, he heard Anna saying coldly in her pristine French:

"Pas le chambre vous supposez!"

Everyone at the table was astonished, Boni said, for Anna never, never was other than circumspect in her conversation.

But Boni had gone too far, he had embarrassed Anna once too often by flaunting his mistress on the avenues. The events of that night served as a warning.

On January 26, Boni arose late, as was his custom, and he and Anna walked for a few minutes together in the Bois de Boulogne as they sometimes did when they were speaking. Then they parted, Boni to go (ostensibly) to the Palais Bourbon on state business, and Anna to go home and care for the children. Anna, for a change, was kind and friendly, giving Boni hope that somehow he might rescue his marriage without working at it.

When Boni returned to the pink replica of the Petit Trianon that evening, the place was dark. He entered the door, and felt for the light switch. The lights had been turned off. He stumbled around the entrance hall and could find nothing that seemed familiar—all the furnishings were gone. He moved through the darkened house attracted by a light at the end of a passageway and there, finally, he met a priest, the Abbé Cagnac, who had been left in the house, sitting in his study illuminated by a single candle. Nothing else remained in the room.

Nor did anything remain in the house, the Abbé informed Boni. Anna had made an astonishing *coup de main*—she had brought in movers and servants for the day, and in four hours, she had stripped the palace, room by room, of everything. The furniture was gone, the rugs were taken up and away, the drapes, even the wall fixtures for the electrical system, chandeliers, beds, and bric-a-brac. The electricity and the telephone had been disconnected. The house was absolutely empty.

How did Boni react? Here is Boni's own story:

> The good priest looked at me with immense pity, but he signed the death warrant of Hope in four fatal words: "She will never return."
>
> Distracted, hardly conscious of what I did, I rushed to the

Hotel Bristol, there to be received like a criminal by the manager and several plain-clothes detectives, who prevented me from communicating with any member of my family. There was nothing for it but to return to the Avenue du Bois, there to be welcomed by the sight of an official application on behalf of Madame de Castellane for a judicial separation.

My first action (when once I had grasped the full meaning of this ominous document) was to quit the palace which had been bought and paid for with Gould money, and leave Anna in undisturbed possession. But I was wrongly advised, as by so doing I contributed to my own undoing, and my consideration for my wife's feelings was construed by her advisers as desertion!

Acting, however, on this purely unselfish impulse, I passed a restless night at the Hotel Laperouse . . . but "restless" is a faint word to describe it. I was pursued by all the Furies, and I wondered to which particular Fury I was destined to fall a victim. I determined, however, not to acquaint my father and mother with the catastrophe, hoping against hope that Anna would return home on the morrow.

Needless to say, she never returned; but when I saw her sometimes afterwards in the presence of President Ditte [of the court] I asked her why she had elected to be so charming to me on the day she left home.

She was silent. She surveyed me coldly. "Because it was for the last time," she replied.

Anna had been in touch with George, and one of his lawyers had come to Paris to see her. She had planned carefully. It was necessary to plan, because, again, Boni was leading them into debt, and new bills of 3,500,000 francs ($700,000) had been presented to Anna, some of them for female finery and goods she had never heard of, much less seen.

Even in 1905, but openly in 1906, the wheels of French justice were beginning to grind. Anna was divorcing Boni.

27

George's Dream Dries Up

While the young were marrying and their elders were divorcing, in the offices of the railroad and telegraph empire on New York's lower Broadway, grand and dangerous plans were afoot. The fortune had been left in such a way that the eldest son had complete power in such matters as this question of business expansion, and he went ahead.

BETWEEN 1901 and the summer of 1905, George's business days were occupied with the move of the Wabash east from Toledo and the move of the Western Maryland into Pittsburgh from the other end. It took four years to build the 60 miles of railroad from the terminus of the Wheeling and Lake Erie at Jewett, Ohio, to Pittsburgh. In the beginning, George had the financial backing of the Equitable Life Assurance people and their allies. But halfway along, their money ran out, and he had to find new financing, which took much time and trouble. Crossing the mountains had been expensive. The Pennsylvania had sewed up the last routes into Pittsburgh, and the Pennsylvania and its allies tried to thwart George Gould every step of the way, ringing the city with railroad bastions and rights-of-way so that he should not enter. But George managed to secure the cooperation of the Pittsburgh authorities (some say it cost him more than a million dollars), and they granted him the right to enter the city and put up a terminal. But with the difficulties, the 60 miles of track became one of the most expensive undertakings in railroad history. There were twenty tunnels in all, and nearly a bridge per mile. The engineers had cut through one mountain a full mile long, and there were hundreds of viaducts, cuts, fills, trestles, arches, and culverts, each of them costly.

There were also many strange accidents attendant on the eastward construction of the Wabash, accidents that might not all have been totally divorced from the political and economic fight being waged by the Pennsylvania to stop George Gould. But aside from industrial accidents, the worst of which cost twenty lives when a bridge across the Monongahela collapsed in construction, there were floods, landslides, and cave-ins, and even a smallpox epidemic that could not be blamed on the Pennsylvania. And the engineers made mistakes in laying out the road and considering its possibilities. George wanted to build a line to carry freight, like the Erie, but he had to bring his line into Pittsburgh on an elevated track, obviously undesirable for freight handling. He wanted to carry freight, but his men built a million-dollar passenger terminal in a little-used section of the city. This foul-up has been blamed on George's airy handling of his business affairs—travelling abroad so frequently, refusing to allow key employees to make basic decisions, and overruling employees when they did make them. When the president of the Wabash, at this critical time, suggested that George let him have some executive authority, George refused, saying he intended to run his property as he very well pleased. The mistakes continued, such as the mistake of not double-tracking the line into Pittsburgh, which cut drastically into the railroad's ability to handle the ten million tons of business available to it the first year.

But with the line built into Pittsburgh, George was a serious threat to the Pennsylvania, and everyone in railroading knew it.

Ernest Howard, in his study of George's railroad operations, *Fifty Years After Erie,* has pointed to a basic difference between George and his father:

> He resembled his father in no important respect. He was free and open and hearty in manner where the father had been reserved, secretive and restrained. Exactly in contradiction to the father George was mercurial in temperament, hasty and uncertain in his judgments, careless and near-sighted in his calculations, extravagant and self-indulgent in business as well as personal habits, and quickly subject to the action of great mental enthusiasms and the reaction to great depressions. The elder Gould was of few words and those cautiously spoken; of plans and market plots daringly conceived and most skillfully prosecuted but never divulged until they divulged themselves in concrete form; of a nature suspicious and so distrustful of others that it may be said that he was never betrayed because no one was ever given the chance to betray him. Pretty much everybody, on the contrary, knew what the younger Gould was up to all the time.

With the move into Pittsburgh, the newspapers began treating George with much more respect. They called him "Titan," and they began chronicling his movements the way they had done those of his father. But unlike his father, George proceeded in the open to display what he intended to do.

In 1902 and 1903, George asked Edward Harriman again to open up the Southern Pacific to the Missouri Pacific for eastern traffic, and again Harriman refused. So George decided to build the Western Pacific.

Once a railroad called the Western Pacific had run south of San Francisco, but this line had been swallowed up by the creation of the Southern Pacific system. The Western Pacific which George envisioned would be an entirely different line. Its backers had gone to the California legislature and secured a charter for a rail line to be built from San Francisco to Salt Lake City by way of the Feather River Canyon and the low-grade route across the Sierra Nevada. The original company had bought almost all the 1,000 miles of right-of-way, had even built some patches of track, and had spent $3,000,000 on the project when George stepped in. The Denver and Rio Grande then purchased control of the Western Pacific. The financing was carried out by a very tricky arrangement which raised $50,000,000 in first mortgage bonds, with George pledging that the Missouri Pacific and the Denver and Rio Grande would ship all their freight and passengers across the Western Pacific route.

While Edward Harriman had cut George off from the rich fruits of the Southern Pacific, when he learned that George was going to build a new line and had *pledged* to cut Harriman off from its traffic, he blew up.

"If you build that line, I'll kill you," he told George one day.

George smiled.

The battle began in the spring of 1905. George resigned from the board of the Union Pacific, and Harriman and his bankers went off the board of the Denver and Rio Grande. If George could pull it off, finish the road, and connect the Wabash to the Maryland, he would have accomplished the grandest coup in the history of American railroading.

When the others in the family learned what George was doing, they reacted characteristically. Edwin was too far out of railroading to care, Helen supported George as the family authority, Howard acceded, Anna did not give a whit as long as she continued to get her allowance each year, and Frank simply was not interested. Since his marriage he had been investing his interest and dividends in electric traction and power companies. He could not disagree more than he did with George's handling of the New York City transit system—letting the subways get away from him

by default because he would not build them when the people
asked, delaying so long in improvements of the elevated railroads
that the people complained. Frank believed in modern traction
methods, and soon he had bought the model Richmond system,
and several other Virginia traction companies, combining them
under the name of the Virginia Railway and Power Company.
Frank had some idea of going into railroading and traction on a
large scale on his own hook, and this company was capitalized at
$42,000,000, although, of course, his investment was nothing like
that.

In this period, Frank's life, perhaps, was more unhappy than
that of any of the Goulds. He and wife Helen simply did not hit it
off from the very beginning. Two children were born to them, but
Helen was not a motherly type, and in 1904, the Frank Goulds
were separated and the little girls came to live with their father for
nine months of the year. Since Frank had no home as such, he
asked his sister Helen to help him out by taking guardianship of
the girls, and she was predictably eager to do so.

Helen's other good works also continued at an unbelievable
pace. She fluttered from one place to another, checkbook open, Bible
in her pocketbook, distributing money and attending meetings.
She had gone to the McKinley inauguration in 1900 and attended
the Inaugural Ball, which seemed a little out of character. More in
character, she went to Ecumenical Missionary Conferences and Bible
study classes, and promoted the translation of religious tracts into
Armenian, Bohemian, Finnish, and some twenty other languages
which to her knowledge were not blessed with a proper Christian
literature. She gave prizes to all the children in the Delaware
County public schools and Sunday schools who could recite selected verses and chapters of the Bible. She helped found the Bib-
lical Seminary of New York, renting four houses for it and then a
nine-story building on Lexington Avenue. She supported the
Nanking Theological Seminary and the foreign mission school at
Foochow. She supported the National Bible Society. She gave
$10,000 to the Istanbul College for Women. She was a Vice Presi-

dent of the American Tract Society, the American Bible Society, and the Woman's National Sabbath Alliance. She was chairman of the Bible Readers committee of the Women's Auxiliary of the New York Bible Society, and so forth. . . . She was a member of the World Narcotics Society before the eradication of narcotics became a popular cause in America. She gave money to Vassar, Mount Holyoke, and Wellesley colleges for religious education, but quarreled with the way the money was spent—the schools were becoming "too liberal" for her—and took back or changed the form of the assistance. A $40,000 endowment at Mt. Holyoke was transferred from the Bible department to Romance Languages, and a $50,000 endowment at Wellesley went from Bible to mathematics. At Vassar, which she regarded as becoming downright dangerous in its approach to female education, her money was returned after many years of her attempt to interfere in the educational process. Underlying this distrust of liberalism was Helen's violent fear that she would be assassinated by an anarchist or some other leftist. She received some threats—but no more than any other millionaire. Her fears actually went back to her childhood days, when Jay had been forced to keep private detectives around the house because of the constant danger from prowlers. The Sages, after all, were Helen's best friends—and Russell Sage had been very nearly blown up by the bomb that exploded in his presence.

In spite of this constant fear of the public, which Helen had cast as a vast monster in her mind, she spent her days and nights in good works for this very same public. In 1905, the year that George was spending millions on railroad building, east and west, Helen sat down and listed her "promises" to charity. There were sixty of them, ranging from gifts of $50,000 each to the Salvation Army, Red Cross, and American Hospital in Paris, to the salary paid for two men to do religious work in the Navy, support of eleven foreign missions, and support or contributions to not fewer than twenty-six YMCAs, mostly in Kansas, Arkansas, and Texas.

These philanthropies crossed George's investments and shored them up in one way at least. During the terrible San Francisco earthquake of 1906, which gravely disrupted George's plans,

Helen's $100,000 for the Red Cross and Salvation Army was put to good use helping his own railroad men among others.

Edward Harriman and his associates, meanwhile, carried on a war against the Gould enterprises that was matched only by the difficulties with Cassatt's Pennsylvania Railroad in the east. In 1906, some attempt was made to regulate interstate commerce, and within the states, to regulate railroads, but these actions did not succeed in preventing the piratical forays that railroad men had always worked against one another. The Southern Pacific–Union Pacific combine charged exorbitant rates for rail shipment of ties throughout the West in order to keep the Gould lines from getting ties from Portland and Seattle. The Harriman roads hired gunmen who peppered the Western Pacific gangs from snipers' nests. They fomented strikes and fights and caused accidents. They hired away the track workers of the Western Pacific line, promising them huge increases in pay, then shipped the poor workers down to the wilds of Arizona and dumped them.

It was a struggle every inch of the way, building through the scenic but difficult Feather River Canyon and across the Sierra. Then came the Panic of 1907.

The Panic began on October 15, when F. Augustus Heinz' Mercantile Trust Company suffered a run and appealed to the New York Clearing House Association for funds to pay depositors —its own funds were widely invested in long-term and sometimes not very sensible schemes. (Heinz had even borrowed $1.5 million from Edwin Gould.) Then one bank after another began to fail, and before the Panic was over, billions of dollars had been lost in bank deposits wiped out by failure and in the depression of stock prices.

Railroad stocks were particularly hard hit, and the battering they took revealed where the weakness of the Gould fortune lay. Had the fortune still been in old Jay Gould's hands, and had he still been playing the railroad baron, the situation might have been different. While Jay was alive the fortune remained monolithic—it existed for the purpose of shoring itself up, of integration and protection. But this was only true as long as the fortune provided the means through which the Goulds controlled the railroad empire. Thought of in another way, the fortune was as exposed as the nerve of a broken tooth, simply because nearly everything was in railroad or other transportation and communications securities. The paper values of the fortune dropped perhaps 50 per cent in the Panic of 1907, but worse than that, the panic and the competitive forays made against the Gould lines, east and west, brought the earnings of the Gould railroads down. No longer could Anna expect to receive $700,000 a year from her share of the fortune, nor could any of the others. In the cases of Edwin, Howard, and Frank, the problem was distressing but not acute because they had taken their accruals and reinvested them in other ways. In other words, these three brothers were earning separate fortunes from the offshoots of the key root.

As for Helen, she was occupied with her good works, she never took all the money coming in each year anyhow, and a cut in her income simply meant a cut in her service to the Lord and the Salvation Army. But with Anna, such cuts could be disastrous because she spent and did nothing else. Frank, the youngest child and not a member of the executive group that held power over the fortune, was openly contemptuous of the way the money was being managed.

The disastrous effects of the Panic of 1907 were far-reaching. It had been anticipated that the Western Pacific would be finished and operable by 1908, but in that year it was necessary to issue another $25,000,000 in bonds to cover the cost of construction. This move tied up the credit of the Denver and Rio Grande, just at a time when the Wabash came into trouble along with the Wheeling and Lake Erie, the line connecting the Wabash with Pittsburgh.

Within a few months, beginning just after the Panic, the Gould railroad empire changed completely. The Goulds were forced out of the Wabash, out of the Wheeling and Lake Erie, and the Western Maryland. The Gould dream of a transcontinental rail line was at an end.

28

How Much Can One Man Lose?

Can a family endure financial disaster, let alone surmount it? What happens to the very wealthy when they begin to see their wealth cut down before their eyes?

IN the next three years, 1908–1911, considerable ferment stirred the Gould family.

Anna divorced Boni de Castellane, and he received a settlement of about a quarter of a million dollars and a yearly income of $30,000 from her share of the estate. Their debts were settled for $.30 on the dollar. Two years later, having secured a dispensation from Rome, or having thought she did, Anna married the count's cousin, Hélie de Talleyrand-Périgord, Prince de Sagan—commonly known as the Duke of Talleyrand. This was a case of wealth meeting wealth, for the duke's holdings were extensive and there was no question of Anna being married for her money. It was a happy marriage, and she had two children by him, Charles Maurice Jason Howard, duc de Sagan, and Hélène Violette de Talleyrand. These children, along with the three de Castellane children, were thoroughly French and involved in the Gould story only as Anna's heirs.

Frank divorced Helen Kelly in 1909, then turned around and married a showgirl named Edith Kelly in 1910. The two little girls came to live with him. Soon Frank tired of making money and decided to devote his life to more pleasant pursuits, so he put his American properties into the hands of managers and moved permanently to France. Frank bought a big old château and farm called Le Robillard in Normandy, once the property of the Montesquiou family, paying $200,000 for the house, grounds, and restoration. His object was to bring the old place back to the splendor of a hundred and fifty years earlier, with the addition of plumbing, of course, and then to settle down to breeding race horses. Upon the death of the horse fancier and Wall Street man James R. Keene in America, Frank bought the pick of his mares, eighteen in all, most of them in foal. Ultimately, the colors of his Maisons-Lafitte stables became famous indeed.

He owned the grand stallion Combourg, son of Bay Ronald out of Chiffonette, who won $67,000 in four years, very nearly a record for that time. Combourg won the Prix de Nice, the Noailles, and the Greffuhle Stakes, placed second in the Grand Prix de Paris, and won the Royal Oak and the Prix du Cadran.

Frank also owned Amphiction, a chestnut gelding, the horse which proved to be his finest. In his first race under Frank's colors, Amphiction won the Prix de Nice. It was also the first time Frank had raced a horse in France, and it was therefore doubly important. Amphiction went on to win sixteen more races in short order, and it was held in France that there was no more courageous horse in the land, not one who could stand up to his finishing pace at the distances he ran.

Then came the 3,800-meter steeplechase at Deauville. Amphiction started strong, but when he came to the hazard known as the

Irish Bank, he fell, breaking his leg at the stifle. So game was he that he rose and took the next jump before he could be stopped. When the jockey caught him he saw the bare end of the thigh bone sticking out through the flesh. Frank offered $20,000 or more to any veterinarian who could save the horse—not make him run again but simply save him—but no one would take on the task, so the horse was destroyed. Then, sorrowfully, Amphiction was taken back to Le Robillard where he was buried with honors.

Angry with his family, annoyed at the bad publicity the Goulds had received over the years, Frank decided never again to return to the United States for more than a visit. He was on the way to becoming a permanent resident of France, a proud expatriate.

In the spring of 1909, Howard had all he could take of Kathrine's shrewishness, and they separated legally, she keeping the house on Fifth Avenue and securing an allowance of $36,000 a year from him. She would not give him a divorce, and he did not press the issue, pleased enough simply to be away from her nagging. Howard then moved to England where he would spend most of the rest of his life, coming home occasionally, keeping up his club memberships in New York and his seat on the New York Stock Exchange. He gladly sold Castle Gould to Daniel Guggenheim, even though he took a considerable loss—every stone of the castle had been fought over by Kathrine and the architect.

George and Edwin, therefore, were the only brothers remaining to manage the affairs of the family, and Edwin had long since declared himself out of the railroad picture.

George's concern, after 1908, was to save the western railroads. He might have sold out his stock at any time, but he knew that mere money, unless it had leverage to make it multiply, could not maintain wealth for a proliferating family.

Noting George's weakness, the forces of John D. Rockefeller and the Deutsche Bank of Berlin and Kuhn, Loeb and Co. bought large amounts of Gould railroad stocks in 1907 and 1908, thereby amassing large minority interests that were thrown on the market at Panic prices. In the old days, Jay would have bought these stocks up himself, but George did not have the capital, his railroads being too heavily mortgaged because of his building programs.

In the spring of 1911, these three forces pooled their interests—perhaps 25 per cent of the total stock—and vowed that they would eliminate the Goulds from the Missouri Pacific, the Denver and Rio Grande, and the Western Pacific. One reason for this decision was the near-success that George was achieving. The Western Pacific was built—although many said it was impossible and the Harriman interests had done all they could to stop it. (Harriman was dead, but Kuhn, Loeb carried his interests in this fight.) The court case brought by the Federal government under the anti-trust laws to dissolve the Union Pacific–Southern Pacific merger as being in restraint of trade (which it certainly was) brought on the struggle. If the courts held that the merger was in restraint, and it seemed likely that they might, then George Gould's dream would be partly realized at least, and by getting a share of the Southern Pacific traffic, he might be able to bring so much strength to the Missouri Pacific and the Western Pacific that he could jeopardize the holdings of all these others, particularly the Union Pacific values in which Kuhn, Loeb was so deeply involved.

So near and yet so far. George was in trouble at this time with the Missouri Pacific stockholders because the railroad had paid no dividends on its stock for four years. So the Kuhn, Loeb and Rockefeller interests were in a strong position to strike a sharp blow. Nothing personal, simply a matter of business.

George saw the handwriting on the wall and prepared in the winter of 1911 to give up the presidency of the Missouri Pacific. But he was not going to give it to these old enemies. He called in the investment banking firm of James Speyer and Company. A railroad man was chosen president. The offices of the Missouri Pacific were moved to St. Louis and a coalition of bankers took control of the line. Here, then, was the culmination of an era, a change begun by J. Pierpont Morgan in the affairs of the railroads.

Like so many roads before it, the Missouri Pacific fell into the hands of the bankers in 1911, and this meant the end of efforts to go beyond the status quo. George and all the other Goulds remained important stockholders and bondholders, but they were no longer important in the operating affairs of the company. For all practical purposes, the Goulds were out of the railroad business. It would be several more years before the Goulds were finally beaten out of the Denver and Rio Grande and the Western Pacific, but the end was in sight. Even as the juggernaut rolled over them, legal deliverance seemed to be in sight. The Supreme Court of the United States held that the Union Pacific and Southern Pacific must be separated because they had been restraining trade. It was true enough—George, for example, had lost millions of dollars in the bottling up of his internal railroad empire by such restraint. Had the fortune been in a condition where it could have been manipulated at the key moments, George might have held on long enough for this restraint to be taken off by law, and his dream of a transcontinental railroad might have come true in spite of all the forces trying to stop him. But the fortune could not be manipulated easily enough, and the juggernaut rolled on.

29

The Tragedy of Edwin, Jr.

———•◆•———

These were new times. Once the rail-road empire slipped away, the newspapers turned on the eldest son and made light of his abilities, comparing him unfavorably with his father. But all these empires were slipping away, railroads were changing in their very nature and, under regulation, they were ceasing to represent the same free-wheeling investments that they had in the past. It was not only the railroads. The world was changing, and changing very fast.

———•◆•———

TWO years after the Goulds were forced out of management of their railroad empire, they were out of Western Union and the Manhattan Elevated Company as well. George, having been badly shaken in his attempt to create the transcontinental railroad, chose to take the family out of these enterprises. He had seen what un-scrupulous capitalists could do to one another—as if he did not know from his father's operations—when A. J. Cassatt had arbitrarily destroyed $5,000,000 worth of Western Union property. It was conceivable that a dozen other railroads could do the same if they felt like it, and there was very little he could do to stop it. Therefore, when power began to fade, he made the decision that William Henry Vanderbilt, heir to old Commodore Vanderbilt, had made before him: get out of business and put a large chunk of the money into convertible securities. When Western Union was sold off to the American Telephone Company and Manhattan Elevated was sold off to the Rockefellers, it was said that the Goulds had the greatest cash nest egg that existed in the United States. George settled down to invest this money in behalf of the heirs, to put it in safe places where it would draw regular interest and dividends.

In 1912, Helen went on tour again, this time in behalf of the YMCA and the YWCA, organizations to which she had given so much money over the years. Her itinerary was planned by the two organizations for a two-month coast-to-coast inspection tour. She would use ordinary travel facilities, for the days of the *Atalanta* were gone. But when Helen reached St. Louis, Benjamin F. Bush, the president of the Missouri Pacific, gave her a special train to carry her over the Missouri Pacific lines to the West Coast and then back to New York. He did not have to give her the train, the Goulds no longer controlled the railroad but were simply big investors, but the Gould prestige in the Missouri Pacific country was still undiminished.

So Helen went touring in style, visiting Mrs. Phoebe Hearst at her California estate, *Hacienda,* and being received in military fashion at San Francisco's Presidio. In Denver, Helen made a major speech, flanked by Missouri Pacific president Bush and his assistant, Finley J. Shepard.

Later that year, Helen was called to Chicago to attend another giant YMCA convention. She was in touch with Mr. Bush again, and again he put a private car at her disposal, and sent two of his officials to escort her. One was a Mr. Pryor. The other was Finley J. Shepard, whom Helen had met in Denver.

There was a train wreck on the trip west. A freight train had buckled in the middle and sprawled across the tracks in the path of the oncoming passenger train. Shepard and Helen worked to free the trapped and comfort the injured, and during their association in the next few days, they fell in love. Imagine Helen falling in love for the first time at the age of forty-four. But she did, and soon Finley Shepard was making many trips to New York to visit at 579 Fifth Avenue.

They were married on January 22, 1913, in the drawing room of Lyndhurst. No champagne party, no enormous reception, just a quiet wedding with the family and friends, and the house, of course, festooned with flowers from the greenhouses. They did not even go away for a honeymoon, unless one could call an hour's motor ride at 5 o'clock a "trip." They returned to Lyndhurst and dined there. The only other excitement came when a river steamer came upriver that night and shined its searchlight on the porch at Lyndhurst until the happy couple came out and waved.

These early years of the second decade of the century were quiet years for George Gould, in a way. He devoted himself to his children, to his polo, and to his horse and dog breeding. In 1910, daughter Marjorie became engaged to Anthony J. Drexel, Jr., scion of the conservative and ultra-respectable Drexel banking family, partners of the Morgans for many years. When Tony and Marjorie were married, George built the young Drexels a big gray house with a high stone wall around it directly across the road from Georgian Court so that the family could enjoy the quiet Lakewood countryside and all the pleasures of the estate.

One pleasure of Georgian Court in those days was so specialized that only a handful of Americans had ever heard of it—the game of court tennis, the ancient pastime of kings and the progenitor of modern lawn tennis. Lawn tennis is played on a single surface—the lawn or court—but in court tennis, back and side walls of an enclosed court are also struck by the ball to give weird bounces. Everyone at Georgian Court played court tennis, but the one who played it best of all was Jay Gould, namesake of the founder of the fortune and inheritor of half a million in his own right.

Jay was twelve years old when the Casino was finished. That year, George hired Frank Forester, a teacher of court games from the Prince's Club at Knightsbridge, England, to come to New Jersey and teach his two older sons the various racquet games for which the family now had courts. Forester arrived at Georgian Court in the spring of 1900, and that year started the boys out playing squash. The next spring, they began to learn court tennis, playing for an hour every day.

George constantly brought athletic people out to Georgian Court for his games, and one day, he invited for the weekend James Henry Smith, one of the best players of court tennis at the New York Racquet and Tennis Club.

"I think my boy can beat you," George boasted to Smith proudly.

So an informal match was arranged to test the proposition.

Jay won, 2 sets to 0, without a handicap.

James Henry Smith was not annoyed. With the true sportsman's instinct, he was delighted to come across so young a lad with so much skill, and that summer, Smith invited young Jay to his summer house at Tuxedo. There Jay played a match with Pierre Lorillard, Jr., which Lorillard won. But next summer, 1903, Jay went back to Tuxedo and defeated Lorillard easily.

Beginning in 1904, then, Georgian Court became a sort of mecca for court tennis players. Only a handful of court tennis courts (or bays) existed in the United States, of course, and George's open-handed hospitality was attractive, but the real reason for their coming was to see and play with young Jay, whose reputation as a court tennis prodigy had crossed the Atlantic.

To Georgian Court came the Englishman Peter Latham, the world's champion, Ferdinand Garcin, the French champion, and a dozen other fine players—all to play with Jay. Every day, Jay practiced for an hour with Coach Forester, then usually spent another hour at night practicing shots at the net. Every Saturday and Sunday morning, he practiced for an hour and a half and then played matches in the afternoon with whomever happened to be on hand.

In 1903, the master player Ernest Thomson came down to Lakewood and beat Jay in a match, but he did teach him the "railroad service." Frenchman Garcin had settled in the United States, spending half his time teaching at Tuxedo and the other half teaching young Jay—and soon Jay was beating the French champion, too. Once Jay even beat Garcin although the boy was suffering from whooping cough during the match.

By 1905, Jay Gould was known as one of the finest court tennis players in the world. That year, when he was seventeen, he played in the Gold Racquet tournament at Tuxedo and reached the finals, finally suffering defeat by Charles E. Sands, the American amateur champion. Later that year Sands came down to Lakewood and beat Jay in singles. There was also a doubles match. Sands played with Peter Latham, the world's champion, against Jay and George Standing, the professional of the New York Racquet Club. Jay and Standing won.

Latham went back to England singing Jay's praises:

> In England the amateurs do not take up tennis until they get to the universities, and I am amazed to find so young and capable a player here. Young Gould is the finest player for his years I have ever known. He lacks only the true tennis finesse, but six months in the London courts against good men would eradicate the tendency to play racquets or lawn tennis instead of the true game.

For many years the court tennis players of Boston and New York had dominated the game. In March, 1906, Jay won the Gold Racquet tournament at Tuxedo, defeating Pierre Lorillard, Jr.

Then came the National Amateur Court Tennis Championship at the New York Racquet Club. Sands was still national champion, and all the others vied until but one was left who would play him for his championship. Sands did not have to compete until the "challenge round" or finals.

Jay marched through the matches, beating one opponent after another. Finally he came to Joshua Crane, against whom he had played many times before. Crane's particular game was well suited to a win over Jay—at least it always had been. It was said that Crane played "half fifteen better" against Jay than against any other player, which meant Crane ought to win. But Jay set out to make every effort to win.

Crane got off to a fine start, and soon was leading 2 sets to 1 and 5 games to 3, one game short of final victory. Jay was badly rattled.

Then a spectator leaned over the gallery and his glasses fell off his nose and shattered on the floor. Play was stopped while the glass was swept up, and in this respite, Jay Gould recovered some strength and skill. When the game was resumed, he drew even with his opponent at 5-all, then forged ahead and won the set, then went on to win the fifth set and the match. Jay then went ahead to defeat National Champion Sands 3 sets to 1 and to become national court tennis champion. He was not yet eighteen years old.

Most of the New York and Boston crowd masked their chagrin by declaring Jay to be "absolutely" the finest player in the world, and insisted that he go immediately to England to compete with the English nationals. George thought the tennis crowd might be trying to push Jay beyond his abilities to see him defeated—but T. Suffern Tailer and Harry Payne Whitney persuaded George to send Jay abroad that spring. So three days after the nationals, Jay and Coach Forester sailed for England.

Jay entered the English national championships, sending his entry by cable, so short was the time. When Jay arrived, he had a month for practice, and then the championship matches began at Queen's Club. Jay breezed through four opponents, including his old friend Crane, then played V. H. Pennell, the winner of the second place in the 1905 tournament, defeated him, and was finally beaten by the English national champion, Eustace Miles.

Next year, Jay returned to become the first American to win the English court tennis championships. In 1908, he repeated the victory, and that year won the Olympic championship as well.

By 1907, Jay's fame had spread across the world, and when he came to play for the English championships, every seat at the Queen's Club was filled and there was standing room only during the match. After the championships, Jay toured France. The crowds were equally large.

For nineteen years, Jay kept the United States championship, and he held the English championship for most of this time as well. In 1913, Jay challenged George F. Covey, professional at Crabbet Park, England, for the world's open tennis championship and played him in March, 1914, at the Philadelphia Racquet Club. Jay won, to become the first amateur court tennis player ever to hold the world's open championship title. World War I came and Jay's family did not want him to risk a trip to Europe, so he did not defend his "open" crown. The next year, Covey took the championship by default, but Jay was still proclaimed the greatest amateur tennis player who ever lived.

Arranging matches and seeing that Jay kept to his work, plus encouraging Kingdon in his polo, Georgie at games, and the girls at dance and other activity—all this kept George and Edith exceedingly busy. Edith also occupied herself with her good works and charities in Lakewood and New York.

The years 1910–1911 marked a kind of high point in the Gould social world, for this was when both Jay and daughter Vivien married. Jay had married Ann Douglas Graham, a girl of a good family, in 1910. On February 8, 1911, with great pomp and circumstance Vivien married the fifth Baron Decies.

Vivien was a striking dark-haired girl with a pleasant face and a very good figure when she met a young—or not so young, he was in his forties—dashing British officer named Jack Beresford during a tour of England. Beresford's perfect manners successfully disguised his drinking and gambling habits. He was a younger son, and could not live on his officers' pay, and he madly pursued this multimillionaire's daughter. Beresford's suit, alas for him, was not encouraged by George and Edith—they thought him too old and not prepossessing enough in his current state of genteel poverty. Then one day Jack's brother died, and plain Major Jack

Beresford became a lord. This great change for the better in his character was noticed immediately by Edith and George, and Jack was transformed overnight into a thoroughly acceptable suitor for their daughter's hand.

The marriage preparations were as lavish as had been those for Anna's wedding into a noble family—perhaps even a bit more so. The ladies were to have gold vanity boxes rather than silver heart-shaped cake boxes. George dug up another coronet for Vivien as a wedding present. Instead of buying a trousseau at dress shops, or even hiring an American couturier, Edith managed a corps of two hundred twenty-five dressmakers who worked for weeks to assemble every piece of clothing and equipment that the new Baroness might demand.

When Jack Beresford, the Baron, came to America to claim his bride, a certain amount of negative feeling about the affair was in the air, especially among those ardent, hopeful young Americans who preferred to see the millions controlled by American misses remain on the States' side of the Atlantic. Beresford was even challenged to a duel by a youth who identified himself as John Madison Turner, a Virginian allegedly from an old Virginia family, who said he would rather die than see the beautiful Miss Gould go into the hands of an English cad. Lord Decies suggested a duel with chocolate éclairs at ten paces.

So they were married in the most impressive Gould ceremony yet, this one at St. Bartholomew's fashionable Episcopal Church in Manhattan, the wedding attended by hundreds of acquaintances as well as family and friends. The happy couple went off from the reception at the Gould palace on Fifth Avenue to live in a manor house in England and raise children: Eileen Vivien de la Poer Beresford, Catherine Moya Beresford, and Arthur George Marcus Douglas Horsely de la Poer Beresford, the heir apparent.

At the wedding, the contrast between Vivien and her mother, once the lady of the hourglass figure, was immediately apparent. Edith had been putting on weight for the last twenty years, and there seemed to be nothing she could do about it. Lord knew, she exercised and she dieted. She walked, and she rode, and she even played tennis with the family. Most of all she golfed, and to please her, George, who had at last given up polo, took the old field and redid it, building a nine-hole golf course on the estate so Edith could have her favorite exercise. Rain or shine, nearly every day Edith was out swinging a club and getting exercise.

Edith, however, was exceedingly fond of sweets. She knew that the local Lakewood confectioner's shop was her nemesis, but she could not stay away from the place. She adopted desperate measures: each time she went into the confectioner's to sniff the wonderful odors, she took her social secretary with her and forced the woman to taste all the confections she bought—for the guests only, of course. Edith bravely forbore the tasting. The servants were instructed to keep these candies under lock and key and bring them out only for guests—but somehow, like a spoiled small child, Edith managed to secrete handfuls of candies around the house, and she kept right on nibbling.

Edith's weight became a real threat to the welfare of the Goulds in the winter of 1913–1914. George was then hovering between his "dangerous forties" and "frightened fifties," and he yearned for something Edith no longer seemed able to give. One night, while Edith remained in the mansion at Georgian Court (as she was to do more and more as the years rolled by), George stayed over in New York to see an opening of a new musical comedy called *The Girl in the Film*. In the chorus and in bit parts throughout the disjointed show, his eye repeatedly fell on an attractive chorine named Guinevere Jeanne Sinclair. She was young, in her twenties. She was 5 feet 6 inches tall, blonde, and she had a figure like that Edith once had shown the world.

One thing led to another, and soon George was backstage with flowers and candy. Not much later, they were sharing a couch, then a town house. Soon after that the lovely Guinevere was ensconced in a mansion of her own in the coastal suburb of Rye. George found it essential, these days, to remain away from Georgian Court for half a week at a time.

Edwin, the mysterious, quiet Gould, took up the new art of flying in those years just before the beginning of World War I. He was particularly interested in "hydro-aeroplanes" which had been developed by Glenn Curtiss, a young man who ran a bicycle manufacturing shop in Hammondsport, New York, and went from bicycles to motorcycles to aircraft. By 1913, Curtiss had manufactured several planes, and Harold H. McCormick, scion of the reaper family in Chicago, had intrigued the world of Edwin Gould by becoming America's first "air commuter." McCormick flew from his summer home in Lake Forest to Bryant Park in Chicago, skimming along the lake front. He made the trip of 30 miles in 26 minutes the first time, and told the newspapers that he was going to fly back and forth to work during the summer months from then on.

Edwin, who knew the McCormicks, bundled Sally up that summer of 1913 and went to Lake Forest for a visit. He, too, became enthusiastic about the hydro-aeroplane, and came home to order two of them for his summer house at Ardsley-on-Hudson. One was a two-passenger plane; the other was the most elaborate flying boat ever built up to that time and carried six people. Edwin was hoping to be able to commute between the northeast and Palm Beach by air, and then from Palm Beach to Jekyl Island, the Georgia retreat. The flying boats worked well enough, but when Edwin also became interested in speed, he bought a French army scout-type plane, which was shipped over to him at Jekyl Island just before the outbreak of the war. By 1915, he had his pilot's license and was flying frequently, even taking up other millionaires of the Jekyl Island Club for rides.

Edwin was also divesting himself of the trappings of the old fortune as he turned his own money in new directions. While George stayed on the board of the several railroads after he had ceased to control them, Edwin moved away, keeping only his interest in the Cotton Belt. George was the *responsible* head of the family, whose obligation it was to see that anything and everything be done to maintain the value of the Gould properties.

George might no longer be king, but he had the same rights and interests that any large stockholder has in maintaining a board seat—to protect his investment as far as possible—and so he remained. Edwin was George's privileged assistant.

George and Edwin had other obligations as heads of the family, such as the one to Howard, which they fulfilled loyally in these last prewar years at the cost of some public embarrassment.

Howard had moved to England, alone, leaving Kathrine as chatelaine of the big house on Fifth Avenue and Seventy-third Street. In England, Howard rented one estate for the winter and, in the summer, took Dunkeld House, which belonged to the Duke of Atholl, for the shooting season. But Howard became tired of paying taxes on the million-dollar property on Fifth Avenue and decided he wanted to get rid of it. He suggested that Kathrine vacate the house. Kathrine claimed her dower rights and refused to get out. That was *not* the end of it, however, when the taxes ran so high. Howard simply let the taxes mount and did not pay—eventually back taxes reached $54,000. George then stepped in and bought the tax lien, which gave him control of the property. He immediately demanded payment of $17.82 in interest on the lien for one month. Howard refused to pay. George then demanded that the property be sold to satisfy his lien. If it were sold, George would get the property (but would of course give Howard back his share of it, and the only one out of pocket would be Kathrine).

Eventually the house was sold. Kathrine lost her right to the house and had to move into quarters elsewhere, but she did get a third of the value of the property, much to Howard's disgust. He carefully refrained from buying any more real estate as long as he had this millstone around his neck.

The Goulds lived relatively quietly in these years, relatively happily, considering that a war in Europe cast deep shadows across the Atlantic, that Frank and Anna in France were virtually on the firing line, and that Howard in England seemed not far away from it.

But tragedy was not far away. The Edwin Gould family consisted then of Sally, and Edwin's two sons, Edwin, Jr., who was twenty-three, and Frank Miller, who was eighteen. The Edwin Goulds had truly adopted Jekyl Island as their winter home. No other New York Goulds had strayed so far away from the area. But Edwin loved the out-of-doors, the rawness of nature, more than any of his brothers or sisters, and Jekyl Island was kept in the rough, except for the little colony where all the millionaires kept houses—Edwin had two houses, one for himself and one for his guests.

Edwin Gould had gone to Jekyl Island for the winter of 1917. Not all the family went to Jekyl Island. Edwin, Jr., was there, but Sally, the social one of the family, had engagements to keep in New York, and she planned to come down early in March to join her husband and son. Frank Miller Gould, the second son, was a freshman at Yale, and so he was in New Haven.

On February 25, Edwin went over to St. Augustine on business, leaving Edwin, Jr., at the cottage with the servants.

For Edwin, Jr., it was to be a sort of "last vacation." He had not gone to college, finding that formal education bored him so much at Pomfret School that he had run away after three weeks. He had considered studying law, but his father decided that whatever he did, it was time that the twenty-three-year-old begin doing something useful. He was going to work for the Guaranty Trust Company, to learn the business world.

So, as Edwin went across the strait, the end of Edwin, Jr.'s, idyll was nearing, and on this particular day, the young man chose to go for a "coon hunt." He checked around the cottages and found that Noyes Reynolds, the tutor to the Tracy Dow children, was free that day and could go with him, so the pair set out in the afternoon in a canoe, headed for Latham's Hammock, a little island two miles away that the Goulds owned, where Edwin, Jr., had set some raccoon traps the day before. They carried shotguns in the canoe with them, just in case they saw something worth shooting.

Edwin, Jr., discovered that one of his traps had been successful —he had caught a big raccoon.

Edwin might have shot the animal with his shotgun, for the gun was loaded, but he was collecting pelts, and so instead of shooting, he picked up the hammer shotgun and struck the "coon" with the butt of the gun. The raccoon shied to one side and he missed—so he took another swipe. This time he hit the raccoon, and the moment the butt came in contact with the animal's skull, the shock caused the hammer to drop on the shotgun shell and fire it. The birdshot in the shell tore into Edwin's groin. The distance was so short that the shot made a gaping wound about two inches in diameter in Edwin's left groin, cutting a great chunk out of the femoral artery. Noyes Reynolds rushed up to help, but there was nothing he could do, the bleeding could not be stopped, and in a few minutes, Edwin Gould, Jr., died from loss of blood.

Reynolds picked up the body and tried to carry it to the canoe. Reynolds slipped and fell in the shallow water, and the body slid down into the shallows. Reynolds leaped into the canoe and rushed over to Jekyl Island as quickly as he could paddle, shouting for assistance as soon as he came into sight of the wharf. Someone heard him, and by the time he had jumped up on the wharf, a small crowd had assembled to hear his tale.

A motor boat was dispatched to Hammock Island to recover the body, and another was sent to the mainland bearing a party instructed to get in touch with Edwin, Sr., in St. Augustine. The body was taken to Brunswick, Georgia, the next day for embalming, and Edwin returned and sent his private car *Dixie* up to Thalmann Junction by special train to pick it up.

When the news reached New York, Sally was prostrate. Frank immediately came home from New Haven, and George and the other members of the Gould family rallied around. It was the first real tragedy of the Goulds, and the first death in the family since Jay's death twenty-five years before.

30

Kingdon and Georgie Go Astray

*It may take three generations of wealth
to make a gentleman, but the son of the
businessman never believed that old saw.
And he sought to exercise his power
over the family's affairs to make ladies
and gentlemen of his children and to
bring about "proper" marriages for them.*

THE first three weddings in the George Gould household had been
magnificent affairs, highly fashionable. When Marjorie married
Anthony Drexel, George and Edith showed their approval by lav-
ishing gifts on the young people. When Jay had married Miss
Graham, it was the same—perhaps even more spectacular because
Miss Graham was related to royalty, and Princess Kauranankoa, of
the last ruling family of Hawaii and a cousin of the bride, attended the ceremony. When Vivien married Lord Decies, no one
considering blood could have any qualms, for the barony went
back some twenty generations.

All was well. George and Edith seemed to be proving that two generations was enough to make a "gentleman"—that is, a man who stood above the crowd, did not soil his hands with business affairs, and spent his days in furious leisure. Edith, having played *la grande dame* for more than twenty years, was beginning to believe it was not just a role.

Alas, what a shock it was, then, when one spring day in 1917, Edith learned that Kingdon was planning to marry *a servant*.

She was the Signorina Annunziata Camilla Maria Lucci, and she was the governess and Italian and French tutor of little Edith. Elizabeth Drexel Lehr, the social lioness, was at Georgian Court the day Edith learned of the affair. Mrs. Lehr reported:

> . . . Edith and I had tea alone in her boudoir. She was unusually silent and preoccupied and after we had finished, she said, "Do stay with me Bessie. I've got a rather disagreeable duty to perform. I am going to talk to the children's Italian governess on the subject of Kingdon. You know he has been having a desperate flirtation with the poor girl, and I am so afraid she may be taking it seriously. I don't want to have any broken hearts here . . . .
>
> A few minutes later Signorina Lucci came in, a handsome girl with beautiful dark eyes and a graceful figure. She stood very calm and unemotional before Edith, and listened in silence to all she had to say. Then she raised her head proudly. Her eyes flashed fire . . . . "So you say you tell me this for my good? You tink he not mean it, he not love me? You are wrong, I will marry heem!"
>
> Very much embarrassed Edith tried to reason with her, pointed out that such a marriage for her eldest son would be impossible, warned her that Kingdon was only *trying to learn Italian* [italics mine]. The girl only repeated more firmly than before, "I will marry heem . . . ." and thereupon walked out of the room, leaving Edith beaten in the field.
>
> Signorina Lucci was dismissed. She left Lakewood and returned to New York . . . .*

* Elizabeth Drexel Lehr, *King Lehr and the Gilded Age,* Philadelphia, Lippincott, 1935.

In her heart, Edith knew that the affair was not ended, but she no longer had the slightest control since the girl was out of her house. Annunziata took an apartment at 27 East Sixty-second Street, joined the Art Students League, and set up a studio at the League headquarters on West Fifty-seventh Street.

Then, on July 1, Kingdon took Annunziata down to New York City Hall and they secured a marriage license in the office of City Clerk Scully. Someone told the reporters that a Gould was about to get married, and Kingdon was accosted before he left the building. It was true, he said. They would be married the next day in the rectory of St. Patrick's Cathedral, not the church itself because Kingdon was a Protestant.

The press on that occasion learned more about Signorina Lucci in ten minutes than Edith Gould had learned in the two years that Annunziata worked for her. The girl was thirty-one, two years older than Kingdon. She was an orphan and the daughter of an old, but impoverished, Italian family. She painted. She was a talented musician. She had come to America eight years ago to study and practice art and had taken the Gould job only when she needed to save money.

Was it love?

"Ask me something about Mr. Gould," Annunziata replied, "and I will tell you that he is the finest man in these United States. Not only I think so, but I am sure everybody thinks so. He is so democratic and plain. Oh, I think he is the finest man in the whole country."

So on the following day, with only Georgie, his brother, representing the Goulds, Kingdon Gould and Signorina Lucci were married at St. Patrick's rectory, and then drove down to the bride's apartment where a reception was held for a few friends. They went out into the country for a brief honeymoon and then took an apartment at Sixty-sixth and Park Avenue. From there, Kingdon went to the office every day and saw his father and his brothers, but after office hours, Kingdon went home to Park Avenue, and he never, never saw his mother.

Was this not enough of a shock for a poor mother who had expected so much more for her oldest son?

Apparently not, for five days later George, Jr., married a Miss Laura Carter of Ardena, New Jersey, in an even quieter ceremony in Philadelphia. This marriage was so truly quiet that the minister, the Reverend Doctor William D. Chalfont, did not even know the identity of the groom, other than that he was "a Mr. Gould," a matter which caused Dr. Chalfont many later regrets since he was Philadelphia's "marrying parson," his house being within walking distance of Philadelphia City Hall. The witnesses at this wedding were Dr. George Coleman, a dentist, a cousin of the bride, and Mrs. D. P. Callahan, her aunt.

The tragedy of Georgie's marriage was far greater than that of Kingdon, any way one examined it. Kingdon was twenty-nine and must be presumed to have known his own mind. Georgie was just twenty-one. Kingdon had chosen a girl of great culture, broad education, and many talents. Georgie had chosen a graduate of Freehold, New Jersey, High School, of the class of 1914. Annunziata knew more about Italian art than any Gould. Laura's main claim to fame was her skill as a dancer, and as dancers went, she was one of the prettiest in the East. Like Annunziata, Laura was an orphan, and she had been reared by her aunt and uncle, Mr. and Mrs. D. P. Callahan, the uncle being well known to Damon Runyon and other chroniclers of the racetrack set as one of the fastest men with a dollar around the eastern tracks. Annunziata spoke four languages, Laura spoke racetrackese and burlesquoise—both fluently.

Was it love?

Well, the press asked the new Mrs. Gould if their wedding had been inspired by the wedding of Kingdon a few days earlier.

"No," she said. . . . "I don't think so. . . ."

The senior George Goulds, of course, knew about the wedding although they did not attend. How could they? Edith was literally sick with her grief, and had she been healthy and bouncing as a young puppy, she would never have lent her presence to Georgie's marriage to a dancing teacher. She and George fled to the wilds of the Catskills. She would not even stay at Georgian Court. Hearing this, Georgie knew he was in for trouble. What was he going to do for a living, the reporters asked him.

"Oh, I don't know," Georgie said with the breeziness of a youth who had never tried to get a job. "Teach school or something."

As it turned out, George was not reduced to making his own way in the cold world. His brother-in-law, Tony Drexel, gave him a job in his brokerage house, Liggett, Drexel and Co. at 61 Broadway. It was not much of a job, because Georgie was not worth very much in the business world at that moment, but it was a job, and it kept the wolves from the door of Georgie and Laura's apartment.

What inspired these marriages? Was it the war and the fever that accompanied it—for, of course, all the Goulds were conscious of the declaration of war against Germany in that spring of 1917. Perhaps. Perhaps it was rebellion against the tight reins that Edith tried to keep on her family, and Edith's growing sense of social involvement with *Society*. Perhaps it was simply young blood rising to fever heat in the spring. But whatever it was, the two marriages shocked and distressed Edith Gould, and she could not bring it to her lips to say that she forgave the boys and would embrace her new daughters-in-law. Either Edith had forgotten the anguish that mother Helen Gould had caused her for years, or she was so busy with her pretensions that human feeling no longer counted.

But however these hasty marriages might have turned out under other conditions, the war tended to heal the wounds between members of the family as the boys went away to war.

Jay was first. He enrolled as a machinist's mate first class in the naval reserve. Kingdon, new wife or not, joined the colors in September and was one of the first 1,000 privates who moved into Wrightstown, New Jersey, to help establish Camp Dix. Kingdon had asked to be included in the first batch of men from his country to go into service.

Such loyalty must be reciprocated, and when Edith thought it over, she decided Annunziata was not so bad after all. So later that month Edith climbed into her Fiat touring car, along with little Edith for moral support, and was driven to Camp Dix where she marched into the office of Colonel Marcus Stokes, the commander, and announced that she had come to see her son.

The army had a system all worked out for mothers who came to see how their little boys were faring under the guidance of the military.

First, the ladies were taken to the office of the Adjutant of the 311th Infantry, Kingdon's outfit. There Edith announced her errand, and Captain Odom, the adjutant, sent an orderly to the barracks to find Private Gould. A few minutes later, Kingdon came ambling in, wearing his golf suit—the suit in which he had begun army life and which had not yet been replaced by olive drab. Then the party was shown into Colonel Stokes' office, and he left so they could talk privately.

They talked. Kingdon put in a call to Annunziata and they all three talked to her, explaining that mother and son had made up and that the liaison included the new Mrs. Gould. They talked until Private Gould was summoned to duty by the bugle, which called an assembly of the new soldiers. Then Mrs. Gould left, Edith trailing behind. They got into the Fiat and drove away, dropping off, by footman, a huge basket of fruit at Kingdon's barracks for the delectation of her boy and his new companions.

Kingdon soldiered well. He rose through the ranks, to become corporal, sergeant, staff sergeant, and last, battalion sergeant major of the headquarters troop of his regiment—no mean honor for an enlisted man. Early in 1918, Kingdon was offered a chance to go to Officers Training School to become a commissioned second lieutenant, but he said he would rather stay with his outfit. In May, he was given a field commission as interpreter, on the ground that he spoke five languages fluently and could read and write two others.

Georgie did not go to war. He tried, but he was rejected from the service on physical grounds, so he stayed on in business in New York. He did not remain long with Tony Drexel, however, but soon moved to Oil City, Pennsylvania, and took a job with the Galena Oil Company. He and Laura had a baby, George Jay Gould III, and Kingdon and Annunziata had one too, Silvia Annunziata, to add to the growing army of Gould grandchildren.

Other babies were being born in the family, not all of them so welcome. Grandpa George was not only grandfather and uncle; now, in his fifties, he became a daddy again—to his children with Guinevere Sinclair. Miss Sinclair had taken a town house in New York as well as a house in Rye. Then she gave up the New York town house and moved to a $250,000 estate on an island that George bought for her. Along came the babies: George Sinclair, born in April, 1915; Jane Sinclair, born in June, 1916. Guinevere's accouchements could not be kept secret, but neither was anything else about the liaison kept quiet. George was seen nearly every weekend in Rye, they said, and his yacht was frequently tied up at the wharf that served the estate. Nor did the arrangement go unnoticed at Georgian Court, and in the family at large, each time Guinevere bore another child it was quickly known that "another one of George's bastards has been born."

These words were spoken plaintively (by Helen), compassionately (by Edwin), humorously (by Howard), and nastily (by Anna and Frank). In far-off Paris, Anna was fretting that her income had been reduced so drastically over the past few years from the old three-quarters of a million dollars a year. Anna was also angry with George because he had seemed to support Helen in her flat opposition to Anna's second marriage to the Duke of Talleyrand. Helen really did not believe in divorce, and more than that, she did not believe in what the Catholic Church had done— given Anna an annulment of the marriage to de Castellane when the marriage had visible results of its consummation in Tippytoes, Pittipat, and Tittimouse. Frank was still angry—furious is the word—that George had attempted to stop his second marriage to

Edith Kelly. Frank had been nursing grudges against one member of the family or another ever since the early days when his father died, leaving him in the care of Helen and George and, consequently, at their mercy. Now, in 1919, Frank decided to do something about it.

31

Frank Falls Out

*In exercising his powers over the rail-
road empire, the eldest son had been
forced to make many arbitrary decisions.
But power and responsibility are inseparable. Having exercised the one for a
quarter of a century, the eldest son then
had to be prepared to account for his
actions.*

FOR half a dozen years, Frank had been brooding. George had
told Frank he was a damned fool to marry that showgirl Edith
Kelly, and George had refused to have anything to do with the marriage. It was bad enough that George had shown such brutal
frankness—it was worse that he had turned out to be right and
that Edith became a more unsuitable wife for Frank than Helen
Kelly had been.

Two years after his marriage, Frank began drinking heavily.
He would wake up early in the morning, drink a quart of whiskey
before 8 o'clock, and then go back to bed and sleep away most of
the day, wake up, drink steadily until dinner, and then go back to

bed again. He kept a large assortment of liquors on his sideboard and would drink first from one bottle and then another, until he passed out. If he left the house, he would often be brought home by his chauffeur or a pair of taxi drivers, dead drunk, and would go to bed to stay for a week, drinking himself into insensibility whenever he aroused sufficiently to do so.

Frank was, in short, a very unhappy man, he had forsaken family, and even country, and now his wife was anathema to him, and his adopted France was cold to his wooing.

But not everyone in France.

Until 1913, Frank's relations with Edith had been decent enough, but one night that year, he left the house in Seine-et-Oise, the Maisons Lafitte, 5 Avenue Picard, not far from Paris, to go into Paris for a meeting with several other men, and did not come home. It was the first night he had been away from Edith. At that time Frank began to frequent the *maisons de joie,* and soon was well known at all the better houses in Paris.

In 1913, Frank also picked up a lady named Sonia to whom he gave 6,000 francs a month ($1200), an automobile, and jewelry. Whenever Edith was on a trip, Sonia was brought to the house in Seine-et-Oise or to the estate at Le Robillard, sometimes for weeks. One time Edith came home while Sonia was in residence, and that caused a fight to remember!

Frank lost track of time. He refused to take a bath for a month, and he would wash out his own underclothes in water without soap—"to save money." He saved string and tinfoil which he kept in a big box. When the box became full, he would throw away all the bits he had collected and start over again.

Twice he was sent to sanitariums to dry out. One night in 1917, he threatened to kill Edith, broke down the door to her room, dragged her from her bed, and beat her. Then he tried to force her to drink a vial of something he said was poison, and when she would not drink, he threw a bottle at her. That same night he called in the fourteen servants and forbade them ever to wait on Edith again. Next morning, he remembered nothing he had done.

That same year, Frank rented an apartment in Paris for Leone

Ritz, a lady well known in the lower circles of night life. Evening after evening, Frank came to the apartment where Leone served up delicious young girls for him, two or three at a time, and he spent his time at these amusements. So scandalous was Frank's behavior that the apartment owner finally forced him to give up the place, whereupon he found quarters for Leone Ritz at the Hotel Meurice and she set up light housekeeping there.

What Leone got as mistress-in-residence and procuress was between herself and Frank; the ordinary girls got 200 francs a night ($40)—for a Paris whore in 1918, it was not bad pay.

In the spring of 1918, Edith Kelly decided that it was hopeless to try to keep on living with Frank Gould, and she moved out. Thereupon Frank decided to divorce her and set the wheels in motion in France. He hired the best lawyers he could find, and they prepared a case of desertion. The papers were served on Edith one day as she was riding in a taxi—they were thrown in the window of the cab. She did not pick them up, and when she got out the papers fell out on the ground. Edith did not know she had been divorced until she read about it in the newspapers. She filed a countersuit to overthrow the decision. Frank hired former Premier Viviani, whose political power was brought to bear, and the decree was upheld. Edith meanwhile filed for separation and divorce in New York, where she said Frank maintained his legal residence. And so the fight went on.

But when he was brooding in his drunkenness, Frank thought long and hard about all the evil, real and imagined, done him by his elder siblings. From time to time, he lunched with Anna, and they shored one another up with tales of the evil-doing of George and Helen. These two convinced each other that George had really been mismanaging the fortune all these years, and in May, 1919, Frank filed a suit demanding the turnover of $25,000,000 to Frank and Anna for moneys lost and misused, and also demanding that George be ousted as chief executor and trustee of the Gould estate.

The suit accused George of losing $25,000,000 by his mismanagement of affairs.

George admitted that the estate had dropped perhaps $12,500,-

000 in value, using the original value of $72,000,000 accepted by surrogate court. But, he said, the drop simply reflected the decrease in value of Missouri Pacific and Iron Mountain Railroad stock. Frank charged that George had never created the separate trusts that the will called for, and Goerge admitted this was true. He said that with the acquiescence of Helen and Edwin and Howard, he had managed the estate as one great trust, paying the others their shares of the interest and dividends each year. It was cheaper, by far, he said, to do it that way.

There were eleven charges in all, the most serious of which involved the manner in which George had sold off control of the Western Union Company without notifying Helen or the others, and taking a commission of $800,000 for himself on the sale of the stock as a broker. The other serious charge was that he had destroyed the books of record. George defended his first practice, saying that he *was* a stockbroker and was entitled to the commission—but he returned the money to the estate. As for the records, he said, he had simply got rid of papers that were cluttering up the office and burned them in his fireplace.

George's attitude—and that of the whole family—toward Frank was revealed in a scrap of correspondence relative to a misunderstanding between Edwin and the youngest brother.

"I sympathize deeply with dear Ed's hurt feelings," wrote Helen to George, "but if we can get Frank really interested in work it would make it easier for you and him and it would perhaps save Frank from frivolling away his life abroad or worse and would be a good thing for the family."

Frank had participated in family decisions until he began drinking in 1912, George said. Then he left the country in March, 1913, and never came back. He gave up homeland and family out of pique and decided to destroy himself and the Goulds.

The case was put up to Supreme Court Justice Whitaker of New York, and after due consideration, he removed George as head of the estate and ordered the estate to be divided into six separate trust funds, one for each of Jay's children.

Jay's will had stipulated that in case of vacancy, Frank would be chosen a trustee to succeed George and Edwin would become head of the family as far as the trust was concerned. But George objected to Frank joining the trustees, and there the matter rested.

George appealed his removal. In the appeal, Edwin's work over the years was revealed. But lately he had moved away from the trust. Helen had had to push George to move into Pittsburgh to build west. He had wanted to undertake more conservative investments. At one point, A. J. Cassatt and J. Pierpont Morgan had offered George a good price to sell out his abortive Pittsburgh investment, but Helen had refused. She was intent on carrying out the will of her father. Helen, perhaps, should have been the heir-apparent, the driving force who would carry on the Jay Gould tradition.

George had lost control of the railroads but he had not lost his stocks. He had not lost control of either the Manhattan Elevated or of the Western Union Company. The first, he had relinquished rather than fight the battle of the subways—he simply did not believe in them. The second, he had given up after making a number of checks on Western Union service, as opposed to Postal Telegraph, and finding that the service of the latter was always the better of the two. Instead of deciding to step in and revitalize the management of Western Union, he had sold his interest to the telephone company, carefully concealing from Helen, until after it was done, any trace of the transaction. Helen would have said it was their father's investment, and since Jay had faith in it, they must keep on.

The truth about George as investor came out in this suit—he was not an excellent conservator. He was freehanded with his own share of the estate at the expense of the general good. George was not the junior railroad baron that everyone believed—he was the unwilling partner of sister Helen in the decisions that resulted in the attempt to build the transcontinental road. Once the course was set, he did not waver. One of the most serious charges against George involved the Missouri Pacific and his shoring up of that unfortunate road at the expense of the fortune. But this activity was carried out in the attempt to realize Jay and Helen Gould's dream of the transcontinental railroad. George, in brief, was neither the lion that Wall Streeters had believed him to be, nor the lamb that Kuhn, Loeb set out to shear, nor the dog in the manger that Anna and Frank now called him. He was simply a well-meaning man who was not up to the responsibility thrust upon him. He was bright enough, and he could be strong minded. He fell short in his insistence on maintaining total authority while delegating much day-to-day responsibility to underlings. They must be on the job while George disported himself in Europe, but they did not have the power to straighten out the day-to-day problems that arose. That was his failing as a businessman.

Once ousted, however, George did not give up. He kept on working to clear his name.

In the summer of 1919, while George was thus involved, Edith was struck by what appeared to her to be another tragedy. Little Edith Catherine fell in love with Carroll Wainwright, son of an impeccable but not overly wealthy New York family.

Like all of George's daughters, Edith grew up to be a good-looking woman. All the daughters were cultured and well educated by any American standards. Edith with her long wavy hair and clear complexion was taller than her mother and less buxom, but these were different times. She was in her next to last year at Miss Spence's school when she and Carroll met—he was then a college boy—and the papers caught up the affair quickly to make a romance of it.

Edith, in fact, had been the darling of the newspapers since her birth on August 3, 1901, aboard her father's yacht *Sybarite* just off Cold Spring Harbor. The news of the unusual circumstances of birth aboard a yacht had been carried by newspapers all over the world. The reason was simple enough. In 1901, children were born at home, not in hospitals. Little Edith might have been born at home, but her mother had been desperately uncomfortable that hot summer of 1901, and George bundled her and her entourage (including Dr. Paul Kimball) aboard the yacht and set out to cruise about the New York area until the baby was born. The smaller children were sent off to Furlough Lodge for the period, and the older ones stayed on at Georgian Court. Every morning, from wherever they were, George went ashore at the nearest railroad station and took the train to the office, making arrangements with his captain to pick him up at night. On the morning of August 3, 1901, the yacht happened to be off Cold Spring Harbor, Long Island.

Eighteen years later came the summer romance. It continued through the fall, while Carroll Wainwright was in the army. Carroll came to see Edith at Georgian Court or at the house at 857 Fifth Avenue. Her mother was aware of the romance and did not entirely discourage it, but she wanted her daughter to go on, to do more with her education, and to make a more suitable marriage, for young Wainwright was an artist, peculiarly unstable financially, and devil-may-care about society. Upon being discharged from the army, he moved into an apartment at 305 West Fourth Street in the heart of Greenwich Village—and it made Mrs. Gould shudder.

So in the summer of 1920, after the family indicated its disapproval of the romance, Edith and Carroll Wainwright eloped to Atlantic City. They were married there and stayed at the Marlborough-Blenheim Hotel, wiring the good news to their parents. Then they went to Wilmington and stayed at the Hotel DuPont. When they came back to New York, Edith would have nothing to do with them, and all was far from forgiven.

That summer the young couple moved into an apartment just off Park Avenue, and young Edith learned to cook and manage a household, which she had never done before in her life. They were poor but happy.

Attending the same parties, the elder Edith would ostentatiously snub her daughter and son-in-law. The newspapers watched the performances each time, speculated on them, and laughed about Mrs. Gould's stubbornness. Finally that winter she gave in and forgave the young sinners. The real reason she had been so angry was that the elopement had made the Goulds look ridiculous for the third time in a row. But all was healed at a dinner-dance given at the Fifth Avenue mansion on January 1, 1921, and the family was more or less serene except for Georgie, whose dancer was still a little too much for his mother.

Poor Edith! She tried hard to keep up appearances and to regain the husband she had at least half lost. Her problem was always the same—obesity.

Medical science had discovered that thyroid extract, taken from cattle, could be dried, powdered, and made into a medicine suitable for the treatment of thyroid deficiency in human beings. In the 1920s, thousands of American women who ate too much believed they were suffering from the dread "hypo-thyroidism," and they began descending on their doctors demanding treatment. They wanted a bottle of pills that would speed up their metabolism and shuck off the unwanted fat. In a handful of cases, where obesity was actually caused by lack of thyroid secretion, the pills worked, and some women actually lost 50 or 100 pounds and then managed, by good eating habits, to keep their weight down to normal. But in most cases, the good ladies suffered no thyroid deficiency at all, and, experimenting with thyroid, Edith discovered, sadly, that she was one of these. Bravely, for many weeks, she took thyroid tablets by the handful, on the theory that if one is good, a hundred are better. Fortunately for Edith and her self-medication program, her body simply threw off the excess thyroid without harm, and all she wasted was the effort and the money.

And she took exercises. She engaged in weight-reducing programs. She was massaged. She went to steam baths. Still the hourglass figure eluded her, and she knew that George spent most of his time away on weekends visiting that strumpet in her house on Long Island Sound. That the strumpet was a good twenty years younger and far more beautiful did not sit easily on Edith's mind either.

In the summer of 1921, at Georgian Court, Edith redoubled her exercising on the golf course George had built in 1912. She played every day, as long as she had time, and when George was at home, he played with her. They began a game on Sunday morning of November 14, after church. When they reached the fifth tee, Edith moved forward, it being her honor, and made her drive. George stood beside her and watched the ball soar down the fairway. Then he turned, and saw his wife lying crumpled on the ground. She had not made a sound.

Edith had fainted, George thought, and he knelt over her and rubbed her hands and face to try to revive her. But she would not revive. George picked her up then and carried her to the nearby Casino and sent a caddy to the house to alert the servants and bring a doctor.

Twenty minutes later, Dr. George W. Lawrence and Dr. Irwin H. Hance arrived from Lakewood. They examined Edith, and reported that she was dead. A heart attack, they said. They also found that she was wearing a rubber suit that encased her like the wrappings of a mummy, from ankle to wrist and to collarbone.

The family rallied. All children came home including Vivien, Lady Decies, who cabled from London that she was sailing as soon as possible. The funeral at the Fifth Avenue house was very simple under the offices of the Reverend Doctor Ernest E. Matthews, rector of the Church of the Heavenly Rest in New York, who had been for many years pastor of All Saints Episcopal Church in Lakewood and as close to a full-time spiritual advisor as Edith possessed. A crowd of a thousand stood outside the big house, crowding in the park across the way, a dozen pallbearers carried the coffin out of the house into the hearse, and the tiny cortege made its way to Woodlawn Cemetery.

Remarkably enough, for a lady who entered marriage with no money, Edith left a sizeable estate—an indication of George's generosity to his wife. The Fifth Avenue house was in her name, and it was left to the children although George had its use during his lifetime. The children also received their mother's million dollars worth of jewelry.

The New York *Times* listed Edith's valuables, as taken from the official records, when the estate was finally appraised several years later:

The most valuable item of jewelry was a diamond and emerald corsage containing twenty-two emeralds and 275 diamonds, appraised at $200,000. A rope of ninety pearls, weighing 1,252 grains, was valued at $127,000. A pearl necklace, containing fifty-one stones with a diamond clasp, and weighing 1,326 grains, was appraised at 100,000.

Other valuable gems were:

Large emerald and diamond pendant, $35,000; diamond necklace, $26,000; tiara, containing seven emeralds weighing seventy carats, with several imperfections, 500 tiny diamonds in bands, sixty-three diamonds weighing twenty carats and 400 small diamonds weighing seventeen carats, $45,000; pearl and diamond crown, platinum and gold, containing twenty-nine diamonds, $22,000; rose diamond and diamond tiara, $3,750; diamond dog collar containing 980 diamonds of 72 carats, $9,100; diamond and seven-pearl festoon, containing three diamonds, fifty-nine square cut diamonds, two round and 240 small stones, $21,000; diamond sautoir of five pendants, $39,500; diamond necklace, sixty small stones, $4,000.

Rope of pearls, 187 stones, weighing 1,700 grains, $85,000; four-strand pearl sautoir, 336 pearls, 1,288 grains, platinum and diamond clasp, $32,000; emerald and diamond cluster rings, $8,500 and $3,000, the latter due to bad flaws; pearl and diamond earrings, $17,000; turquoise and diamond necklace, $4,100; heart-shaped opal brooch, $350; diamond collar, $6,650; miniature of Mrs. Gould, $200; collar of small diamonds, $700; sapphire and diamond brooch, $1,650; diamond and rose diamond bowknot collar, $4,650; and three turquoise rings, $425.

An interesting item in the collection of gems was an amethyst and diamond set, consisting of the following pieces: corsage, containing 384 diamonds and 74 amethysts, $3,300; heart pendant chain, 380 small diamonds and cabochon emerald, $950; four bowknots, each set with 58 brilliants and one amethyst, $1,400; pendant from bow, 93 small diamonds and one cabochon amethyst in centre, $650; and bracelet set with 9 amethysts and 9 small diamonds, $300; total value of set, $6,600.

Mrs. Gould owned a watch containing a large rose diamond

in the back surrounded by small diamonds, valued at $2,000, and had two other watches appraised at $75 and $50. A gold chain and locket containing a picture of Mr. Gould is valued at $100. A diamond chain of fifty-four stones with fifteen pearls was valued at $40,000. A square diamond ring was valued at $4,000, and a gold mesh bag $1,500.

The list of Mrs. Gould's clothing included the following: Ten evening gowns, $350; eight street dresses, $125; two sport suits, $25; three silk afternoon dresses, $75; negligee and lingerie, $50; summer evening wrap, $25; green velvet evening wrap, $25; black satin day coat, $30; monkey fur cape, $100; old style green velvet evening wrap, $20; and purple velvet evening wrap, $75.

The furs included a Russian sable small cape of twenty-three skins, $1,500; sable stole, $2,200; and three sable chokers, $200. She had a fitted traveling bag valued at $600.

The list of furnishings in the Fifth Avenue residence showed that Mrs. Gould's room contained a Mme. du Barry bed of carved and gilt wood, with modern silk draperies and antique tapestry spread, all valued at $3,500. The bed in Mr. Gould's room was a four-poster of Italian carved walnut with a canopy, and was appraised at $200.

So much for the $500,000 pearl necklace, so much for the huge wardrobe that Edith was always supposed to have had. The newspaper reporters had smoked strong stuff when they wrote the stories of the grandeur of 857 Fifth Avenue and of Georgian Court, even to relating that Georgian Court's impressive but moderate-sized great hall was 250 feet long, perhaps six times its actual size. The newspapermen were not primarily to blame, of course, for few of them found entrance to the Gould houses, and they were forced to rely on such unreliable reporters as Elizabeth Drexel Lehr, who exaggerated sizes and costs and the expenditures of her rich friends beyond measure. Mrs. Lehr was scarcely alone. Over the years, Edith Gould had gained a reputation for being a spendthrift, and so had George, and no one would believe otherwise. This assessment of Edith's estate puts the picture in perspective, perhaps.

That autumn most of the jewels were sold to divide the estate more easily.

That same autumn, and in the spring, George continued his running battle with Anna and Frank. An attempt was made to disbar George's attorney at the time, Thomas L. Chadbourne, on the grounds that he stood by while George "looted" the railroads, particularly the treasury of the Missouri Pacific, of several million dollars. When it came time to share out the interest and dividends of the estate for 1921, Anna and Frank again tried to make trouble. On the basis of the estate's earnings and his share of it, George was to have $664,904. His brother and sister sought an injunction to prevent payment unless George allowed the outside examination of his assets and finances. Anna and Frank had been plotting this move for some time. They had demanded—not asked—that Edwin, Helen, and Howard bring the action as trustees. These three older siblings had refused to have anything to do with the unpleasant fight, and the family took the shape it would keep from that time on: the four older children allied against the younger two. George had mixed the finances of the Jay Gould estate with his own, and that could not be contradicted, but Edwin, Helen, and Howard knew enough about the manner in which business was done that they did not complain. Anna and Frank simply used the financial excuse to even old personal scores.

The struggle cost George dearly in health and peace of mind. Worried and upset as he was, he turned even more to Guinevere Sinclair, and in the summer of 1922, he married her and moved to England. They travelled in France, stopping at the Hotel Meurice in Paris, and motoring to Aix-les-Bains with Tony Drexel and Marjorie for a brief vacation. It was a celebration, at least, if not a honeymoon. The couple's third child, Guinevere, had been born in April.

Howard, who had decided that he would never again live in the United States, had taken an estate at Wallingford-on-Thames, and for a time, George used this as his English headquarters. But he soon leased Castle Grant in the Scottish highlands, the principal seat of the Earls of Seafield, chiefs of the Clan Grant, and a truly beautiful place so rustic that the red deer played on the lawns and no lawnmowers were needed.

Soon the village of Grantown-on-Spey in Elginshire was buzzing with activity. The old castle was spruced up for the season. The place had deteriorated in the last few years with the impoverishment of the family following the death of the old Dowager Countess, a friend of Edward VII, and the death in action during World War I of the next count.

Run down or not, the castle was a splendid house. The dining room was 47 feet long and 27 feet wide, and contained priceless paintings—or at least they had never been priced—including a Van Dyke portrait of Charles I and Henrietta. The long halls were filled with ancestral paintings and suits of ancient armor that had belonged to the men of the Clan Grant stood here and there on pedestals. The grounds were stocked with grouse, and the stream was full of salmon. A mile away at Grantown was a golf course which George and Guinevere could visit for exercise. Golf was now George's game since he had given up polo. It appeared that he and Guinevere would have many happy months in their castle.

But it was not to be. George and Guinevere had not been married a year when, on a trip to France, George fell seriously ill in Mentone. At first, his illness was reported as serious, and Jay and Kingdon booked passage on the *Majestic*. Anna was also in New York then, and she and the Duke were going home on the *Majestic*. She denied that she was going to see her brother, and it was quite true, Anna and George had not spoken for several years. The boys were ready to sail, but they did not when cables brought word of George's great improvement. George, Jr., was on hand in France—he had been living there for several years but was now busy divorcing Laura. (She received custody of little George Jay Gould III and Maugham Carter Gould.)

A week later, Kingdon and his family did sail after telling reporters that George was improving steadily. But they did not go immediately to Mentone because the reports were so favorable.

The illness had begun as a chest ailment in the winter, shortly after George and Guinevere had taken the Villa Zoralde at Cap Martin. His health had gone up and down for months as he suffered from pneumonia and other fevers.

From France, George and Guinevere had taken the children to Egypt and had engaged a dahabiyeh on the Nile for the trip from Cairo to Assuan, to see the ruins. Before they could reach Thebes and the tomb of King Tutankhamen, George caught a cold, which turned into pneumonia. He returned to France ahead of the family, and his health grew better and then worse. Suddenly on May 16, 1923, without any member of his first family at his side, George collapsed and died.

Then the family did rush to Mentone by ship and train. The funeral was held May 19 at Mentone, and Guinevere and their children and Howard, along with several new friends, were present. The others had not yet arrived, and Frank and Anna refused to come. The body was taken to Paris and, by liner, to America. For the first time it was now revealed that George had been ill with high blood pressure and heart ailments for eight years, and that these had become so serious in the winter of 1922 that he knew his days were numbered when he went to Mentone.

His body was brought back to America, additional services were held, and his coffin was placed in the catacombs of the Gould mausoleum next to Edith's.

The fortune was now officially in its third generation. Its first custodian was dead, and the future did not look bright.

32

The Great Estate Fight

---◄●●●►---

The estate had been left intact to pre-
vent quarrelling, but there was quarrelling
anyhow. The fortune had been left in the
hands of the eldest son, but the others had
grown to dislike the arrangement. The
whole had been left in complicated trust
to preserve its integrity, but the integrity
was lost. All this had occurred in thirty
years. Now that the principal guardian
was disgraced and had gone to his maker,
what would happen to the powerful
fortune?

---◄●●●►---

AFTER George's death, some fair appraisal of the value of the
Gould estate-in-trust after all these years of George's supervision
could take place, and the indications were that George was about
as bad a manager as Anna and Frank had indicated. The residuary trust in George's estate, that part which had to be disposed of
according to old Jay's will, came to an estimated $10,000,000. Mul-
tiplying this sum by six, to give the total value of Jay's estate, one
arrives at the figure of $60,000,000, which represents a value drop of

$12,000,000 according to tax figures, but much more in reality because of the vast difference in approach to finances between 1892 and 1923. Almost to the end of the nineteenth century, the United States government had been self-supporting through customs receipts and sales of public lands. The idea of a sustained financial deficit, or of heavy personal taxation, had always been repugnant to Americans. But World War I and the heavy demands on the government along with the growing call for social services by government were already changing the attitude of the federal and state authorities toward taxation of large estates. Talk of income tax was in the air, and in a year, an individual income tax would be levied at rates shocking to multimillionaires.

Beginning in 1924, a married millionaire with $500,000 a year in income, with two children as dependents, could be taxed $199,535 of his $500,000, or just about 40 per cent! One can imagine how the children of Jay Gould felt about that, since they had all been receiving half a million dollars or more each year from the estate for thirty-one years.

But the point, in 1923, was that government was valuing such estates as the Goulds at far more nearly their actual worth than had been the case in 1892, and so the $12,000,000 figure indicating a drop in value of Gould securities actually represented losses to the estate of more nearly $40,000,000 in values. Frank was shrewd enough to see this fact and he convinced Anna. Thus the suit against the George Gould estate was renewed and dragged on.

Another bit of litigation began. Under Jay's will, only blood-Goulds were entitled to share in the estate. The children of George's second marriage, although recognized by him in his will as his own children, were still illegitimate because they had been born to Guinevere while George was still married to Edith. So the children of George and Edith went to court to be sure that the children of George and Guinevere did not get any money. In the will, George left a total of $30,000,000, first dividing up the Jay Gould trust among his first set of seven children, then setting aside a trust fund of $4,000,000 for Guinevere, then dividing the residuary estate of $16,000,000 into ten parts (one for each child of each marriage). If the will were executed as George wanted it, each child would receive about $3,000,000. Almost immediately suits developed in addition to those of the children: Guinevere could not get the interest on a million dollars worth of securities that had been turned over to her before George's death and she sued. Edith Kingdon Gould Wainwright sued the eldest son, Kingdon, and asked his removal as an executor of the George Gould estate because he did not put into the estate certain moneys she said he should have. It was as if the case of Anna and Frank were being opened for the first time—and to add complications, Anna and Frank continued to sue.

The heirs squabbled busily. Then one day, Gloria, the youngest child of George and Edith, married Henry A. Bishop, Jr., and in her behalf, guardian William A. W. Stewart filed special motions before the court that was trying to straighten out George's extremely complex affairs.

When Justice Davis of the New York State Supreme Court considered the matters at hand and figured out what might be coming to each child, there was a rude shock. Each of George and Edith's children was to have $562,000 from the Jay Gould estate— less than half of what they expected. Justice Davis found that the market value of one-sixth of the Jay Gould securities was $8,411, 379, plus interest for several months of $42,000. *Then the judge took out $2,800,000 for taxes and expenses,* and the reporters, putting the facts together, figured that the judge estimated that the total taxes, litigation costs, and other expenses of settling George's total estate would come to $16,000,000.

All the children of George Gould, legitimate and later legitimate, were aghast. So were the children of millionaires everywhere. Over half the George Gould estate to be lost in the settlement? What was the world coming to?

Worse, the litigation continued for four more years, eating up the time of fifty happy lawyers, who collected $2,703,635 in fees. Finally Anna and Frank won their case against the four trustees, who were ordered to pay back $16,000,000 to the estate. By this time, an *appreciation* of the securities made George's investments look millions of dollars better than they had before, but the attorneys and referees concluded that George and his fellow trustees had violated the letter of the law regarding trusteeships. Helen testified and continued to believe that George and the others had done what Jay had wanted them to do—but Jay was not there to say, and the court ruling held.

While all this litigation was going on, the various Gould heirs to George's share were trying to make ends meet, and the court awarded them various sums of money. Guinevere, within a year, married Viscount George St. Johns Broderick Dunsford and moved to England with her children to fight the battle of the Gould fortune by long distance. (She got $1,000,000, finally, in 1925). When anyone tried to move pictures or do anything else with property she thought she might own in part, she complained. Everyone else also complained about everything. The lawyers earned their money; that much is apparent. But matters ground to an end. Harry Payne Whitney bought the big mansion on Fifth Avenue for his mother, Mrs. William Kissam Vanderbilt. The house at Lakewood was sold to the Sisters of Mercy who turned it into a college, first buying up part of the furnishings, which sold for $91,000 at auction.

The Gould children sent representatives to the auction and purchased a few keepsakes. Edith and Gloria were there, and each bought furnishings and draperies to remind them of the dear, dead days. But as for the big buyers, they were Mrs. John Ringling, wife of the circus owner, Julian Noyes, an old friend of the Goulds, and Arthur Brisbane, the editor, who bought the Gould grand piano for $2,575.

When Georgian Court became a college, the court tennis court became a storage area, the racquet courts inside became the college girls' paint shop where they fabricated decorations for their proms, and the indoor polo field was floored over and became a combination assembly hall and dance hall for the girls—still as big as

Madison Square Garden. Little by little, the old place went down-hill because the college could not afford 20 gardeners. The funerary urns that lined the walks were overturned by boys coming to visit the girls. Inside Georgian Court itself, matters were left fairly much alone, except that in the drawing room off the dining room, the lovely Roman nudes were carefully clothed by the embarrassed nuns. A one-story strictly utilitarian library was erected on one side of the grand drive leading from Georgian Court to the Casino. Dormitories were built. One night part of the stables burned down —the rest were turned into a dining hall, classrooms, and utility rooms. The golf course was let go and eventually much of the 450 acres was sold off in part to finance building programs in a more expensive century than that in which Georgian Court was built. By the 1950s, like all the old mansions except those marked for preservation as historic sites, Georgian Court had been cut down to size in a world that found the imperial opulence of an earlier time insupportable.

With George's death, Jay Gould's heirs were reduced to five, and they prospered according to their bents. Edwin was perhaps the most prosperous, for he was the most industrious of the boys. He had for years been investing the interest and dividends from his share of the estate. When Edwin, Jr., died in 1917, the boy left an estate of nearly half a million dollars, obviously property given him by his father, which then reverted to the father. Edwin Gould put the money to use along with his other funds. In the early 1920s, he went into real estate speculation and development in New York City. He bought raw land along the Pelham Parkway in the Bronx—then a "suburb" of New York. The land consisted of 100 acres fronting on the parkway for more than a mile, begin-ning at Eastchester Road and running along the north side of the road to the bridge to the New Haven Railroad. Soon brick build-ings went up, and Edwin was deeply involved in multiple hous-ing. Two years later, Edwin sold out of these speculations, auction-ing the property off in lots which went for as high as $13,000 (for the corner of Pelham Parkway and Eastchester Road). He had expended a million dollars on development of the area, and this sale represented the seventeen houses and the eight hundred and twenty one lots that had not been gobbled up earlier. The sales of that day alone paid out the investment.

Edwin also dealt in midtown real estate, such as the old Hotel Sturtevant on Thirty-fifth Street just west of Broadway, which he bought, held, and then sold for $200,000 to other real estate operators.

Edwin was doing very, very well, and his fortune was increasing rapidly. And with the tragic death of one of his children a few years earlier, it was not likely to be dissipated by spreading out among a large number of heirs.

But Edwin's thoughts were not just for wealth. He organized the Edwin Gould Foundation, which established a large home for children at Pelham Parkway Gardens, where he had built the housing development. This home was what Edwin called his "clearing bureau"—an apt title to describe a peculiar charity. Edwin was always finding orphans and other underprivileged children, and sending them off to various institutions which he supported. But before a child could go to an institution he had to be vetted—that is, put into quarantine to see that he did not have measles or any other disease that could raise havoc in a children's home. Edwin's "clearing bureau" was a quarantine, no less, but what a quarantine! He had rooms filled with every imaginable toy, and other rooms filled with new clothing of every imaginable child's size. The urchins were brought to Edwin's clearing bureau where they were kept for a week or two, fed, and petted, and given any toys they wished, newly clothed, and sent off with money in their pockets to their new homes with the blessing of Edwin and the support of his foundation. The clearing bureau grew and grew until Edwin was reported to have perhaps $7,000,000 invested in plant and property.

Edwin also supported dozens of other charities, nearly all of them concerning children. It was said that nearly every children's home or camp or colony in the United States had a Gould cottage or some sign of Gould participation in its finances. He gave $30,000 to the Berkshire Industrial Farm School for Problem Boys to build a kitchen and laundry. He gave $10,000 to the Salvation Army. And he gave thousands to children's hospitals and other children's institutions.

In the 1920s, after nearly two decades, Edwin decided the area around Ardsley was becoming a little common and that it was time to get out of the Hudson River valley and down among his fellow millionaires on Long Island or in Connecticut. Agawam, the estate of 80 acres with its Spanish stucco house, was sold, and Edwin went to Oyster Bay, keeping his own Fifth Avenue house, of course. At first, Edwin leased a 30-acre estate belonging to William Vander Poel while his own house was being built. He chose 38 acres in Oyster Bay Cove, and upon them built Highwood, a two-story twenty-four-room brick house with marble fireplaces and hand-carved doorways, six bedrooms and six baths. The estate also had a seven-room servants' house, flanked by two guest cottages, a two-story gatehouse, a greenhouse, stables, and a swimming pool. Here Edwin lived until he died in 1933. Even before his death, the importance and even the artifacts of the Gould family were beginning to disappear from the American scene. After 1930, most of the articles in the newspapers that dealt with the Goulds concerned either scandal or the internal litigation over the residue of George's fortune (it was finally reduced to $5,000,-000 and most of the heirs received around a million dollars each). In 1927, Columbia University's historic Gould boathouse at the foot of One-hundred fifteenth on the Hudson River burned. It had been abandoned for several years, but, even so, the story made the front pages of the newspapers. Somehow there was in the end of this old place, which had housed so many successful Columbia crews, a concomitant feeling of an "end of the era."

Edwin was probably the happiest of the Goulds, and he might well have been the richest of them all had he not persisted in giving away huge sums of capital and much of his annual income each year. Happiest? Almost certainly, for he had one wife who

cherished him to the day of his death. True, he had suffered the
tragedy of his eldest son's death in the hunting accident at Jekyl
Island, but that pushed him into even greater gifts to children
everywhere in America.

In his later years, Edwin gloried in obscurity. He often disappeared from the house early in the morning, went to his office, and
then went out to some home he had founded for children to talk
to the social workers and play with the children. Many times, Sally
had to track him down by telephone to be sure he came back for
an engagement, and on one occasion, speaking to a social worker,
Edwin remarked ruefully that the social worker did not know
how lucky he was not having to put on white tie and tails that
night and go out to dinner with a lot of people he cared nothing
about.

His one son, Frank Miller Gould, was nearly as retiring as
Edwin. On the day that his father died, July 12, 1933, Frank was at
his camp at Ashland, Maine, and came down from there to the
house. Ashland, Maine, was not even Bar Harbor, and certainly
not the Hamptons or that resort passé, Newport. Frank had enlisted in the service during World War I, but few heard about it.
Frank would secure a captaincy in the Army of the United States
in World War II, and few would hear about that—certainly not
the collectors of tales about the very rich. Like his father, Frank
was a quiet investor all his life. Yet he had had his pranks: as a
young man he was once held in the Tombs overnight for speeding
in Manhattan.

In 1933, Edwin had made sure that the name of Gould would
continue to be connected with charity by allocating half his large
fortune to that end and by listing ninety of his favorite charities to
which the foundation ought to contribute. The amount was not
made public, but it was believed then to be higher than the residue
of Jay Gould's estate before it was distributed among the children,
for Edwin had saved his money, his Continental Match Company
had merged with Diamond to become the largest match company

in America, and his railroad investments had earned him a million dollars before he was twenty-one years old.

So the second child of Jay Gould was dead. The heritage as of 1933 might be assessed thus: George had tried to become the important capitalist, and, failing, had left upon his death a mess of litigation among family members. Edwin had retired early from public life (he retired from business only seven years before his death) and devoted himself to real charity, but it was so little known that the Goulds received little credit for it. In 1933, when Americans considered the Goulds, they did not think of Edwin, but of George, and the excesses of Georgian Court, and $500,000 necklaces that never existed, and the "swindles" of Jay Gould.

33

Helen and the Night-Blooming Cereus

———◆•••◆———

A detached observer could look at the Gould fortune in the middle of the American Depression and say that it represented, oddly enough, more concern for good works than most of the other fortunes, at least in terms of percentages. Edwin was spending his money on charity, and so was Helen. But not all the people who read the newspapers in the 1930s were detached.

———◆•••◆———

MANY sad stories about the Goulds and the mismanagement of their money in the 1920s and 1930s could be told. One day, for example, Lord Decies came back to the English estate that Vivien Gould's dowry had bought for the Baron and his family, and announced that he had just lost the place at cards. Howard Gould helped them out, and the Baron and Baroness were not left to walk the streets—although for some months they had a sticky time of it living in a dinky flat in Pall Mall.

An even sadder tale is that of young Edith who married Carroll Wainwright. They had three children, Stuyvesant Wainwright II, Caroline DePeyster Wainwright, and Carroll Livingston Wainwright, Jr. They were very much in love, the tempestuous daughter of millions and the temperamental artist, but they quarrelled frequently.

During the late years of the Roaring Twenties, they fought so often that they were seldom seen together at parties. She grew fat. At one time, she elected to lose 70 pounds for the opening of the opera season. They had built a handsome $350,000 house at Easthampton, the fashionable Long Island summer spa, and Carroll stayed there or at their New York apartment, while Edith went off alone to parties and house parties.

At one such party she met a charming Englishman named Hector MacNeal, a gentleman whose expensive tastes matched her own and whose temperament seemed more suited to her. Edith went to Lake Tahoe, set up residence in Nevada, divorced Carroll, and married Sir Hector.

They went to the Riviera to live. They took a villa, a handsome red and white villa with high cement walls topped by broken glass to assure privacy. They had privacy, so much of it that, having no playmates, the children played fantasy games among themselves. There were no neighbors except a bad-tempered old duke in the next villa who was constantly complaining about the noise from the MacNeal place. When they returned to America, Edith grew estranged from MacNeal, too, and she took to drinking much, eating little, and living so frenzied a life that she died at thirty-six, leaving the children to be supported by her trust fund. The house as Easthampton, Gull Crest, was sold to Juan Trippe, the Pan-American World Airways entrepreneur, lock, stock, and furnishings, for less than $.10 on the dollar. These were Depression years, and the bank's trust department was more interested in shedding an expensive white elephant for the children than in preserving the generous way of life for their future.

Another social tragedy—Howard Talleyrand-Périgord, Duke de Sagan, Anna's son by her second marriage, committed suicide in 1929 after a frustrating love affair. How shallow these lives could be!

The world heard and read much of this life but knew little of the life of Helen, Mrs. Finley J. Shepard, who lived a quiet existence in the old Jay Gould mansion at 579 Fifth Avenue, surrounded by the Victorian pomps of her father and mother, and who moved up to Lyndhurst in the summer, again to live with the past.

Yet did she live with the past? There has seldom been a woman more dedicated to life and living than Helen Gould. Married late, she adopted and raised four children, Finley J. Shepard, Olivia Margaret Shepard, Helen Anna Shepard, and Louis Seton. When Seton was married in 1934, he chose as bride a young woman named Celeste Andrews who was blessed with a sharp curiosity and an excellent memory.

In her book, *Helen Gould Was My Mother-In-Law,* Miss Andrews recreated life with Helen Gould as it was lived, day in and day out, at the old house where no liquor was allowed. Sitwell, the butler, always did have gin on hand for the youngsters at Lyndhurst, where they had to go to church twice on Sunday and swim in the big pool wearing black stockings because the Bible said something against swimming in bare legs, and at Roxbury, where Finley Shepard, a fine understanding man, went off to dynamite obstructions in the countryside while Helen held a sewing class for the girls of the community.

One tale, perhaps, tells of the gentleness and old-fashioned purity of Helen's life better than any other—the tale of the night-blooming cereus.

Late in spring or early in summer, the night-blooming cereus was supposed to perform in one of the many greenhouses at Lyndhurst. Each year Helen went to Lyndhurst early, some might even call it winter, and while there, she sent back a barrage of notes to her friends and relatives, one of her favorite topics being the state of the night-blooming cereus.

In the spring of 1934, Celeste and Louis, her husband-to-be, drove down to Lyndhurst. They came to the gatehouse, and there encountered Mr. Allan, the superintendent:

Louis called out: "Hello Mr. Allan," and a pleasant-looking middle-aged gentleman in a tweed jacket and gray flannel slacks walked briskly over and greeted us in a thick Scotch burr.

"Hello Mister Louis. I maun say yer lookin' braw the noo. Yer puir mither is aw a dither o'er the wee blawsoms comin' oot the nicht. The cereus, ye ken."

Celeste did not understand this greeting but Louis Seton did, and soon they were driving into the estate, past what seemed to be endless lawns and gardens, the gravel drive lined with old elms and linden trees. After a quarter of a mile of driving up the hill they came over a crest, and there stood the Gothic castle, Lyndhurst.

Miss Stebbins and Miss Davis, Helen's companions and secretaries, met them, along with ten dogs, but not by Chinky (who was the sixth Chinky at that point). Celeste was shown to her room, and there she picked up a slim black volume:

Bible Verses to Memorize
Selected by
Helen Miller Gould Shepard

She went for a swim, and then she met Helen just before dinner. The conversation turned to nature.

Mrs. Shepard was voluble on any subject to do with nature—at times, even lyrical. This was so different from her limited conversation in the city. On almost every subject at 579 she talked in isolated words and phrases. With people, even with her own immediate family, she often seemed a stranger; but at Lyndhurst among the birds and the flowers, she was always at home.

"Of course, Celeste," she went bubbling on, "you knew what we are all waiting for?"

"I think so—the night blooming cereus."

"Exactly my dear, the Hylocereus undatus."

"Last year the blossoms were rather small," Louis said.

"Yes," she said, "but they did their best."

Louis apologized. "I meant no offense."

"Of course you didn't, but we shouldn't talk about our flowers without thinking, should we?"

At dinner Celeste stepped on Chinky No. 6, and soon learned why there were so many Pekingese in the succession—Chinky was picked up and pampered and fed bits of chutney and other hot condiments. Much of the art of living at Lyndhurst was taught to Celeste that evening by her adoptive sister-in-law, Olivia, who was also weekending at the house.

At 10 o'clock everyone in the household kissed Helen good night quite ceremoniously and went trouping off to bed. Then, sometime in the middle of the night, the household was aroused— it was time for the night-blooming cereus. All except Helen assembled and waited.

And then we heard Mrs. Shepard's voice inside: "At last! At last! Isn't it thrilling? Isn't it wonderful," and she toddled through the door looking like an apparition. She wore a white, wooly bathrobe, and on her head at an angle a lace night cap. To help guide her through the night, she carried an enormous flashlight.

"There is not a moment to lose," she cried. "Follow me. We must all hurry down the path to the greenhouse."

The street lamps along the cinder paths had been lit, and it was as bright as day. We hurried along after Mrs. Shepard who trotted as fast as her little feet could carry her. We made a strange ghostlike procession hastening to our destination. When we approached the entrance to the greenhouse, a shrill piercing voice—half alto and half scream—cut through the night: "Wait for me. Heaven-a-day, wait for me."

It was Miss Davis, whom we had all forgotten in the excitement. "Wait for me," she cried, and she ran up wheezing and out of breath. "I didn't hear the bells," she gasped. "Thank Heavens, I'm here on time."

"Don't worry, there is time," Miss Stebbins said putting her arm around her companion for support.

We all quieted down when Mrs. Shepard opened the door to the greenhouse, turned, faced us, and said solemnly:

"Now we will enter and proceed quietly and orderly to the south wing."

The greenhouse was a long building subdivided into many sections. In some were coffee and cinnamon plants, in others roses and lilies. One contained endless varieties of ferns, elephant ear, and other tropical plants. In another were tier upon tier of orchids, and I recognized an old friend—*Cattleya trianae*. Finally, we arrived at the last section. Mrs. Shepard hesitated a moment—then quickly opened the door and looked in. Her expression told us we were not to be disappointed.

"How beautiful! How divine!" she said.

We walked inside. The entire end wall of the greenhouse was a foam of white. Hundreds of white flowers were born and being born. Hundreds of white flowers were unfurling and unfurling. This was the night-blooming cereus in its white radiant glory. This is what made Mrs. Shepard say: "How beautiful! How divine!" This was the white vision that rang the bells in the ivory tower.

No one spoke. Sitwell and the gardeners stood off quietly to one side. Soon the other servants in the house began to arrive in little groups and took their places along the edge of the wall. It was a strange, unearthly, pre-dawn gathering. I looked at Mrs. Shepard.

Her face was fatigued. There were lines of anguish in it. Tears were streaming down her face. She made no attempt to hide them. Suddenly she perked her head up, straightened her bent figure, and said loud enough for everyone to hear: "Thank you—thank you all very much." Then she left hurriedly by herself.

Soon the rest of us followed, and we walked slowly and silently back to the castle. As we started up the marble steps to the door I glanced back over my shoulder. One by one the little lights on the cinder path to the greenhouse were slowly blinking off.

This event occurred in the autumn of Helen's life, when she had mellowed much from the earlier days. She suffered six strokes, over six years, beginning in 1932. Each stroke forced her to cut down a bit more on her activity, until the last one, in 1938, which brought on the end. She died December 21 at Roxbury.

Could it be? Upon her death, the New York *Times* devoted an editorial to Helen Miller Gould Shepard and her works, noting that she was often called the "best loved woman in the country." There was a change for the Goulds—from most hated father to best loved daughter.

"She not only reached forth her hand to the needy," said the *Times*. "She gave constructively to institutions of learning, to patriotic movements and especially to the memory of the Republic's great souls. Her own works will long be 'praised in the gates.'"

34

How Frank Came Back

---

*Helen was religious, her brother Frank
was very nearly apostate. Helen was virtuous, Frank was a rake. Helen was loyal,
Frank brought about the final dissolution
of the family. Helen was sober, Frank was
a drunk. Helen was a bore, Frank was a
card. Could one see the image of the father
in either child?*

ODDLY enough, the younger generation seemed to have less vitality
than the elder. Vivien, Lady Decies, died in 1931 after a most
difficult life. Jay Gould, namesake of the founder of the fortune,
died in 1935 after a lifetime spent largely in court tennis, with
some excursions into real estate development. The estate he left
was small—it could hardly have been otherwise since he was not a
"producer," and he had started with only around a million dollars.

So, while the unspectacular third generation was dying off, the
most spectacular of the Goulds since Jay himself was flourishing.
Frank, who had spent the first forty years of his life as a profligate,
suddenly began to sit up and notice the world around him. Per-

haps it was the character of the third woman he married—
Florence LaCaze. She had been an actress and she was a woman
of strong character. Whatever the cause, Frank suddenly ceased
drinking and became, of all things, an up-and-coming business-
man. He began buying real estate, particularly in the south of
France. Whether Frank's initial success was dictated by business
acumen or money and luck is debatable. He decided to go into the
gambling business on the Riviera, and soon was known back in
New York to an amused society as the "King of the Croupiers."
He built a casino at Nice, the Palais Méditerranée, for $5,000,000.
He built a casino at Juan-les-Pins. He took on hotel investments:
Le Provençal Hotel and the Majestic at Nice, and the Mont
Mournier Chalet at Beuil. He restored the spa at Bagnoles de
L'Orne, 150 miles from Paris, and built a casino there. He kept
going and going until 1930 when his real estate holdings in the
Riviera and particularly the Côte d'Azur were said to be worth
more than $20,000,000. He was responsible for the introduction of
the chain ownership idea in France and was the forerunner of the
"mob" in the ownership of chains of casinos.

The trouble was that the casinos were gambling houses and, as
such, required a special type of management that Frank did not
understand. Take the Palais Méditerranée, for example: Frank
opened that marvelous casino in 1929. It was built of glistening
white marble over two acres of ground and furnished with the
utmost in *luxe*. It was, in short, "a palace the Caesars could not
have built," the most impressive gambling casino in the world. But
in its first five months, the casino *lost* $800,000.

He built the hotel and developed the resort of Beuil, and lost
money in his operations. He took over the opera house at Nice,
announcing that he was going to stage operas with seats at $1
top—pop opera, in other words.

But in 1932, feeling the press of his American investments, no
doubt, in the general depression, Frank decided to turn over the
operation of his various enterprises to experts and simply to retain
the ownership—to take his profits in exploiting real estate values.

Frank certainly suffered during the Depression. In 1934, his Palais Mediterranée was damaged by fire, and, when repaired, had so few gambling customers that it shut down for the winter season. Growing annoyed when the lessees closed down his business, Frank took it back from them, then reopened the casinos himself in 1934 after declining a bid to operate them by the Monte Carlo company. The Monte Carlo company was *the* gambling operator of the Riviera, and Frank's decision took a certain amount of courage—it was tantamount to declaring war on the Mafia.

The Monte Carlo company had a good laugh, however. For Frank's resort at Beuil, 60 miles inland from Nice, flopped like a French pancake. He had spent $2,000,000 there to create a vacation spot for Europeans that would rival St. Moritz. He had built a beautiful resort hotel, the Chalet de Mont Mournier—and it was bankrupt. That summer of 1934, Frank showed that he knew how to do business on the Riviera: he leased his Palais Mediterranée to the Monte Carlo Company for thirty years at a million francs a year.

That year, Frank also gave some indication that he might consider returning to America and American life. He bought a house at Ardsley for $250,000, and Florence, quizzed by the press, announced that they would retain their French financial interests and spend part of the year on the Mediterranean, but that their principal home would be in the United States.

But then Frank ran into the new American income tax system—he had been away for nearly 30 years, after all. He liked neither the system nor what it portended for his fortunes, so he turned back toward France while still keeping a foothold in America. When war came five years later, Frank was in France and he stayed in France, not bothered by the Germans.

Florence spent much of the war in Paris, working publicly in hospitals and secretly for the Resistance. In 1944, when the Americans were sweeping through France, the Germans suddenly had the idea they might better their position by kidnaping some Americans, and one of those they considered was Frank Gould. Florence then carried out a series of financial maneuvers and investments and managed to save her husband. After the war, the Goulds were investigated by everyone in sight, by the American government, the French government, and the government of Monaco. When all the investigations were finished, it was agreed that the Goulds had not collaborated with the enemy, although that charge had been made in the excitement of the early days of peace.

Frank, who was over sixty and in poor health, had lived quietly, and the Germans had regarded him as French because of his long residence in France. Only when they began fortifying the Riviera had he been forced to go up into the mountains to live because, technically, he was an enemy alien.

In 1948, Frank was sued by the Baroness Anne Vilbert de Sairigne, who claimed that she had sheltered him from the Gestapo from 1943 until the end of the war in her villa at Juan-les-Pins, and that he had given her a check for $400,000 for her efforts which, later, he had ungratefully stopped payment on. The case was tried in America because the check was drawn on an American bank—and it went as far as the United States Supreme Court, which refused to hear it, just as all of the lower courts had.

The war over, Frank and his wife continued the development of Juan-les-Pins. They opened two hotels, and they bought more real estate. In 1952, their reputation as wealthy investors was so well known that they were burglarized—thieves forced their way into the offices at the Hotel Alba and stole the hotel payroll of $3,000 along with $286,000 in negotiable bonds.

In 1952, Frank Gould began disposing of his estate rather than have it go to the governments of the countries in which he lived and held investments in the form of death taxes. He gave $1,500,-000 to his alma mater, New York University. In return, the university gave Frank a Doctor of Engineering degree, which was presented by Chancellor Henry Heald at Juan-les-Pins since the eighty-year-old Frank could not come to America.

In 1954, New York University staged a ceremonial opening of the student center that had been built with Frank's money, and as three hundred and fifty people watched, Frank's New York representative walked up to Chancellor Heald and gave him another check for $1,000,000 for the university. That same year, Frank gave his estate at Ardsley to New York University for use as a conference center.

Two years later, Frank died at Juan-les-Pins. His estate quite possibly rivalled that of his father, but no one would ever know (at least outside the family) because in a world of high taxation, much had been done to keep quiet the extent of this estate. In 1925, he sold a small part of it—the Virginia utilities—for $11,000,000. Most of it went to his wife and daughters, Mrs. Helen G. Marat of Lausanne, and Mrs. Dorothy Burns of Mexico City. The girls were not mere professional expatriates but highly Frenchified ones who had also married into the French nobility. But no matter the extent of Frank Gould's holdings, he had never touched the capital of his father's trust bequest, and he kept piling up new capital of his own for nearly forty years after his initial profligacy. When he died, he left the hotels, the gambling casinos, the resorts, and the land to Florence and his daughters, and Florence had in addition two villas in Juan-les-Pins, one to live in and one to entertain guests. As for the amount, who could estimate it? It was said that Frank Gould owned Juan-les-Pins.

35

Poor Gloria

------◆◆◆------

Fewer than sixty years after the death of the middle-aged millionaire, affairs in the United States had changed so much that the story of his life and times was ancient history. Nearly all the methods he had used to garner his huge fortune had been declared illegal—largely because Gould, Sage, Harriman, Vanderbilt, and countless others so abused the privileges of business that government stepped in to protect the general public. The bankers came under equally tight scrutiny—the Morgans, Kuhns, Loebs, and all the other investment bankers—because they had added a new element to the American scene: cartelization. And so the world changed.

------◆◆◆------

BY MIDCENTURY, only two of Jay Gould's children still lived, Howard and Anna. Howard lived very quietly in England, spending much of his time salt-water fishing and receiving old friends. He was particularly taken by the children of Edith Kingdon Wainwright —and they needed a friend, having been pushed from pillar to post all their lives by the peculiar ways of their mother. So Stuyvesant, Caroline, and Carroll Wainwright spent much time with their great uncle. From this association, oddly enough, only Caroline emerged with much interest in the Goulds as a family. She became something of a student of the Goulds and a fierce defender of the oft-maligned name. Stuyvesant Wainwright grew up to become a lawyer and to serve in Congress from Long Island. Carroll Wainwright went into business in New York. Most of the young American Goulds became professional people. Young George Gould became a broker. Young Jay Gould became an insurance executive.

There were scandals among these younger Goulds, but their age was a more scandalous age, and from about 1900 on, the newspapers took a positively fiendish approach to the scions of the old millionaire families, viewing their marital excursions with alarm. The Goulds were far from angels—like other children of the very rich. They could create their own morality because, with their money, they were responsible to no one except the law.

In the last half of the twentieth century, morality came to be divorced from success and money. But prior to the 1950s, an American who wanted to get ahead in the worlds of business, government, or the professions had best remain relatively subservient to the popular mores of political and social life and relatively sober, relatively quiet, and relatively restrained about his sex life. The Bohemians and the very rich alone were able to live as they wished before this time.

Gloria, the baby of the George Gould family, probably received the most attention of any of her generation of Goulds as far as the press was concerned, at least while she was growing up. Gloria was fifteen when George died in Mentone, and she was taken in by her brother Kingdon to be reared in society. She married Henry Bishop when she was seventeen against the wishes of nearly everybody in the family. Henry expected to live in Bridgeport, Connecticut, and commute to New York. Gloria quickly disabused him of this tranquil dream, insisting that they stay on in New York. They stayed and Gloria pursued her career of teaching dancing. How her mother would have hated it! But Edith was long gone, and Gloria had her way.

On March 12, 1925, her daughter Gioa was born. "She will amount to something in spite of being born a Gould," said Gloria, who was suffering from the publicity given the family errors. "If she wants to be a laundress, I'll help her be a good one. I want her, first of all, to be a real human being."

With so independent a turn of mind, Gloria was bound to be unhappy in her world. A few months after Gioa's birth, Gloria rushed off to Paris, intending to get a divorce, then changed her mind and came back to New York. But she did not settle down. She became managing directress of the Embassy Theater, an upper-crust movie house. That lasted a few months, and then Gloria went to Lake Como with Gioa and without Henry Bishop. Gioa and the governess fell ill with typhoid. The governess died, and the doctors were not sure that Gioa would live, but Gloria nursed the little girl back to health. Then she divorced Henry Bishop, who was very civilized about it, saying it was his fault because she had been a spoiled child and he had not asserted himself enough in the beginning of their marriage.

Bishop married again immediately, but Gloria was single until 1930 when she married a man outside the brittle society in which she had grown up, Wallace MacFarlane Barker, a paint contractor. They moved to Phoenix where Gloria bought an estate and seemed to be very happy. Barker adopted Goia, and it seemed that they were settling down to live really new lives. But the old way, the yearning for distinction without earning it, was too great, and in 1940, Gioa was sent east to "make a proper debut" at Kingdon's home in New York. Exposed to society, Gioa reacted as her mother had years before. She met a young Harvard man named William Grimditch. In June, 1943, Gioa and Grimditch were married and went off on their honeymoon.

Two months later, Gloria and Mac Barker, who went out frequently in Phoenix society and drank heavily, went to a party, returned home at 1 o'clock in the morning, and stayed up most of the rest of the night talking and drinking. Gloria woke later and decided to go for a swim. She did not come back.

At noon, Barker began searching for her. He found her at the bottom of the swimming pool. The coroner decided that Gloria had slipped on wet leaves, struck her head on the edge of the pool, slipped in, and drowned.

Gloria left $50,000 to her husband, plus the income on a $100,-000 trust fund. Gioa was to have $25,000 when she became twenty-one, $50,000 when she was twenty-five, and perhaps another half to three-quarters of a million dollars was put in trust for her children.

Gioa became pregnant in 1944, and a son, William, was born in 1945. Then she became pregnant again just before William Grimditch went overseas with the army to Korea. Gloria Joia was born in May, 1946.

Gioa was also the victim of money, loneliness, and the "society syndrome." When Grimditch came back from Korea, he read in her diary the intimate details of her relations with Blake Brophy, the son of a local bank president. And so the divorce action began.

36

The Return of the Duchess

————◆•••◆————

*Not all the stories about the Goulds
were quite so gamey. One could find
whatever one was looking for within the
confines of this large family.*

————◆•••◆————

DURING the 1930s, Anna, Duchess de Talleyrand, became one of
France's best-loved figures. Anna was middle-aged then, the
storms and stresses of her early life largely forgotten, the last bit-
terness wiped out by George's death and the settlement of the
claims against the old estate. A very wealthy woman in her own
right, she had perhaps $12,000,000 when Jay Gould's affairs were at
last settled. But her husband, the Duke, was also well-to-do, and he
was not the spendthrift that Boni had been, so her life was more
tranquil than that of most of the Goulds. She was honored by
France for her work in the war and for her work after the war

with its relicts. She founded Le Phare de France (The Lighthouse of France) for work among the blind. And she had other charities.

When Helen died, Anna inherited Lyndhurst, probably because she was the only one, aside from Howard and Frank, who could afford to keep up the place, and neither of the brothers had the slightest interest in taking on the huge house.

Anna came to America in 1939 and took over. She left the house very much as it had been in Jay's time but removed many of Helen's religious articles that filled the rooms. During her occupancy, the house became celebrated for its parties. During World War II, when rationing cut into the living of most in America, Anna had *paté de foie gras aux truffes de Périgord* flown in from France, along with Guinea hen which would be served under glass, and cases and cases of champagne. She served these meals at the big table in Jay's dining room, on golden service with golden implements. One might say that Anna ran the last great opulent house in the United States.

But that was not all Anna did during the war. She did help with war work, and she invited some refugees from France to live on her estate. She gave considerable sums to the YMCA, and especially to the naval branch which was assisting the young men, merchant seamen and sailors, of France. And she gave parties at Lyndhurst for the French sailors.

Anna continued to be the duchess, to live the noble life, until her death in 1961. Her money, of course, went to her own children, the three by de Castellane and Hélène Violette, née de Talleyrand, who had married Count Joseph de Pourtales, her last son having died by his own hand years earlier.

When Anna died, she left Lyndhurst to the American people if they wanted it, along with a trust fund for its preservation, and after some discussion, Congress voted to accept the gift. The old estate was turned over to the National Trust for Historic Preservation. A discussion was begun by the mayor and village trustees of Tarrytown, New York, who did not want to accept the gift because, they said, Jay Gould was one of the old "robber barons" and should not be honored by American society.

The trust established, the house was opened to the public, but so queasy were the officials of the National Trust, that they did not live up entirely to the spirit in which Anna left the house to America. She had stipulated that Lyndhurst was to be a memorial to her father and mother. The guides who took the people through Lyndhurst were loath to discuss Jay Gould or his family—except the Duchess—and tried to confine the conversations in the tours to matters of architecture, even though the house was almost entirely as Jay had left it, even down to his crystal ball gazing equipment. So much for the impact of the "robber baron" myth.

37

Poor Little Rich Kids

———◄•••►———

*The heritage seemed to go on and on.
The sons, the grandsons, and the great
grandsons were tainted by the Gould
name. These children resented the hypoc-
risies of American society, and tended to
believe that they were mistreated in everything they did because they were Goulds.
How they comported themselves had nothing to do with the facts. Some of them,
however, comported themselves with considerable dignity, and some others quite
amazed the world with what they
produced.*

———◄•••►———

SOCIALLY speaking, by the 1890s the Goulds were accepted within
that brittle group known as New York society, and by the end of
the first decade of the twentieth century, not even Vanderbilt com-
plaints stood against them. Society was largely a question of money,
at least one generation removed, and it continued to be that way as
long as it lasted. The fact was that by the fourth generation, the

Goulds were interested in their Gould ancestry only faintly, and usually did not like to talk about it unless someone began a conversation about "robber barons."

Caroline DePeyster Wainwright, daughter of Edith Kingdon, granddaughter of George, and great granddaughter of Jay, did have some hopes of recreating the picture of her family in more gentle colors. She did all the things that girls are supposed to do in polite society, went to private schools, to Miss Porter's Finishing School, to Pine Manor Junior College.

In the whirlwind of society life, Caroline at one time became acquainted with Gloria Vanderbilt, "the poor little rich girl" who, in the 1930s, was shoved about by members of her family who were quarrelling over her trust fund. Caroline and Gloria never became fast friends, though, because one day when Gloria wanted Caroline to come to a party, she had her social secretary call. Caroline was affronted, and that ended the friendship.

Caroline lived a busy social life between the activities of New York and those at Uncle Howard's estates in England and in Easthampton. She met many young men in short order, and she was married, after a whirlwind courtship, to Edward Townsend Shean, a handsome young naval officer, in 1945, and they had five children. They divorced, she married again, and this husband died within a year. All this while, Caroline made it a point to keep in touch with the other Goulds—farflung as they were. She visited Georgian Court. She visited Lyndhurst. She went around New York, locating the spots where the family houses had once stood. She took a real interest in the story of the Goulds, and she was one of the few to make it a point to become associated with the vanishing splendor. Years after Juan Trippe had bought the big house at Easthampton from her mother's estate, Caroline purchased it back and made it into her summer home and a kind of Gould museum. The house did not go back very far in Gould parlance—really only to Edith Kingdon's generation—but it symbolized, in a way matched only by Lyndhurst, the glory of the past. Caroline was the curator of this past, as far as Gouldiana was concerned.

Three other members of the family contributed to another kind of heritage. One was Howard, the last of Jay Gould's sons to die. Howard's wife, Kathrine, died in Virginia in 1930 after a long life and an interesting career which included some success as a novelist and magazine writer. Seven years later, Howard married a Berlin actress named Margaret Mosheim, one of the most promising students of Max Reinhardt in the Deutsches Theater, and former wife of Oscar Homolka, the well-known actor. Ten years later Howard and his second wife were divorced, so when Howard died in New York in 1959, at the age of eighty-eight, he left no children at all. Under the terms of Jay Gould's will, his share of the estate was split up into tiny pieces. The surviving heirs of George, Edwin, and Frank all received parts, as did Anna, who outlived Frank. Since Helen had left no children of her own, her share was also split among the others. But the Jay Gould part of Howard's estate was nothing compared to all that he left—for by not having a huge family, by working at his investments, and by living quietly if luxuriously (he chased actresses all his life but with some circumspection in the later years), Howard left an estate of $62,000,000 to twenty-eight heirs. The trouble again was taxes, and as it turned out, $50,000,000 of the total was eaten up by the state and federal tax authorities because Howard had not left his money in a manner that would take advantage of the loopholes!

When Howard Gould died, he had proved several hitherto unknown things about the Goulds—that a Gould could make a huge fortune without becoming a public figure outside the society pages, that a Gould could become the No. 1 member of the New York Yacht Club, an honor he achieved by longevity (he was No. 2 on the New York Stock Exchange, which is not nearly so significant in society), and that a Gould could make as much money as his father had made.

Edwin had done almost the same. Given less time, and given his proclivity for charity, his fortune was not so spectacular as Howard's, but it was large. And Edwin had left his money to his son, Frank, who in turn had left it to his two children, Marianne and Edwin. Marianne married a young man named John Wright McDonough and went off to spend her patrimony domestically. But what of Edwin, who could be supposed to be one of the new millionaires of America, receiving a larger slice of the Gould fortune because he came from a line that had not spread out?

Edwin became what the French would call a banker, and what Americans call "an investor." He did not take a seat on the Exchange. He married a Bermuda girl and was divorced a few years later. He opened an office in New York, employed several secretaries, an old family advisor named Hubert Longua (whose father had served his father and grandfather), and established the Edwin Gould & Co. investment firm, of which Daniel W. Hofgren was president in the 1960s. Then Edwin went fishing. Or on safari. Or to Bermuda.

Edwin's great love was the out-of-doors, and particularly the Caribbean. While others stayed at home and invested, Edwin spent as much time as he could hunting big-game fish, and in 1968, he dedicated himself even more to sport, building not a yacht, for yachts were passé, but a big modern sport-fishing craft which was equipped with every conceivable luxury.

As for investment, the Edwin Gould Company was not involved in railroads or anything nearly so puerile. The Gould Company invested in controlling interests, if possible, of producing industries. The company, in 1968, was looking into a huge cane sugar plantation in Florida, which had netted $1,500,000 for two or three years running before the Gould Company took interest, and which had an unused crop allocation that was worth many thousands of dollars in cash. The owner was an elderly man who wanted to get out of business. The plant was up-to-date, and it had been checked out by industrial engineers and investment analysts as an A-1 investment.

Edwin was what in modern American parlance could be called a "sportsman." His life was dedicated to pleasure and to cautious retention of the fortune by reinvestment of the moneys.

The old Jay Gould way was being followed, fittingly, by the eldest son of the eldest son of the eldest son of Jay Gould—Kingdon Henry Gould.

Kingdon was the eldest son of Kingdon and Annunziata. He grew up in and around New York and at the retreat in the Catskills, Furlough Lodge. He attended proper private schools (Buckley, Milbrook) and grew up like the other Goulds, with all their apparent advantages and hidden disadvantages.

Kingdon was a small, wiry boy who had a great interest in music and considerable talent in playing the violin. In time, he went to Yale to study for his bachelor's degree. World War II began just after he was eighteen years old, and Kingdon enlisted as a private in the army. He served in an armored unit through the war, as an enlisted man, was wounded twice, for which he received Purple Hearts, and won two silver stars for gallantry in action. He also was so badly wounded in the arm in one engagement in Europe that the violin became a matter of history except for his own amusement.

After the war, Kingdon Gould went back to Yale, finished his course, made Phi Beta Kappa, and was graduated from Yale Law School. He then joined the law firm of a brother-in-law, Guy Martin, in Washington.

There Kingdon encountered a bright young Italian-American named Dominic Antonelli, who had grown up in the streets of Washington and had gone into the parking lot business. Seldom had two men seemed more different: Gould was urbane and moneyed, and Antonelli was the Gould of four generations earlier, a high-school dropout, a self-made man. But the two men shared many attitudes and interests—Gould's mother was Italian—and soon they were in partnership in Washington and building a parking empire.

Their first firm, called Auto Centers, was formed in 1953. They went on to build more parking buildings and to buy lots. In the three years between 1961 and 1964, for example, they bought one hundred and thirty-four separate pieces of property in the District of Columbia. They took a long-term lease with an option to buy on the Capital Garage, Washington's largest. They bought half interest in the Mayflower Hotel. They went into parking ventures in Los Angeles and Baltimore, and in Washington, one of the nation's fastest growing cities in the 1960s, they kept buying and buying.

From parking, Gould and Antonelli branched into apartment houses and office buildings, and in a fashion characteristic of Jay, they rounded out their investment picture by going into banking, organizing the Madison National Bank which is closely connected with their ventures. They also organized a bank in Conway, New Hampshire, the home town of Mrs. Gould, the former Mary Bunce Thorne.

In the parent company and their subsidiaries in the 1960s, the Antonelli-Gould holdings were estimated to be worth around $25,000,000, and in 1968, the partners were moving ahead so that the values might easily triple in a decade.

This Gould, then, displayed the talents of his great grandfather. Taciturn, slender, and dark like his great grandfather, for some reason he brought down on himself the same wrath on the part of the press. In 1966, the Washington *Post* published a six-part series of articles about the new parking multimillionaires, complaining that their activity was scarcely in the public interest and recalling that Gould was the great grandson of "the Mephistopheles of Wall Street."

"He's the scion of one of the wealthiest dynasties in American history, and one of the heirs to an $82,000,000 fortune."

Perhaps, but what Kingdon inherited could scarcely be called a large part of an $82,000,000 fortune. As one of three children of Kingdon Gould, this Kingdon was lucky if he inherited a million dollars, so great was the fragmentation of the fortune, and although the fortunes of Helen and Howard went back into the general fund, by the time the tax collectors were finished with them, there was little to be distributed among twenty-five to thirty heirs.

Kingdon Gould, like so many of the other Goulds, was, in the 1960s, quite used to living with the public image of the "robber barons" thrust upon him. Yet he did not like the image. "Why are we Goulds always chosen to play the heavy?" he asked one day. But he was prepared to live with it, to avoid the press and publicity, and to go his own way in the manner of his great grandfather.

Kingdon Henry Gould, like his old ancestor, also believed in a large family, and as of 1968, there were nine children's rooms in the big Gould house atop a pleasant hill outside Laurel, Maryland. Not all the nine were in residence, the eldest daughter was married and some were at college or at school, but there were the nine Gould children, each to be provided with an inheritance. Their prospects have perhaps been indicated by their family's past.

The Social History

AS A whole generation of muckrakers would have it, the great American fortunes were conceived in Hell and acquired almost entirely by evil-doing at the expense of the American people. This theory, which still dominates the teaching of American history, holds that somehow a great nation grew, industries arose, capital suddenly appeared, and the national product burgeoned, *in spite of,* and not *because of* the men who exploited iron, steel, communications, rails, shipping, merchandising, and the other materials of a powerful civilization.

The exploiters are called "robber barons." The term was widely publicized, if not invented, by Gustavus Myers in his devastating, socialist history of the great American fortunes. This period is vaguely fixed by historians, but essentially, it begins with John Jacob Astor, who created a fortune in the fur business and then invested it in New York City real estate. There were rich men before John Jacob Astor, but most of them owed their fortunes to position and prestige under the British crown, or going back further, under the Dutch, whose grants were later honored by England. Historians somehow do not equate skullduggery and scheming at the royal courts to secure huge grants of property with the skullduggery of business operation. If they do make the comparison, the businessmen always come out worst. The difference is hard to discern between the exploitation carried out by an Astor, for example, whose rent collectors were sorely hated and dreaded by the poor of New York City, and the exploitation of the colonists of Pennsylvania by the family of William Penn in England, a situation so painful that long before the Revolution, Benjamin Franklin and others were sent to England to try to secure relief for the colony from excessive taxation by this family.

The period of the "robber barons" runs—and there is little argument about the end of it—until men of social conscience began to assume control of American government, that is, beginning with the 1880s and coming to a climax in the administrations of Theodore Roosevelt and William Howard Taft when the trusts were brought under a degree of effective regulation.

One might say, then, that the great American fortunes considered in the "robber baron" class were acquired from the 1830s until about 1900—a date that must be used to include the full unfolding of the Rockefeller financial dynasty. Depending on the historian, the class may or may not include Astor (who defied even President Jefferson's Embargo in his search for fortune). But it would include Commodore Vanderbilt, the steamship and railroad entrepreneur, George Law, who was known as "King of the New York Horse Cars," Daniel Drew, Jim Fisk, DuPonts, Guggenheims, Pierpont Morgan, Bet-A-Million Gates, Andrew Carnegie, the Mellons, the Rockefellers, and most certainly, above all others, Jay Gould, who has come down in history as the vilest "robber baron" of them all.

It is not necessary to hold that Jay Gould was a spiritual descendent of St. Francis of Assisi to believe that he was not as black a fellow as he has been painted. In his personal life, for example, he was the superior of most, and especially of such as Vanderbilt, Morgan, and the Guggenheims, several of whom were known for their mistresses as well as their millions. In his business life, he was certainly no trickier than Carnegie and Rockefeller, both of whom used the under-the-table rebate as a cornerstone of business, and his stock watering ventures were small compared to those of Vanderbilt and the refunding operations of Morgan, which virtually destroyed one whole class of railroad investment in favor of another.

Can any of these men be faulted for what they did?

Not unless historians are ready to condemn the entire business community, the entire political community, the entire social community of the time. Thus the dragging forth of the most successful simply becomes an exercise in muckraking, which may have served a useful purpose in the early years of the century in securing reforms, but which, half a century later, is no better than small town gossip.

Still, the historians of high and lofty tone have a point: the business and political communities were exceedingly immoral to those who expected businessmen to abide by the Golden Rule. The fact is that businessmen then and now were and are forever doing unto others what they would prefer *not* to have done to themselves, and that total honesty in business was and is likely to leave the businessman with empty pockets. (Honesty, for example, would demand absolute truth in advertising.) Standards of morality were low everywhere in Jay Gould's day—for a homely example, take the case of the drover who herded his thirsty cattle to a point just short of town, fed them salt to increase their thirst, then watered them to add perhaps 10 per cent to their weight. The next step was the wholesale butcher, who cheated on his weights and sold old beef for choice steer meat. Finally, the retailer carefully watered his hamburger and his whiskey, sanded his sugar, and shortweighted the customer.

Or take politics. Among Jay Gould's most serious malpractices, as seen by the moralist historians, was his buying of the New York Legislature during the Erie fight, his purchase of the judgment of two or three New York judges, and his bribery and attempted bribery of members of President Grant's "kitchen cabinet."

Until the Civil War, the standards of morality of the small United States federal government were regarded as pure enough for practical purposes, yet the question of conflict of interest did not arise often except in political matters. Thus was Daniel Webster able to plead cases before the United States Supreme Court as a lawyer, then cheerfully, and without thought of dishonesty, turn around and help legislate on matters in which he was a special pleader and for which he had taken high fees. James Monroe was accused of overcharging the government for expenses when he was envoy to France and Spain, but the base for these charges was his breach with the Jeffersonian wing of the Republican Party. Andrew Jackson's "kitchen cabinet" was notoriously loose with funds. Nicholas Biddle fought with Jackson, Biddle upholding the *right* of certain wealthy Philadelphians and others to manipulate the National Bank for the benefit of their personal fortunes—but even this was not the basic issue in the bank fight. It had long been accepted practice—and it still is—that men who rise high in public office achieve fortune as well as fame. (How many poor United States Senators are seated in Congress, and precisely how did Lyndon Johnson acquire his fortune of some sixteen million dollars before he became President without once in those climbing years having his foot out of the public trough?) The point is not raised to condemn American practice but to note how little it has changed in essence no matter how much attention is now given to the form of "conflict of interest."

Occasionally, of course, men have been accused of every dishonesty and thrown to that great beast, the aroused public. Aaron Burr was one, although his case was complicated by possible treasonable intent. Schuyler Colfax was another. He did nothing as Vice President that others had not done and have not done before and since, yet he was casually discarded as a handy "fall-guy" for President Grant in the break of the Credit Mobilier scandal during the first Grant administration. Or take the classic case of James G. Blaine, "the man from Maine" who should have had the Presidency some time in the 1880s. The highest office in the land was denied a man who might well have succeeded in it because of his associations with railroad and other industrial leaders. Blaine legislated in behalf of interests in which he had a financial part. In the roar of outrage that arose in the 1880s against unrestrained financial and political power, Blaine's distinguished career came to an end. It is easy for moralist historians to curl their lips in speaking of James G. Blaine, and they often do. He was the horrible example of his time, thrown up by politicians to cover their own tracks.

Look at those tracks for a moment. In the 1860s and 1870s, virtually every state government in the United States was crooked, the legislators could be bought, and more, they openly sought purchasers of their votes. In Congressional testimony long after the fact, Jay Gould said wearily that he could not remember how much money he had parcelled out to legislators during the Erie fight. Commodore Vanderbilt's spending during that struggle was on the same level, and, later, both men found it less expensive and less wearing to buy William Marcy Tweed and let that New York political boss do their legislative buying in Albany for them. Should Gould or Vanderbilt be blamed for the sins of the legislators? Knowing that these men were up for sale to the highest bidder, would any other businessman have failed to purchase? The New York legislator was not bought only by Gould and Vanderbilt, but by every industrialist with an axe to grind. The price of legislation for business purposes as far as Boss Tweed was concerned was laid out in hard cash. Gould was simply one of the contributors to the machine.

Another affair for which Jay Gould is often flayed is the Great Gold Scandal of the Grant administration. It is held that Gould based his hopes for cornering the gold market on corrupting President Grant and those around him. A careful study of Gould's actions here, however, indicates that he was playing the gold market both ways in this transaction, that he was trying to "persuade" Grant to his point of view, working on the President's dishonest in-laws with cash, flamboyantly entertaining the President on the trip on the old Fall River line, and doing his best to keep the government out of the gold market. But the fact is that there was much sentiment in favor of the government staying out of the marketplace no matter what the consequences; that when the crisis began, Vanderbilt tried as hard to get Grant into the picture as Gould tried to keep him out; and that Gould was selling gold short and buying outright at the same time, figuring a narrowing margin as the crisis continued. Jim Fisk was the fool in this action, the conman conned. Jay Gould was simply playing his cold-blooded business game, as always, making the best use of the materials at hand—and if those materials included corrupt government officials, then who is to be blamed?

As for the Gould descendents, a study of Jay's attempt to establish a dynasty by laying out a careful financial plan should leave all of us in awe of the Egyptian dynasts, and the Hapsburgs, the Plantagenets, and the Windsors. When one sees how badly Gould failed, one realizes that the systems of sibling marriage and primogeniture had something to offer him who would be founder of a long and powerful line. Amenhotep 1 knew what he was about. Jay Gould only thought he knew.

In the case of the Goulds, it might be said that the wrong character got the reins. Jay's spiritual heir was daughter Helen. She spent more time with him, and she knew his thinking better than any other member of the family. From her mother, Helen inherited a leavening or perhaps ennobling snobbism (Jay was the most democratic of men) and a sense of *noblesse oblige* that sometimes descends on the second generation of money-making families. Helen accompanied Jay on nearly all of his later tours of the western railroads, and she was thoroughly familiar with his dream of a real transcontinental railroad for America. After Jay's death, it was Helen who insisted on holding onto every one of the major properties Jay had secured.

George Gould was a very complex character. Since he left little written information about himself, his motivations may never be entirely known. In his early years, George showed such a degree of loyalty and business acumen that his father had no hesitation in turning over the Gould financial empire to his son—and the imprimatur of Gould was never something to underestimate.

Are we to assume that Jay Gould was so sentimental about his family that he allowed himself to be duped in assessing business matters? It seems most unlikely. Most likely, George was as astute and even brilliant a businessman as his father believed. But only as long as he had the guidance of his father. It may well be that even

Jay underestimated his own ability and his leadership of the boys.

Or it may be that George was bemused by the life of leisure which he loved dearly, engrossed with social affairs and with women, and pushed and pulled by his own business judgments which represented the here-and-now and those of Helen which represented the spirit of Jay. Who knows what Jay would have done had he been faced with the successful Morganization of the railroads? Jay might have sold out, or bought, rather than face the open competition with the Pennsylvania in Pittsburgh. He might have reached an accommodation with Harriman and Kuhn, Loeb to prevent the Union Pacific–Southern Pacific combine from forcing the Denver and Rio Grande into disaster. He might even have sensed the direction of growth of communications and used his hold on Western Union to acquire a leading position in the Bell Telephone System.

Yet, in spite of all George's misdemeanors and what the courts chose to regard as improper use of the powers left him by his father, he was victim of bad luck for the most part. His holdings were hard hit by the Panic of 1907. The panic came on top of the depredations of Kuhn, Loeb and the Morgan-backed Pennsylvania. George might have weathered any two of these storms—even Jay might not have survived all three of them.

As for the rest of the tribe, there was not a leader in the lot except for Helen, and being a woman in a man's world, she never tried to enter business. (It took an entirely different type to be a Hetty Green.) Edwin was a recluse by nature. In another society, he might have joined the church and become a bishop. Howard and Frank were playboys whose ambitions went only slightly beyond the self-gratifications of the moment. Their fortunes increased simply because they did not spend all the money that came in. After all, 5 per cent of $12,000,000 is $600,000 a year, without compounding interest, and if a Gould could get along on only $1,000 a day, he might increase his *income* by $15,000 each year while increasing his capital by nearly $300,000. In other words, it was very nearly impossible to spend as much money as the Goulds took in every year, although except for Edwin and Helen they tried manfully, and even George managed to spend all his share by keeping two full households going.

As for the third generation of Goulds, their stories tend to become a dreary recital of the peccadilloes of a fragile and undisciplined society which was beset by too much money and too little purpose in life. Of this third generation, it can be said that all of them followed their own bents and that none of them committed a heinous crime. Most of them were part of that useless froth of America that was called "the cream"; they did nothing particularly to harm or help the course of the republic.

The fourth generation of Goulds was much reduced in power and wealth, and with the exception of Kingdon Gould, none of its members showed any spark reminiscent of Jay's acquisitive nature. They had nothing to be ashamed of, but they were simply average American citizens but with more money and consequently fewer controls on their behavior. They behaved then much like their peers in this ever-upward-oriented society, permitting themselves license in the matter of marriages and liaisons. As for Kingdon, his flair for acquisition seemed to be limited to the making of money and not pointed in any particular direction. Making money, honored as it is by Americans, is not necessarily a lovable or redeeming characteristic from the standpoint of social history. As for their distribution of the wealth, the Goulds, after Jay, showed a remarkable lack of intuition or foresight. Of course, Kingdon's story is not finished as of this writing.

Jay thought he had established a dynasty, but he ought first to have given his children lessons in birth control. George lived at a time when he might have come to greatness, either by acquisition or by spending. In George's lifetime, old John D. Rockefeller established his remarkable foundation dedicated to promotion of world health. Other millionaires assured the preservation of their names by foundations: the Guggenheims, for example, served the cause of art, scholarship, and aeronautics. A relatively unknown plumbing equipment manufacturer named Crane practically financed the Czechoslovakian republic at one point, and established a foundation which has educated thousands of Americans in matters of foreign affairs.

This is not to equate the Rockefeller and Crane contributions, but simply to note that there are a thousand ways to leave money. A great splash can be made—as with the Ford Foundation, which has billions of dollars at its disposal. But the point is that for every fortune earned in America or elsewhere, there is a concomitant responsibility laid down, and the view that history takes of any given fortune depends on what public service the money renders in the aggregate. For the Rockefellers, who have given widely and wisely and who have trained their sons to public service, there is one kind of accounting. The Roosevelts, with much less fortune but more history behind them, behaved in the same manner. The DuPonts chose to become business leaders, and have bettered society in their way through the development of a multiplicity of products that contribute to the standard of living. The Fords, having engineered huge private wealth, are turning to the new public sector of foundations as a means of giving money, not for direct accomplishment, but to encourage accomplishment by others. If this move is developing a new governing factor in the public sector, and one that might, eventually, threaten to be more bureaucratic than useful, at least it is a new approach to the problem of justifying fortunes achieved by exploitation. It is hard to see how the Goulds could do such public work, with the small remnant of the great fortune that exists, but if they are, it remains to be done.

Index